THE COURTS, THE PUBLIC,
AND THE LAW EXPLOSION

The American Assembly, *Columbia University*

THE COURTS, THE PUBLIC, AND THE LAW EXPLOSION

Prentice-Hall, Inc., *Englewood Cliffs, N. J.*

A SPECTRUM BOOK

Copyright © 1965 by The American Assembly, Columbia University, under International and Pan-American Copyright Conventions. All rights reserved. No part of this book may be reproduced in any form, by mimeograph or any other means, without permission in writing from the publishers. *Library of Congress Catalog Card Number 65-23292.* Printed in the United States of America—C. P 18511 C18512

Preface

Each new American Assembly program opens with a meeting at Arden House, on the Harriman (New York) campus of Columbia University. Seventy participants, representative of a variety of occupations and geographical areas of the United States, were in session from April 29-May 2, 1965, in the Twenty-seventh American Assembly on *The Courts, the Public, and the Law Explosion*. At the close of the discussions a statement of findings was approved in plenary session. It has been published in a separate pamphlet by The American Assembly.

Under the editorial supervision of Harry Willmer Jones, Cardozo Professor of Jurisprudence at the Columbia University School of Law, the chapters which follow were prepared as background reading for the Arden House Assembly, for subsequent regional and local Assemblies, for college and university classes, and for general readership.

With gratitude the Assembly acknowledges support from The Rockefeller Foundation and Walter E. Meyer Research Institute of Law specifically for the preparation, publication, and some circulation of the volume; and from Laurel Foundation for the general program. None of these institutions is to be associated with the views in the pages following or with the recommendations of any meeting on this subject; and The American Assembly, a nonpartisan educational institution, takes no stand on the subjects it presents for public discussion.

Clifford C. Nelson
President
The American Assembly

v

Table of Contents

THE COURTS, THE PUBLIC,
AND THE LAW EXPLOSION

Harry W. Jones

Introduction

      This is a book about the courts and about their problems in con-
temporary American society. Some of these are old problems; others arise
from new burdens imposed on the legal order by technological change and
present-day social tensions. It is no exaggeration to speak, as some of our
writers in this book will, of a crisis in judicial administration. To understand how this crisis has come about, it is necessary to know more than
is commonly known concerning the organization and staffing of the
courts, the workloads they carry, and the procedures they use in disposing
of their business. The essays in this book are not technical studies for
lawyers—although most lawyers know far less than they should about
the facts of life in the lower criminal and civil courts, where the pressures
and strains are heaviest—but efforts to describe the realities of court
functioning in terms that will be intelligible and meaningful to all
citizens. For it is the underlying premise of this book, as it was of The
American Assembly for which the book was originally prepared, that
every American has an important stake in the fair and efficient administration of justice.

In a decent legal order, it is not enough that justice be done; it must
also be seen to be done. This common law maxim is a shorthand way of
saying that the rectitude and humaneness of the law's workings must be
manifest to all members of the community and particularly to those whose
interests are adversely affected by the operations of legal institutions. It
is an indispensable element of our legal tradition that everyone has the
right to his day in court—that is, fair opportunity to state his claim or
defense and assurance that his assertions will be considered carefully and
in high seriousness before the decision comes down.

Traditional court procedures, when working at their best, accomplish the kind of patient hearing and discriminating investigation that we associate with the just administration of the law. But this takes time and sufficient resources in adjudicative personnel to handle the flow of work. The arts of the judge, like the arts of the sculptor and the cabinet maker, are most perfectly performed when the craftsman has no assembly line to rush him and can give full and painstaking attention to one commission at a time.

Our courts are now confronted by the mid-century law explosion. This, to some extent, is a function of the population explosion—twice as many people, therefore twice as many disputes to be settled, twice as many civil claims to be heard and weighed, twice as many criminal charges to be tried and determined. But that is by no means the whole story of the law explosion; the full truth is that we have a society that is far more complex and vastly more demanding on law and legal institutions. New rights, like those of social security, have been brought into being, and older rights of contract and property made subject to government regulation and legal control. New social interests are pressing for recognition in the courts. Groups long inarticulate have found legal spokesmen and are asserting grievances long unheard. Each of these developments has brought its additional grist to the mills of justice.

Two aspects of the law explosion are of central importance for contemporary judicial administration. In court congestion, the automobile is the villain of the piece, as Maurice Rosenberg makes plain in Chapter Two. Technological advances and dramatic gains in prevailing income standards have put tens of millions of cars on the roads, and one result has been an astronomical increase in accident figures and personal injury suits. This tide of litigation has inundated our trial courts of general jurisdiction. In the great cities, delays run into years, and courtroom adjudication becomes a painful last alternative, to be resorted to only when a tolerable settlement cannot be secured from the insurance company out of court. There is no inherent reason why this must be so. We put up with the situation only because we are used to it and fatalistic about it. How long would the public tolerate comparable delay and inefficiency in the furnishing of any other public service?

Edward Barrett's essay (Chapter Four) provides abundant evidence that the quantitative pressures on the courts are even greater in criminal law administration. There has been a massive increase in crime and other phenomena of social instability. Scholars of society have varying explanations, but all seem to agree that two of the major factors are 1) the waning influence of the family, the church, and other nonlegal agencies of social control, and 2) the vast migrations of population from the small towns and rural areas to the great cities that have taken place in the United States since World War II. Whatever the causes, the consequences for the legal order are manifest. The great mass of criminal cases, divorce proceedings, and adjudications in matters of mental illness, alcoholism, narcotics addiction, and juvenile delinquency are disposed of in any major city on an assembly-line basis, so many cases to the hour. What are the implications for law and social order when untold thousands of people charged with criminal offenses are handled in the lower courts as if they were mere blanks for processing?

Can justice be administered on a mass-production basis? Are there no middle ways between the glacial slowness of the court process in personal injury suits and the frantic speed of the magistrates' courts in misdemeanor cases? So far we have made only a little progress in recasting our judicial institutions to meet the quantitative burdens imposed on them by the law explosion. There are widening discrepancies between the formal law in the books and the law in action in the courts. These are not cracks to be painted over but faults that imperil the structure of American justice. We are going to have to be searching and candid in our appraisal of existing judicial procedures and boldly imaginative in reconstructing traditional institutions to meet the challenges of our own time.

What has been said so far in this introduction should account sufficiently for the emphasis of this book on the *trial courts* and what they do. The law explosion has its greatest impact on the trial courts. It is there that the workloads are most unmanageable, the civil delays most tedious, and the criminal process most harried and rushed.

This is not to say that appellate-court processes can be left out of the appraisal. Milton Green is quite right in his insistence that the "inferior" trial courts, the "courts of general jurisdiction," and the other trial courts described in his guide to state and federal judicial organization (Chapter One) can be seen in proper perspective only when understood as components in a system of courts which, in its turn, is a part of the structure of government. Geoffrey Hazard's essay (Chapter Three) demonstrates the many ways in which appellate-court functioning affects the operation of the trial courts and shows that the appellate courts, too, have their problems of workload and delay. His discussion of "discretionary review" and other devices to keep the number of appeals down to a volume that can be handled by the appellate courts with reasonable deliberation and dispatch suggests analogies that might conceivably be drawn on in devising ways and means of reducing lower court caseloads. These are significant variations on our central theme and necessary to its development, but the focus of this book is on the realities of the judicial process in the trial courts.

Our stress on the work of the trial courts carries with it an emphasis on procedures for the adjudication of what might be disparaged as "ordinary" cases, that is, controversies which, taken one by one, appear to have no profound implications for legal theory or constitutional law. If we seem to be slighting high doctrine in this emphasis on ordinary cases and how they get decided, it is not that we are insensitive to the importance of the principles enunciated in such great cases as the Supreme Court's recent decisions on school desegregation, legislative districting, and freedom of expression. Authoritative pronouncements and binding legal precedents are made, however, not by trial judges but by appellate courts of last resort. Appellate judges are the general staff of a legal system; trial judges are the officers in the field who decide the final fate of the overwhelming majority of cases that never go on to appeal. There is a rich scholarly and popular literature analyzing high court doctrines and decisions; by contrast there is painfully little in print on what goes on in the trial courts. A good many authorities on the formal doctrines of the law of torts know as little about procedures in actual use for the settlement of personal injury claims (Chapter Two) as Emily Post would have known about behavior at a country picnic or a Coney Island clambake. A Justice of the Supreme Court, fresh from collegial deliberation in Washington on the procedural privileges of accused persons, might get the shock of his life if he spent a day listening to arraignments (Chapter Four) in a magistrate's court in any great city of the United States.

Certain distinct notes run through the several essays that make up this volume. The task of law in the conditions of the law explosion is characterized, as law's task would not have been characterized two decades ago, as a vast enterprise in public administration (see Chapters One, Two, and Four). A new philosophy has gained ascendancy: "It is as much a part of judicial responsibility to administer the courts effectively as to decide the cases wisely" (Maurice Rosenberg in Chapter Two). There is agreement on the underlying diagnosis: too much work for too few judges to do in the ways they are traditionally supposed to do it. Means must be found either to reduce the inflow of cases drastically, or to augment present adjudicative resources in a very substantial way, or both. There is a shared concern (discussed in Chapters Two, Three, and Four) that undue preoccupation with problems of delay may lead to widespread adoption of expediting gimmicks that can impair judicial deliberation and affect the quality of justice by distorting case results in wholly unanticipated ways. There is optimism, particularly in Maurice Rosenberg's essay (Chapter Two) about the use of social-science research techniques to identify critical disorders in existing trial court functioning and to appraise experimental programs designed to ease the strains of volume processing. There is emphasis (in Chapters Four and Five) on the often neglected point that respect for law can be undermined and social order impaired if court processes *seem* callous, mechanical, or unjust to persons caught up in them. Again, justice must not only be done; it must be seen to be done.

The prescription for the ills of the trial courts has many necessary ingredients: better planned administration, drastically modernized procedures, and systematic reductions in the workload along with more judges to handle it. But there is another indispensable ingredient, this one purely qualitative. Whatever the course of court reform may be, much will turn on the character, personality, and intellectual quality of the men and women who preside over our trial courts. My own essay (Chapter Five) undertakes to analyze the trial judge's role as a decision-making official and his further role as justice representative, that is, as the most important bearer of law's witness to society. It is not easy to assess a man's moral and intellectual qualifications for effective service as a trial judge, as Glenn Winters and Robert Allard make clear in their essay (Chapter Six) on judicial selection and tenure in the United States. But nothing is more urgent in a society under law than that men and women of genuine quality be called to the bench and that judicial office be withheld from those who, whatever their professional ambitions or political connections, are insufficient to the task in energy, mind, or character. Of all the measures now under way to revitalize the role of the trial courts, none is entitled to priority over the accomplishment and maintenance of far higher standards of judicial selection.

This book embodies an effort to engage the interest of a wider public in the trial courts and their pressing difficulties. Someone may ask whether these are not problems for the legal profession and for it alone; why not let the lawyers put their house in order? The answers are several. The legal profession itself is sharply and hopelessly divided on certain of the central issues. Many lawyers of great distinction are high-level business counsellors and do not see a courtroom even once a year. A proposal like the intermittently active one to substitute a liability-without-fault compensation system for court determination of automobile personal injury cases (discussed in Chapter Two) is likely to strike a Wall Street lawyer as an eminently sensible way to get rid of court congestion, but half the members of the bar will recoil violently from it as threatening their bread and butter. Even where lawyers stand united on issues within their competence, the legal profession has been singularly ineffective in influencing public opinion. Bar association polls on the qualifications of judicial candidates have no substantial political influence in most cities. A realist in metropolitan politics once put it in these terms: "I would rather have my district leader on my side than all three bar associations in town," and he was quite right in his appraisal.

The legal profession's ineffectiveness as a political force is not due entirely to the ineptitude it shares with the medical profession in matters of public communication. Other factors contribute to the indifference of the public to lawyer-sponsored proposals for court reform: among them are lack of public information concerning the realities of trial court functioning and limited public awareness of society's stake in the effective administration of justice. If judicial institutions were autonomous, this lack of public interest and support might be of relatively little consequence. A private hospital can reorganize its clinical and out-patient services without getting prior approval from the city council or the state legislature. But courts are agencies of government, and fundamental court reform can be achieved only by political action. Our trial courts will never be structured and reinforced to sustain the burdens of the law explosion until it is brought home to the public at large that justice is everybody's business.

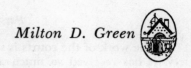

Milton D. Green

1

The Business of the Trial Courts

Court organization is terra incognita *for even the best informed members of the public, and there is need for a road map if the general reader is to find his way around in a lawyer's world of separate federal and state court systems, of "jurisdiction," "pleading," and "pre-trial procedure," and of "inferior trial courts," "trial courts of general jurisdiction," "intermediate appellate courts," and "courts of last resort."*

Court structures differ greatly in plan and nomenclature from state to state in the United States, and in most states court organization is more a jig-saw puzzle than an orderly and consistent system. Often the adjudicative authority of one of a state's courts overlaps with the authority of another. In many states, coordination of judicial business and effective court administration are made flatly impossible by the planlessness and lack of integration of existing trial court arrangements. Excellent blueprints for a simplified state court structure are available, as in the Model State Judicial Article of the American Bar Association, but inertia and vested interest are in the way, and effective political action will have to be marshaled, as in Illinois in 1963, to secure the necessary amendments to present state constitutions.

This chapter is designed as an introduction and guide to the complexities of the remarkably unsystematic American court system and provides, among other things, a kind of glossary of court designations and procedural terms that will appear often in later chapters of this book.

MILTON D. GREEN *has been a professor of law at New York University since 1959. He began his academic career in 1937, after eight years of law practice in Denver, and was dean of the law school of Washington University (St. Louis) from 1953 to 1959. He is a nationally known authority*

*on civil procedure and judicial organization and has been prominent in
the work of the Institute of Judicial Administration, particularly as a
director of field studies of court administration in a number of states.*

Perspective

The work of the courts is such an important facet of our modern
society, it has received so much attention from news media, from the
entertainment world, and from literature, that the average citizen has
gathered a general idea of how our courts operate. Nevertheless, more
specific and accurate information is necessary for fruitful discussion of
contemporary problems in the administration of justice.

The emphasis of this book is upon the trial courts. In order to bring
them into proper focus, however, they must be understood as components
in a system of courts which, in turn, is a part of the structure of government. The United States of America is a sovereign state in the community
of nations. The states of which it is composed are also sovereign, even
though they do not possess complete autonomy. They are free to enjoy
the privileges of self-government except in regard to those matters which
have been delegated to the federal government, and subject to limitations
imposed upon the states by the federal constitution. Thus a resident
citizen of the United States is subject to the governmental powers of two
sovereigns: the United States and the particular state in which he lives.

Unlike the British, from whom we have inherited so much, we live
under written constitutions which define the powers of government,
powers which are traditionally classified under three headings: legislative,
executive, and judicial.

The judicial power of the federal government, and of each state, is
exercised through its courts. Each state is free to fashion its judicial
machinery and distribute its judicial power among its courts as it sees fit,
subject to federal constitutional limitations, the chief one of which is the
clause of the Fourteenth Amendment which provides that no state
shall deprive any person of life, liberty, or property without due process
of law. As might be expected, great variety exists among state court
systems. Some are relatively simple and some unbelievably complex.
Nevertheless they all exhibit certain common traits. All of them make a
distinction between trial courts and appellate courts, and all of them
arrange their courts in some sort of a hierarchical system.

Our dual system of courts is unique and is not found in most nations
in which governmental units are combined into a federation. The usual
pattern in such countries is to entrust the enforcement of the federal law
to the state courts. At the time of the adoption of our constitution, however, the states and the federal government were too jealous of each other

to accept a unitary judicial system. Consequently we are burdened with two complete sets of courts—state and federal—which may have some advantages but which, as we shall see, exacts a high price in terms of time, money, and efficiency.

The Federal Court System

Article III of the Constitution vests the judicial power of the United States in "one Supreme Court and in such inferior Courts as the Congress may from time to time ordain and establish." Under this grant of power Congress has created a simple three-deck hierarchy which, in the order of ascendency, consists of the District Courts, the Courts of Appeals, and the Supreme Court. A few specialized courts, such as the Court of Claims and the Court of Customs and Patent Appeals, are supplementary. Unlike all of the state court systems, there is no inferior trial court, although United States Court Commissioners (appointed by District Court judges) perform some of the duties of committing magistrates in criminal cases, such as releasing a defendant on bail.

THE DISTRICT COURTS

The United States covers a vast area which must be subdivided for the purposes of efficient judicial administration. Accordingly, Congress has divided it into districts and has established a District Court for each of them. It seemed desirable to follow state lines as far as possible; hence approximately half of the states are defined as federal districts with but one District Court. Thus there is the United States District Court for the District of Alaska, the United States District Court for the District of Colorado, and so on. However, some states are so populous and have such a volume of judicial business that one court could not handle it. In such cases the state has been divided into two, three, or even four districts with a corresponding number of District Courts. As population (and judicial business) continued to grow, Congress began adding more judges rather than creating new districts. This made sense, especially where population was concentrated in small geographical areas such as New York City, which lies chiefly in the Southern District of New York. This district contains one District Court, but this court is served by a complement of over twenty district judges.

Aside from the specialized courts, previously mentioned, and the rare occasions when the Supreme Court exercises original jurisdiction, the District Courts are the only trial courts in the system. In the vast majority of cases, a trial in a District Court is presided over by a single judge. There are situations, however, where a three-judge court is convened.

These are the cases in which it is sought to enjoin the enforcement of a statute of a state or of an Act of Congress on the ground that it is repugnant to the Constitution of the United States. The maintenance of the delicate balance of state-federal relations involved in such litigation, in the opinion of Congress, warranted the special three-judge court.

THE COURTS OF APPEALS

The principal appellate courts in the federal system are the Courts of Appeals. There is one such court for each of the eleven judicial circuits into which the country is divided. Each of the Courts of Appeals is the proper appellate tribunal to review the actions of the District Courts which are located within that circuit. There is great variation in the geographical size of the circuits. The largest is the Ninth, which embraces the states of Alaska, Arizona, California, Idaho, Montana, Nevada, Oregon, Washington, and Hawaii. The smallest is the District of Columbia. The number of judges in the Courts of Appeals also varies. The Ninth Circuit and the District of Columbia have nine each while the First Circuit, which is composed of Maine, Massachusetts, New Hampshire, Rhode Island, and Puerto Rico, has only three. The reason for the variation is the volume of judicial business. The Court of Appeals for the District of Columbia has an extra heavy load since it also reviews the action of many of the federal administrative agencies, such as the Federal Trade Commission and the National Labor Relations Board. Any dissatisfied litigant in a federal District Court may appeal his case as a matter of right to the appropriate Court of Appeals.

THE SUPREME COURT

The highest court in the federal system is the Supreme Court. In rare instances, in cases involving ambassadors or in suits between states, the court exercises original jurisdiction. In other words, it then sits as a trial court, but unlike the usual trial court it does not take testimony in open court but appoints a master to hear the testimony of the witnesses, put it into written form, and submit it to the court. During the last three years there have been but two cases in which the court has exercised original jurisdiction. Most of the work of the court is devoted to reviewing the action of lower courts in the federal system and the highest courts in the state systems.

The Constitution does not define the appellate jurisdiction of the Supreme Court, but instead delegates that task to Congress, a power which Congress has exercised from time to time by enlarging or restricting the jurisdiction of the court. Congress has been conscious of the fact that if the court is to function well its work must be kept within manageable limits. Consequently, it has delegated to the court a large measure of control by investing it with discretionary power to decide whether or not to review a case. This power was granted by Congress in 1916 and greatly enlarged in 1925. It does not, however, give the Court complete discretion. Where a federal court holds an Act of Congress unconstitutional, or where a United States Court of Appeals holds a state statute unconstitutional or invalid, there is an appeal to the Supreme Court as a matter of right. Likewise, where the highest court of a state holds a federal law to be invalid or upholds a state statute which is challenged as unconstitutional there is an appeal as a matter of right. In all other cases, even though federal questions are involved, the Supreme Court may exercise its discretion in taking or rejecting the case. As a matter of practice, if four of the nine justices vote to take a case the Court will "grant certiorari" and the case will be set down for argument. The extent to which the discretion is exercised is disclosed by the fact that during the last three years 5,967 cases were filed with the Court but only 322 were disposed of with full opinions. Of that number 224, or 69 per cent, were appeals from lower federal courts and 98, or 31 per cent, were appeals from state courts.

THE JURISDICTION OF THE FEDERAL COURTS

In theory, at least, the federal government is a government of limited powers. It has only the powers which the states have ceded to it and which are spelled out in the constitution, expressly or by necessary implication. The judicial power of the United States is defined in Article III and is confined to three types of cases: 1) those which involve a question of federal law, and this includes the Constitution, statutes, and treaties; 2) cases of admiralty and maritime jurisdiction; and 3) controversies involving certain categories of parties. The latter include (a) ambassadors and public ministers, (b) the United States, (c) a state, (d) citizens of different states, and (e) foreign states or citizens thereof. This is the sum total of the judicial power of the United States and is a limitation upon the jurisdiction of all federal courts.

In actual practice the cases which find their way in and out of the federal courts are usually of three kinds and are about equally distributed. They are 1) cases in which the United States is a party, 2) civil cases involving a federal question, and 3) civil cases involving diversity of citizenship of the parties. In the first category are civil as well as criminal cases, but the latter are very numerous since the federal courts have exclusive jurisdiction in enforcing the federal criminal law. Falling within the last two categories are most of the civil cases in the District Courts. In each of these classes of cases a minimum amount of $10,000 (exclusive of interest and costs) must be involved before the case is eligible to be brought into the District Court.

State Court Systems

Each of the fifty states, exercising the prerogative of sovereignty, has set up its own system of courts. As might be expected, great diversity exists. No two state court systems are exactly alike and none is as simple as the federal system; but all of them exemplify, in more or less degree, a hierarchical arrangement.

"INFERIOR" TRIAL COURTS

Every state has made provision for a set of "inferior" or "petty" trial courts to handle minor matters of a civil nature and minor violations of the criminal law. Their civil jurisdiction is frequently defined in terms of a maximum pecuniary figure, which may be as low as fifty dollars or as high as a thousand dollars or more. Their criminal jurisdiction is also frequently defined in terms of the maximum jail sentence which may be imposed, which is commonly six months. Sometimes there are geographical limitations, specifying that the events giving rise to the litigation must have happened within the precinct, town, or county in which the court is held.

Such courts go by a variety of names, the most common of which is Justice of the Peace Court, or Justice Court, or J.P. Court. The court and the name are part of our English heritage, as of a time when life was rural and relaxed, and the business of a J.P. (Justice of the Peace) was regarded as a part-time job. It is still a part-time job in many states, the incumbent of the office sometimes being paid a small salary and sometimes being compensated on a fee basis, so much for each case he tries. The latter arrangement has led to the wry remark that J.P. stands for judgment for plaintiff, since satisfied customers bring more business. In the more populous areas such inferior courts are often called Magistrates Courts, and there is not infrequently some specialization, even on this level, such as Police Courts, whose jurisdiction is limited to minor criminal matters, or Traffic Courts, whose function is limited to hearing cases involving violations of the traffic laws. In some states the organization of these inferior trial courts is on a local basis. In other words, in a single state there may be Justice Courts in the counties and Magistrates Courts and Police Courts in some of the cities. A growing number of states are attempting to remedy this confusing and unsatisfactory situation and to reorganize their court systems on a symmetrical state-wide basis. This would result in the abolition of the Justice of the Peace Courts (or their equivalents), and the creation of a state-wide set of inferior courts staffed by full-time and qualified judges. Such movements, of course, meet with political resistance, and progress comes with glacial speed. The new states of Alaska and Hawaii, however, have organized their lower trial courts on this basis.

Whatever name they go by, the inferior trial courts of the several states exhibit certain common characteristics: 1) they are all trial courts, or courts of original jurisdiction, or courts of first instance—three ways of stating the same thing; 2) their jurisdiction, or judicial power, is sharply limited, whether that power be in relation to civil matters, or criminal matters, or both; 3) they are not ordinarily courts of record (this means that no detailed record of their proceedings is kept, merely a brief entry identifying the parties, perhaps noting the names of the attorneys—if there are attorneys—and a notation of the final disposition of the case; this is sometimes referred to as a "blotter," especially in Police Courts); 4) the procedure is usually summary and informal; and 5) the losing party usually has the right to appeal the case to a higher trial court where he can obtain a whole new trial under more formal proceedings.

TRIAL COURTS OF GENERAL JURISDICTION

Above the inferior trial courts are the courts with authority to try all types of cases, civil or criminal. These are known as trial courts of general jurisdiction. Even if there are some limitations on the power of a superior trial court, if, for instance, its jurisdiction begins where the jurisdiction of the inferior trial court leaves off, at $500, for example, it is still frequently referred to as a trial court of general jurisdiction. With this qualification in mind, it is safe to say that every state, in addition to its inferior trial courts, has a set of superior trial courts, or trial courts of general jurisdiction. Such courts are variously named in the different states. In some they are called Courts of Common Pleas, still following the ancient English tradition; in many states they are called Superior Courts; in others they are called District Courts, or Circuit Courts, taking their names from the circumstance that the state is divided into judicial districts, or circuits. In the state of New York the state trial court of general jurisdiction has the curious title of the Supreme Court, which is confusing to outsiders because that name is usually reserved for the highest appellate court of a state.

As in the case of the inferior trial courts, trial courts of general jurisdiction are distributed geographically throughout the state so that citizens will have easy and convenient access to them. This is done by dividing the state into judicial districts or circuits and establishing a court for each geographical unit. There is a district or circuit judge for each geographical unit, and in districts where judicial business is heavy, more than one judge is appointed or elected. Perhaps the largest trial court of general jurisdiction in the world is the Superior Court of Los Angeles, which has 120 judges. In multiple-judge courts in the large metropolitan areas it is quite common to have specialized parts or divisions or departments, such as criminal, civil-jury, civil-non-jury, domestic relations, juvenile, and probate divisions. In addition to the original jurisdiction which such courts exercise, and which is their principal function, they also usually act as appellate tribunals for the decision of appeal from the inferior trial courts. They frequently also act as appellate tribunals to review the action of state boards and commissions, such as the industrial accident board and the public utilities commission.

TRIAL COURTS OF INTERMEDIATE JURISDICTION

In all but a few of the states there is also a trial court of intermediate jurisdiction, usually organized on a county basis, and commonly called the County Court. As in the case of the inferior courts, there is customarily a pecuniary ceiling upon the civil jurisdiction of a trial court of intermediate jurisdiction, and it may or may not have concurrent jurisdiction with the inferior trial court or the superior trial court where monetary limitations overlap. Frequently it is also invested with jurisdiction in some specialized area, such as administration of the estates of decedents, minors, and incompetent persons.

SPECIALIZED TRIAL COURTS

In the states which cleave to a simple court structure there is often a degree of functional specialization in the superior trial court. This is especially true in areas of large population. Where there is a multiple-judge bench, a certain judge is assigned a particular job at the beginning of the term, such as handling probate matters, or divorce matters, or criminal matters. Many states have solved the problem of specialization, however, by the creation of special courts. Perhaps the most common type of special court is the one designed to administer estates, variously named Probate Court, Orphans' Court, or Surrogate's Court. Another common type of special court is the court whose jurisdiction is restricted to criminal cases. It too goes under many names, some of which have a strange medieval sound, like Court of Oyer and Terminer and Jail Delivery, or Court of Quarter Sessions. There are also Divorce Courts, Courts of Domestic Relations, or Family Courts, whose specialized jurisdiction is indicated by the name of the court. Some states, following the federal pattern, have a special Court of Claims, which tries civil cases brought against the state. At one time in this country it was customary to have one set of courts to try common law actions and another set to try equity cases, but reform movements for the simplification of procedure have all but eradicated this historical anomaly.

INTERMEDIATE APPELLATE COURTS

Every man is entitled to his day in court. This is one of the proud boasts of the Anglo-American legal tradition. It must be admitted that historically this merely meant that every man was entitled to his day in the *trial* court. Appeal was not a matter of right but of grace which the legislature could grant or withhold, and this still remains the law in the absence of a specific right to appeal found in a constitution. In the famous case of *Ex parte McCardle* the defendant, who was being held in military custody, petitioned a federal court for *habeas corpus,* which was denied, and he appealed to the Supreme Court. After the case had been argued before the Supreme Court and was under consideration on the merits, Congress repealed the statute which authorized the appeal, and the Court held that it thereby lost the power to proceed with the appeal. That case was decided in 1868 and may still be valid as a matter of constitutional law, but our ideas of fair play and substantial justice have changed considerably since that time. The present trend is that in every case provision should be made for review of a judgment by a court other than the one which rendered it. There have been side-effects of this view that appeal is a matter of right. Many appellate courts have become overburdened and appellate dockets congested. This situation, at least in the densely populated areas, has led to the creation of intermediate appellate courts in order to relieve the burden upon courts of last resort.

Intermediate appellate courts exist in fifteen states, but there is nothing resembling a uniform pattern. Structurally they are of two types: those in which the court is an entity, distinct from both the trial court and the court of last resort and lying between them; and those in which the intermediate appellate court is a branch or division of the trial court. There is a wide variation in the number of judges composing such courts, with a low of three in Alabama, a high of thirty-three in Texas, and a median of about thirteen. Such courts are generally found only in heavily populated states, none in states under 3 million. The jurisdiction of state intermediate appellate courts is usually broad, encompassing most appeals but excepting certain classes of cases which may bypass the intermediate court and go directly to the Supreme Court. Here again there is no uniformity, but the most common types of cases in which a direct appeal to the highest court is allowed are, in the order of frequency of provision therefor: criminal cases involving the death penalty; cases involving the constitutionality of a state or federal statute; cases involving the title to land; civil cases involving an amount in excess of the monetary jurisdiction of the intermediate court; cases involving taxation and revenue; and criminal cases, variously defined. In some states certain of these matters first go to the intermediate appellate court but a further appeal is allowed. In a substantial number of states the highest court may exercise discretionary jurisdiction in permitting or denying the further appeal.

THE COURT OF LAST RESORT

At the apex of the judicial system in every state is a court of last resort. It is usually called the Supreme Court, although here again the states have exhibited some individuality: in Kentucky, Maryland, and New York it is called the Court of Appeals, in Connecticut the Supreme Court of Errors, and in Maine and Massachusetts, the Supreme Judicial Court. Whatever the name, its function is the same: to review the action of the lower judicial tribunals of the state. There are two ways in which this is done. By far the most common is to entertain appeals at the behest of dissatisfied litigants on a case-by-case basis. This is the exercise of appellate jurisdiction. In the United States the scope of judicial review which the court exercises in such cases is relatively narrow; it does not retry the case on the merits and it does not substitute its ideas of justice for those of the trial court; what it does is to review the record of the proceedings to determine whether or not the lower court committed error in its procedure or in applying the substantive law to the facts of the case. Rarely does an appellate court review the facts if there is only a conflict in the evidence, but it may set aside a verdict if it feels that it is unsupported by the evidence. The other method by which a court of last resort reviews the action of the lower courts of its system is to exercise a superintending control over them. This it usually does by issuing court orders, or writs, directed to the lower courts. The principal ones are 1) *mandamus,* by which a lower court is ordered to do something, such as grant a change of venue or grant a jury trial; 2) prohibition, by which a lower court is forbidden to proceed in a case in which it does not have jurisdiction, or in which it is exceeding its jurisdiction; and 3) *habeas corpus,* by which a lower court is directed to justify its action in holding a person in custody alleged to be illegal. The highest state court will issue such writs only upon the petition of an aggrieved party who makes application directly to it. The highest court of a state may also exercise superintending control over lower courts in the system by promulgating rules of procedure which they must follow.

State-Federal Interaction

The delicate balance of state-federal relationships exists in many areas of our governmental structure but it stands out in bold relief in our overlapping court systems. Our present purpose is not to plumb the more difficult problems, such as the use of federal troops to enforce judicial decrees, but to sketch in light detail the routine and recurring situations in which the federal and state court systems become intertwined.

We start with the basic fact that superimposed on the same geographical territory there are two court systems. In many civil cases this presents the plaintiff with a choice of forums, state or federal, and presumably he will bring his case in the court which offers him some advantage. If a plaintiff sues in a state court the defendant may be able to have the case transferred to a federal court. This will be true if the case involves a federal question or if the plaintiff and the defendant are citizens of different states and the defendant is a nonresident of the state in which the suit is brought—provided that the amount involved exceeds $10,000. There are some cases, however, which meet these specifications but are not "removable." For instance, the Federal Employers Liability Act provides a remedy for injured railroad employees, gives them a choice of forum— state or federal—and prohibits the railroad from removing such a case from state to federal court. Over the years Congress has done considerable tinkering with "removal jurisdiction" and as a result much time, effort, and money has been spent on litigating borderline questions in this area.

Another type of situation in which there is a conflict of jurisdiction between state and federal courts exists when litigation between the same parties is pending in both state and federal courts at the same time. A classic example of this was provided by the dramatic litigation involving the validity of the alleged marriage of Senator Sharon of Nevada. Sarah Althea Hill claimed to be his wife by virtue of a written contract, which Sharon claimed was a forgery. He sued her in a federal court seeking cancellation of the alleged contract. She countered by suing him for divorce and alimony in a California state court. The state courts (trial and appellate) held the contract valid, but the federal courts (trial and appellate) held it to be a forgery. The protracted litigation lasted for almost a decade. Perhaps there is no ideal solution for avoiding such an unseemly struggle under our dual system. Congress has eased the situation, however, by prohibiting the federal courts from issuing injunctions against state court proceedings save in exceptional circumstances. The federal courts themselves have also developed the doctrine of "abstention," under which they will frequently stay their proceedings and await the decision of the state court.

Jurisdiction

JURISDICTION OVER THE SUBJECT MATTER

Up to this point we have concentrated on a description of the structure of the court systems, state and federal, which exist in the United States. We now turn to a consideration of the operation of the courts. A court is an arm of the state, created for the purpose of settling controversies which the parties are unable to settle by themselves. It must be invested with authority to render a binding decision whether the parties like it or not, and one of them probably won't. This authority, or power, which a court exercises is called *jurisdiction*. When we ask whether a court has jurisdiction over a particular type of case we are, in legal parlance, inquiring whether the court has jurisdiction over the *subject matter*. If it is a divorce case we ask, Has the state granted *this* court power to hear divorce cases? If it is a personal injury suit seeking $1 million damages we ask, Has the state granted *this* court power to try this type of case (personal injury) and one of this magnitude (possible pecuniary limitations). In other words, a court is said to have jurisdiction over the subject matter when it has been invested with power to try the type of case to which the instant case belongs. It is basic that a court must have jurisdiction over the subject matter in order to render a valid judgment.

To determine whether a court has jurisdiction over the subject matter, one must consult the statute or constitutional provision which created the court. That should settle the matter, one way or the other. It is not, however, quite that simple. For example, the statute creating a court may state that it is invested with power to try cases involving the title to land. Does this mean that the court may decide a title dispute over land located in another state? It does not; it is clearly settled that only the courts of the state in which land is located have jurisdiction to try cases affecting the title to it. This is common law, that is, law established by court decisions, and goes back to the time when all actions were considered local actions. In other words, the courts of a state were held to be without power to entertain cases which involved events occurring beyond the territorial boundaries of the state. By a process of evolution, however, this provincial conception of jurisdiction has largely disappeared. Today there are very few strictly local actions. Land litigation remains local, and so does divorce, in theory if not in practice; but most actions are not territorially circumscribed if the court is otherwise competent. They may be brought in any court which can acquire jurisdiction over the parties, which brings us to the second basic aspect of jurisdiction.

JURISDICTION OVER THE PERSON

In the early days of the English common law, civil cases as well as criminal cases were begun by arresting the defendant. He was not only arrested, he was kept in prison until the case was decided. Some one has said that in those days if you wished to find out if the court had jurisdiction over the person of the defendant, you looked in the dungeon—if the defendant was there, the court had jurisdiction. This system was hard on the defendant, especially in cases in which he ultimately won, but it does mark the beginning of the "physical-power" theory of jurisdiction, the idea that, lacking physical power over the defendant, a court has no jurisdiction to try him. In a later and more enlightened age the theory was retained but the practice modified. Initial arrest was discontinued in civil cases and jurisdiction obtained over the person of the defendant by having the sheriff serve him with a summons ordering him to appear and defend. Although the defendant remained at large the physical-power theory was satisfied because the sheriff could have arrested him at the time of service of the summons. This was the system we inherited when our colonies became a nation; a court did not acquire jurisdiction over a defendant unless and until he was personally served with a summons within the territorial jurisdiction of the court.

Today the physical power theory of jurisdiction is a shadow of its former self. In 1927 the Supreme Court of the United States upheld as constitutional Massachusetts' nonresident-motorist statute, which gave its courts jurisdiction over nonresidents who caused motor accidents in the state and provided for service of the summons on a state official. The theory was that by operating an automobile in the state the nonresident was deemed to have consented to the jurisdiction of the state's courts. Following this case, many states adopted nonresident motorist statutes. In 1945, in another famous case, the Supreme Court upheld the jurisdiction of the courts of the state of Washington over the International Shoe Company, a Delaware corporation with its principal place of business in St. Louis, even though the company was not doing business in the State of Washington in the traditional sense in which that term is used. The Supreme Court said that "due process requires only that in order to subject a defendant to a judgment *in personam,* if he be not present within the territory of the forum, he have certain minimum contacts with it such that the maintenance of the suit does not offend 'traditional notions of fair play and substantial justice.'" The theory enunciated in this case stimulated many states to enact so-called "long-arm statutes," investing their courts with jurisdiction over nonresidents who do certain prescribed acts within the state, such as entering into a contract or committing a wrongful act which causes injury. Presumably there is a constitutional minimum in contacts, below which a state may not go in acquiring jurisdiction over nonresidents, but it is not yet clear exactly where the Supreme Court will draw that line.

Profile of Civil Litigation

INVOKING JURISDICTION

In order to invoke the jurisdiction of the court and put the machinery of justice into operation, the plaintiff must file his complaint (petition) with the clerk of the court, pay the statutory docket fee, and have the defendant served with "process," which, in a civil case, is a summons. A summons is a court order commanding the defendant to appear and defend the action within a certain number of days (usually twenty or thirty from the date of service) and warning him that, unless he does so, a judgment by default will be taken against him. In some states the summons is issued and signed by the clerk of the court, and in others the attorney for the plaintiff has authority to issue and sign it. A copy of the complaint must be served with the summons or, if it is not, the summons must contain a short statement of the plaintiff's grievance and what he is asking for in the way of a remedy. Normally the summons will be served by a court officer, usually the sheriff or a deputy, but most states also provide for service by private process servers under certain conditions. After a copy of the summons has been served upon the defendant, the officer who made the service will write (in a space upon the back of the summons) a notation of the date, time, and place of the service. This is usually called the "sheriff's return," and serves two functions. It officially establishes the fact that jurisdiction has been acquired over the person of the defendant, and it starts the time running within which the defendant must answer. If he does not answer in time a default judgment may be taken against him. Most states provide that if the defendant cannot be found, process may be served upon a member of his family at his usual place of abode. Under the "long-arm statutes" a defendant may be served outside the state.

THE PLEADINGS

The "pleadings" are the formal written contentions of the parties. There was a time in early English law when pleadings were oral, but this proved unsatisfactory. The underlying philosophy of the common law in this matter was that the parties should frame the issues which they want the court to try. This was accomplished by a series of alternate written allegations designed to narrow the issues to a single one, if possible. This drive to narrow the issues led to more and more technical and formal rules of pleadings until, in some cases, "justice was smothered in her own robes." In this country the revolt against procedural technicality bore fruit in a simplified code of civil procedure adopted in New York in 1848. It abolished the technical forms of common law pleading and provided that thereafter there would be but one form, a civil action, and that the pleadings should state the contentions of the parties "in ordinary and concise language without unnecessary repetition." The lead of New York was rapidly followed by many other states. Another impetus for reform came in 1938 with further simplification of the rules of pleading in the federal courts. Today most states are operating with very simple and uncomplicated pleadings, which do not give adequate notice of the contentions of the respective parties, one of the purposes of pleading in a former era, because they are too general. They are not unfair, however, because other devices are now available to enable either party to find out what his adversary's case is all about, devices far beyond the dreams of the common law lawyer.

PRE-TRIAL PROCEDURES

The pleadings never were an effective means of notifying the court and the lawyers of what a case was about, because pleadings were formal and dealt with generalized issues and not with the actual evidence. It has often been said that the pleadings merely outline the skeleton of the lawsuit, which is filled in later by the evidence introduced at the trial. Unfortunately, the skeleton does not give a picture of the flesh that is to be added to make up the body of the case. As a consequence, either side in a lawsuit is apt to be surprised by the evidence introduced by the other. A diligent lawyer could come into court well prepared on his own case, but he was frequently in the dark as to the exact nature of his opponent's case and consequently unprepared to meet it. Surprise was a legitimate trial tactic. A lawsuit was viewed as a game or a joust in which counsel for each side strove mightily for his client, and the theory was that justice would emerge triumphant when the dust of combat settled in the judicial arena. The flaw in this practice was that the decision would frequently be a prize awarded for the prowess of counsel, instead of an adjudication of the case upon its merits. Dean Pound has called the process the "sporting theory of justice."

The common law remained indifferent for centuries to the injustices implicit in this system. It did provide feeble remedies to enable a lawyer to obtain evidence to support his client's case, but, if he sought to find

out details of his opponent's case, he was denied relief on the ground that
the court would not be a party to a "fishing expedition."

It was not until the first quarter of the present century that a new philosophy emerged, one which has drastically changed the trial of a lawsuit.
In summary form it may be stated thus: the goal of a trial should be a just
decision on the merits; this requires that all relevant facts be presented
to the court; this demands complete pre-trial disclosures; and this means
the elimination of surprise as a legitimate trial tactic. The implementation of this new philosophy occurred with the promulgation of new rules
of civil procedure for the federal courts in 1938. The new rules furnish
counsel with a complete set of tools for the discovery of the truth prior to
trial. Under these rules the old cry of "fishing expedition" is no longer
available. Each party to a suit is required, upon proper request, to furnish the other party with full factual details. The scope of pre-trial discovery under the federal rules is very broad and covers:

> any matter, not privileged, which is relevant to the subject matter involved
> in the pending action, whether it relates to the claim or defense of the exam-
> ining party or to the claim or defense of the other party, including the
> existence, description, nature, custody, condition and location of any books,
> documents, or other tangible things and the identity and location of persons
> having knowledge of relevant facts. It is not ground for objection that the
> testimony will be inadmissible at the trial if the testimony sought appears
> reasonably calculated to lead to the discovery of admissible evidence.

The principal "discovery" tool under the federal rules is the deposition, which consists of answers to questions and cross-questions put to a
witness under oath. Either party may take the other party's deposition
and ask him everything he knows about the case, including the names
and addresses of his witnesses, and may also require the opposite party
to answer written question under oath. A party may require his opponent
to admit or deny written propositions relating to the case and may require his opponent to produce documentary evidence in his possession
or to submit to a mental or physical examination by a physician appointed by the court if the case involves this mental or physical condition.
If a lawyer displays any diligence in using the discovery tools available to
him, there is very little excuse for him to claim surprise at any evidence
offered at the trial.

The federal rules also provide for a pre-trial conference called by the
judge and attended by the parties and their lawyers. The purpose of the
conference is to simplify the issues, secure agreement on facts which are
not really in dispute, and give the parties another opportunity to see if
the case can be settled without trial.

The discovery and pre-trial procedure has been in operation in the
United States District Courts for over twenty-five years and has served

as a model for reformed state court procedure in a majority of the states. There is no doubt that it has produced beneficial results: cases are better prepared, actual trial time has been saved by pre-trial processing, settlements without trial have been encouraged, and probably the quality of justice has improved in the cases which do go to trial. The procedure is not, however, an unmixed blessing. Critics claim that it is not appropriate in all types of cases, that it is subject to abuse, that it has increased the costs of litigation, and that it has contributed to court congestion by increasing pre-trial delay. Further study and experience will be necessary before a balance can be struck between the merits and demerits of the system and a determination made as to the modifications indicated.

THE RIGHT TO A JURY TRIAL

The Constitution of the United States "preserves" the right of trial by jury in civil cases and says the accused "shall enjoy the right" of jury trial in criminal cases. The Supreme Court has held that these provisions of the Constitution apply only in the federal courts. Every state constitution, however, contains a provision (more or less similar to the federal one), guaranteeing jury trial in the state courts.

It will be noted that the federal and state constitutional provisions merely "preserve" the right, but do not create it. The scope and extent of the right to jury trial must, therefore, be determined by scrutinizing the right as it existed at the time the constitutional provisions were written. When we look to the situation as it existed in 1787, we find that under the law of England, from whom we borrowed, the right to jury trial in civil cases extended only to "actions at law" (where the demand was usually for money damages) and that it did not extend to "suits in equity" (where the relief prayed was commonly an order compelling a defendant to do or refrain from doing an act). As long as we retained the distinction between law and equity, there was little difficulty in applying the constitutional guarantees of the right to jury trial, but under our reformed procedure, which merges law and equity, we ran into perplexing problems. When the same case involves both legal and equitable issues what happens to the right to jury trial? Different courts have given different answers. Some states hold that the "legal" issues must be tried by a jury and the equitable issues by the judge. Others hold that the case must be treated as a unit, and a jury trial will be ordered only if it is predominantly "legal."

At common law a jury consisted of twelve men who were required to arrive at a unanimous verdict. This is the type of jury which the Supreme Court has ruled must be used in the federal courts. The only modifications to the rigidity of the rule are that women are now eligible for jury service and that the parties may agree upon a jury of less than twelve or for a majority verdict. Some state constitutions specifically authorize juries of less than twelve or verdicts by some specified majority of the jurors.

Although jury trial is a guaranteed constitutional right it may be waived. In civil cases in the federal courts it is deemed to be waived unless a written demand for a jury is filed within a specified time. To dispense with a jury trial in criminal cases in the federal courts the defendant must file a written waiver and secure the consent of the court and the government. There is considerable variety in the state courts as to the procedure required to effectuate a waiver of jury trial.

THE TRIAL-COURT CALENDAR

When a case has passed through its pleading and pre-trial stages it is put on the trial-court calendar. This does not mean that the case will be promptly tried. It may be if the court is in a rural area, but it may take four or five years for the case to work its way up the calendar if the court is in a metropolis. Efficient management of the trial court as a means of combating court congestion is one of the problems of judicial administration. Should jury and nonjury cases have separate calendars? Should contract cases share the same trial lists with personal injury litigation? Where there is a multiple-judge bench, should there be centralized calendar control or should each individual judge be responsible for the cases assigned to him? These are questions which are receiving different answers in different courts, and there is considerable experimentation in an effort to find better ways to reduce or eliminate the backlog of untried cases. Voices are also being raised—as yet unheeded—suggesting more radical measures, such as abolition of the jury in civil cases or the removal of automobile personal injury litigation from the courts and placing it in an administrative tribunal under a system similar to workmen's compensation.

PROCEDURE AT THE TRIAL

Nonjury trials are in most respects similar to jury trials, the most significant difference being that the judge, in addition to his normal duties, performs the fact-finding function which is the traditional province of the jury. We shall, therefore, consider the jury trial.

The first step, when the lawyers for the parties have answered "ready," is the selection of the jury. (By way of flashback it should be remarked that weeks or months before the trial date, court officials have been at work to select a list of persons who meet the statutory qualifications for jury service, have sent out notices to them to appear for examination, have screened them for disqualifications, exemptions, and excuses, have chosen by random a sufficient number of the survivors to make up a panel, and sent them summonses to appear in court at the opening of the trial term.) When counsel answers "ready" the judge tells the clerk to "call the jury." As names are called at random from a jury wheel, the prospective jurors take their places in the jury box, where they are put under oath to answer questions touching their qualifications to serve. These questions may be put by the judge as well as by the two lawyers. A prospective juror whose answers disclose a relationship or business interest with one of the parties or a strong bias or prejudice about the case will be removed. This is called a *challenge for cause.* The number of challenges for cause is unlimited. Each side also has a certain number of *peremptory challenges,* fixed by local statute, which may be exercised by counsel without assigning any reason. When finally a total of twelve jurors have survived both types of challenge, they are sworn to try the case.

The party who has the burden of proof has the right to open and close. This will normally be the plaintiff. It is an important right, since it gives the plaintiff the first opportunity to make an impression on the jury and the last word in argument after the evidence has been presented.

The opening statement of counsel for the plaintiff is primarily for the benefit of the jury. The judge is presumably familiar with the case, but the jury has been selected for its impartiality, and it does not know about the case. The purpose of the opening statement is to give the jury an outline of what the plaintiff intends to prove at the trial, so that the jurors will understand the relevance of the testimony as it is introduced. When the plaintiff's counsel has finished, counsel for the defendant may make an opening statement or, with the permission of the court, may reserve his opening statement for a later time.

The introduction of the evidence is the most time-consuming part of the trial. Each party is permitted to produce his witnesses and question them regarding their knowledge of the case, and each is entitled to cross-examine the other's witnesses. As a general proposition, any evidence relevant to the case is admissible, provided that the witness is a competent one, and speaks of his own knowledge. "Hearsay" evidence is not admissible unless it can be brought within certain well-recognized exceptions. Photographs, letters, bills, receipts, hospital records, and other documentary evidence may be admitted, if relevant, after they have been properly authenticated. Expert-opinion evidence may be received in relation to medical and scientific matters.

When the plaintiff has completed the presentation of his evidence he "rests." At this point, if the defendant feels that the plaintiff has failed to prove a case, he may move the court to dismiss the case or to direct the jury to return a verdict for the defendant. Such motions are made and argued outside the presence of the jury to prevent any possible prejudice if the motions are denied. In ruling on such a motion, the judge is required to view the evidence in the light most favorable to the plaintiff and is permitted to grant the motion only if he feels that reasonable minds could not differ on the inadequacy of the plaintiff's case. If the motion is granted, the jury is discharged and the trial is over. If the motion is overruled, the jury is recalled, and the defendant proceeds with the presentation of his defense. At the conclusion of the entire evidence the defendant may renew his motions.

Summation, or closing argument by counsel, follows the normal trial sequence: plaintiff, defendant, plaintiff's rebuttal. There are no limitations upon eloquence, but counsel are required to "stay within the record." In other words, they may not argue matters which do not find some support in the evidence introduced at the trial. They may not argue points of law. That is the province of the judge, who supplies the jury with the necessary law of the case in his *charge* to the jury. The charge is usually given following the arguments of counsel, and the jury then retires to consider its verdict.

There are two types of verdict, general and special. A *general* verdict is one which simply finds for one party or the other. If for the plaintiff, it fixes the amount of his recovery. To render a general verdict the jury is supposed to assess the conflicting evidence and "find the facts," to which it then applies the law which has been given to it by the judge. How well or how poorly the jury performs this function is difficult to say, since the deliberations of the jury are secret, and it is not required to give reasons for its verdict. A *special* verdict is one in which the jury simply finds the facts (usually in the form of answers to questions formulated by the court), leaving to the judge the task of applying the law to the facts. Theoretically, the special verdict is superior since it eliminates the chance of misunderstanding or misapplication of the law by the jury and minimizes the influence of prejudice and sympathy. Curiously, however, the special verdict has never been popular and it is seldom used.

Even after the verdict has been returned and filed, there is a limited amount of time available within which the losing party may prepare and file motions to set aside the verdict, to grant him a new trial, or to grant him judgment notwithstanding the jury's verdict. The court will permit counsel to argue in support of these motions, but if they are overruled the court will then enter a judgment in conformity with the verdict. From this judgment the losing party may appeal, or he may negotiate a settlement of the case even at this late date, or he may pay the judgment. If none of these things happens, and if it was the plaintiff who won, he must go about the business of trying to collect the judgment, which should not prove too difficult if the defendant is insured or is a person of substantial means. The processes of the law are there to help him collect the judgment. There are times, however, when a plaintiff must reluctantly admit that you can't get blood out of a turnip.

Before We Sleep

The foregoing description of our court systems and our judicial process suggests two things: 1) there has been improvement over the years, painfully slow at times, but happily greatly accelerated in recent decades; and 2) there is still much room for improvement. We still suffer from serious defects and weaknesses. Jurisdictional disputes between state and federal courts have plagued us from the beginning. Some friction is inherent from the very nature of our dual system, but it can and must be further minimized. The American Law Institute is engaged in a study in this area which shows promise. Complexity of structure in state court systems, resulting in intra-state jurisdictional disputes, waste, inefficiency, and confusion remains a serious problem. Here, again, reform is proceeding, but at a pace which is too slow in this modern day and age. The American Bar Association has prepared a Model State Judicial Article which may encourage states to undertake the difficult task of constitutional amendment, which is usually necessary for court reform.

It is not enough, however, to redraft a state constitution to provide for a simplified court structure. It must be made to work. The administration of justice is now big business and can profit from the introduction of modern business methods. This was recognized in the federal court system in 1938 with the creation by Congress of the Administrative Office of the United States Courts. The movement to centralize responsibility for court administration has spread to approximately half of the states. One of the many things which a court administrator can do is to make the most efficient use of judicial manpower by transferring judges to places where they are most needed; but this he cannot do unless the state has an integrated court system. The two types of reform should go together.

In addition to these matters of court structure and administration, and of paramount importance, is the matter of the quality of the judiciary at all levels in the system. This requires a restudy and re-evaluation of our current methods of judicial selection, together with the related problems of tenure, compensation, and removal. Finally, there remains the never-ending task of improving the rules of procedure which the judges must use as tools in fashioning justice in individual cases. Judges, lawyers, and law teachers, in their public utterances, often point with pride to the reforms in judicial administration which have occurred during the past fifty years. Viewed in the perspective of the sluggish centuries of the common law, such pride may be justified, or at least pardoned. Progress, however, is a relative thing, and pride in the past should not blind us to the needs of the present and the future. If we might borrow and adapt a phrase of a great American poet, we have "miles to go before we sleep."

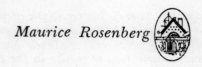

Maurice Rosenberg

2

Court Congestion:
Status, Causes, and Proposed Remedies

"The sooner the courts settle down and deal on the basis of fact and actuality with a vehicle which has revolutionized the business and the pleasure of the civilized world, the better it will be, not only for society but for the courts." These words are taken not from a contemporary treatise but from an opinion of the Supreme Court of Kansas in an early automobile accident-personal injury case, decided forty-seven years ago. How far are we, almost a half-century later, towards fair and administrable solution of the problems imposed on the trial courts of the United States by the remorseless flow of automobile accident-personal injury litigation?

This chapter is a comprehensive analysis of the many and varied procedural devices that have been tried or suggested to reduce the congestion and delay that prevail in the trial courts of every great American city. The drive against court delay has accomplished no breakthrough, the author concludes, but that has not been for want of trying. The quest for solutions continues, determined and undiscouraged. High-court judges and university legal scholars are working in closer partnership than ever before, and the new techniques of behavioral science research are being made use of in intensive studies of the delay problem and in the experimental testing of proposed "delay killers."

MAURICE ROSENBERG *is a professor of law at Columbia University and was for many years Director of the Project for Effective Justice. He is a co-author of casebooks in civil procedure and conflict of laws and has written many articles analyzing the causes and possible cures of court delay in personal injury litigation. His most recent book is* The Pretrial Conference and Effective Justice: A Controlled Test in Personal Injury

Litigation *(1964)*. *Justice Clark of the Supreme Court, in his preface to this book, said of Professor Rosenberg that "he is truly an extraordinary man whose efficacious methods have left a tremendous imprint upon the administration of justice in the trial courts of our country."*

On the twelfth day of 1965 a *New York Times* headline made it official that courts spiritual are also burdened by an affliction well known to courts temporal. It said:

POPE PAUL EXHORTS MATRIMONIAL COURTS TO REDUCE DELAY

The dispatch reported that the Pontiff, in opening the judicial year of the Sacred Roman Rota, warned that "culpable delay" in the tribunal's dispensing of justice is "in itself an act of injustice." The court members, he urged, must strive to avoid delays in handling matrimonial cases.

If the pace of justice lags in the Sacred Rota in Rome, it is a fair surmise that it also limps at times in the courts of Islam and Israel and everywhere else. It is also a fair guess that the spiritual courts, like their secular opposites, are not encountering lagging justice for the first time in their history. Court congestion—delay, strictly speaking—is not something that came in with sputnik. Hammurabi denounced it; Shakespeare immortalized it: Hamlet, in compiling his dolorous list of the burdens of man, sandwiched the "law's delay" between the "pangs of dispriz'd love" and the "insolence of office." English Chancery delay made Bleak House one of the best known edifices in English literature and made Dickens a leading law reformer. Paradoxically, German court delay, scholars tell us, led Goethe to give up the law for letters.[1]

For all its long, disreputable history and its ubiquity, court delay as a problem never before reached the pinnacle of notoriety it has achieved in this generation in this country. In the nineteenth and early twentieth centuries there had been sporadic commissions of inquiry into court delay, which even then was recognized as a chronic disease. These flurries of interest tended in the main to agitate changes in the general rules of procedure; then they subsided. The present furor is different both in its intensity and its stress on specifics and betterment of court administration as the key approaches.

By about 1950 the impact on courts of the explosions of the human and the case populations became manifest. Manifest at the same time was the ascendancy of a new philosophy of the role of judges, holding that it is as much a part of judicial responsibility to administer the courts effectively as to decide the cases wisely. In part, the new outlook is a complement to basic changes in procedural doctrine to permit easy

[1] Zeisel, Kalven, and Buchholz, *Delay in the Court* at xxii-xxiv n.6 (1959) [hereinafter cited *Delay in the Court*].

pleading, easy amendment, and easy discovery, with attendant risks that a lawsuit may produce waste or abuse if left to the unsupervised control of the lawyers. In 1938 the Federal Rules of Civil Procedure had confirmed the coming of age of the new procedural philosophy. It was in that context that a decade or so later the custodians of American justice looked closely at the way the civil courts were discharging their duties—and recoiled. Major tribunals in urban centers appeared in danger of being swamped by waves of new lawsuits as these added their volume to an overabundance of old ones already clamoring for judicial attention. In some populous counties litigants with serious disputes were forced to wait several years to bring their case before a judge and jury. Among eminent judges and bar leaders the conviction grew that unless quick action were taken many courts would capsize in the flood of their work. In 1958 the Chief Justice of the United States used crisis language to describe the situation:

> Interminable and unjustifiable delays in our courts are today compromising the basic legal rights of countless thousands of Americans and, imperceptibly, corroding the very foundations of constitutional government in the United States.

It is a comment upon the intensity of the hubbub over congestion that those words of the Chief Justice are probably cited more often than any other statement he has made. Scarcely a book or article on court delay fails to quote it—more perhaps, to inspirit the faithful than to portray reality.

It was true in 1958 and it remains true today that a lot more is said about court delay than is known about it. But how thick a supporting dossier need one collect to take a stand against sin? And that is what, by common repute, delay is—an unmitigated evil. Typical assertions are that:

> Delay causes hardship. Delay brings our courts into disrepute. Delay results in deterioration of evidence through loss of witnesses, forgetful memories and death of parties and makes it less likely that justice will be done when a case is reached for trial.[2]

> . . . Excessive delay may result in the denial of reparation for wrongs. It may force parties into unjust settlements.[3]

> Prolonged and unjustified delay is the major weakness of our judicial systems today.[4]

[2] *O'Donnell v. Watson Bros. Transportation Company*, 183 F. Supp. 577, 581 (N.D. Ill. 1960).
[3] [1957] 4 N.Y. Temp. Comm. on the Courts 9, N.Y. Legis. Doc.6(c).
[4] *Ten Cures for Court Congestion*, 9.

Besides permitting evidence to deteriorate, memories to dull, witnesses to vanish or die, and besides forcing parties into unfair settlements, delay is said to nurture a sense of injustice because of long periods of "denial and uncertainty." When a man suffers deprivation of money this year, the wrong is not erased by paying him his due in three years. Delay breeds cynicism about justice. We become used to the wrong and accept it.

Everyone understands in a general way what is meant by delay in reference to the court process: the period of waiting litigants must endure as they take their place in a long queue inching its way toward judgment. Although it is the vogue to equate "delay" with "congestion," I prefer to reserve the latter term to describe the condition of a court with a huge volume of cases, regardless of whether or not they experience delay as they wend their way to termination. A good example of "speedy congestion" is to be found in metropolitan traffic courts, where a hundred alleged violators may pack into one courtroom and be adjudicated guilty with hardly more delay than it takes to tell. High-volume courts may find it positively useful to accumulate masses of cases on their trial dockets in order to prevent breakdowns or gaps in the flow of cases to courtrooms. In the interests of efficiency, some courts may purposely create congestion. No court would deliberately create delay.

Defining and Measuring Delay

Colloquial meanings aside, the term "delay" in the context of courts and court calendars is used in two different senses. One refers to the waiting time exacted of litigants who are ready and eager to go ahead when the court is not because other cases have priority. That is court-system delay.[5] The other kind is the delay which the lawyers create through their own unreadiness or unwillingness to proceed. That is lawyer-caused delay.

COURT-SYSTEM DELAY

With regard, first, to "systemic" delay, it is an oddity of the subject that there is no shorthand way of stating with meaningful accuracy how much of it exists in the federal and state courts of the country.

[5] Kalven, *The Bar, The Court, and The Delay*, 328 Annals 37, 38 (1960): ". . . What we mean primarily by the problem of court congestion is the problem of 'system' delay, such that even though the parties are ready and anxious to try their case the court system cannot accommodate them promptly because there are other controversies waiting ahead of them for the court's time. . . ." Systemic delay also exists in obtaining decisions after trial and in appeal proceedings, but these affect relatively few cases compared to delayed trials. See generally Vanderbilt, *Improving the Administration of Justice—Two Decades of Development*, 26 U. Cin. L. Rev. 155 (1957).

It would be simple if each jurisdiction decreed that all cases entering its courtroom must form a single line, advance in the sequence of their filing and receive a trial in regular turn. That does not happen. No court can make the statement: "Delay in this court is one year; every case assigned for trial today was filed just twelve months ago." That would be a clear and uniform measure of delay, but it is an ideal we must do without.

To begin with, there are differences from court to court regarding the stage of its career when a case first comes to the court's attention. In most jurisdictions a lawsuit must be filed and entered on the court's docket at the very outset. In other states, notably New York, it is not brought to the Supreme Court's attention until the litigants formally demand a trial. Moreover, some categories of cases—particularly jury personal injury suits—are segregated from other categories and move at different rates toward trial. Besides, some cases in the same line become involved in lengthy pre-trial skirmishing—motions, discovery, even appeals—while others do not. Some cases are adjourned by consent of the litigants and lose their places on the conveyor bound for trial; others the court places on an express line by awarding them preference for prior trial.

Even if there were no different lines for different types of cases and even if there were no dropping back or leap-frogging, it would not be possible to describe court delay throughout the country except in the most relative, temporary, and general terms. Further, in a given court and in a given category of cases the interval from ready-for-trial to actual trial may fluctuate markedly from year to year, or indeed at various terms in a single year. Delay is a complex matter, and it is necessary to deal with limited aspects of it in order to make meaningful statements about it.

Among groups seriously engaged in measuring court system delay, views vary regarding the proper starting point. Some say from time of filing, others from the date the case is ready for trial. The yardstick which has gained wide acceptance is the one used by New York University's Institute of Judicial Administration, the nation-wide leader in compiling court delay statistics since 1953. Rather than reckoning delay from the time a lawsuit is commenced, the Institute and most other authorities use the interval between the date when the case is "at issue" and the date when it reaches trial.[6] For a given court the reported figure

---

[6] Green, *The Situation in 1959,* 328 Annals 7, 9 (1960): *cf.* [1957] 4 N.Y. Temp. Comm., *op. cit. supra* n.3, at 10. As of 1959 Professor Green reported (*supra* at 19):

> . . . In the federal courts this period varies from 4.1 months to 39.1 months. During the seven-year period from 1953 to 1959 the trend in individual federal courts has varied, but on the whole there has been an increase of delay from 7.5 months to 11 months. In the state courts, where the delay varies from 1.0 month to 52.9

commonly is based upon the time required by cases which reach trial in "normal" or "regular" order—that is, cases proceeding as fast as the line moves, with no artificial lags and no preferential speedups. Alternatively, the reported figure may show the average waiting time of *all* cases, including the ones that dallied or received priority.

But since it is true in every civil court that the vast majority of suits are terminated short of trial, it turns out that none of the routinely compiled figures on delay deal with the larger part of the case population. It is as if life expectancy tables for humans were based on only those who died with their boots on.

Besides differences of view regarding the proper point to begin and the proper cases to count when measuring delay, opinions split on how long the delay must last in order to be rated "excessive." In the personal-injury field—where delay is mainly centered—some lawyers urge that a lapse of a year, far from being excessive, may be indispensable because a serious injury does not show its full extent and effects for a year or more. Yet the over-all judgment of the leaders of the Attorney General's Conference on Court Congestion and Delay in Litigation and of the Judicial Conference of the United States was that delay is excessive if it exceeds six months. This was found too strict a standard by a special American Bar Association committee, which concluded that a court has a delay problem when the "lapse between filing and judgment exceeds 2 years."

Focusing on personal injury suits, I suggest that a meaningful measure of delay must convey two dimensions. It must not only tell how long the "normal" or "average" delay is for cases that persist all the way to trial. It must also disclose what percentage of all injured suitors who ultimately received payment had to wait x months, 2x months, 3x months, and so on, for their money. The figures must tell us how many people waited how long for reparation.

For New York City those figures, and more, are available as a result of research by the Columbia University Project for Effective Justice. They show that in a recent year, of 193,000 persons who tried to get compensated for negligently caused injuries, about 23,000 had to wait more than twenty-four months for payment. That was 14 per cent of those who ultimately recovered something. Giving further depth to the figures is the finding that the more disabling the plaintiff's injuries (and hence the greater his probable need for quick payment), the longer

---

months, there has also been a variance in individual courts, but the over-all picture shows a decrease in delay from 11.5 months to 10.1 months. As of 1959, both the federal courts and the state courts are suffering from excessive delays in the trial of civil cases, but the state courts are showing more progress in solving the problem than are the federal courts.

his wait was likely to be.[7] In Michigan, research by a University team has developed a similar pattern—longer delay for serious than for trivial injuries.[8]

It seems clear, in summary, that most statistics on court-system delay do no more than feel the patient's forehead, without regard to whether it has been standing in the sun or the meat cooler. The trouble is that the skin temperature readings are then treated as if they were diagnostically infallible. Worse, they form the basis for prescribing powerful nostrums, some of which are themselves likely to give the patient hot flushes and high fever.

DILATORY LAWYERS

Even in a court which dispatches its business promptly, vintage cases are often uncorked at trial. The aging was done by the litigants or their lawyers. Plaintiffs have been known to dally before getting or following advice to sue and, for their part, defendants are not notorious for efforts to avoid slowdowns and stalling in bringing cases to trial. From studies so far made, however, it does not seem that clients' delay is a major factor in slowing justice, and we may put it aside.

The same is not true of their lawyers' practices, certain of which slow the disposition pace seriously, and do so even in undelayed court systems. A recent noteworthy study of the Pennsylvania courts, *Dispatch and Delay,* found that in five of nine randomly picked cases in Pittsburgh, attorneys added an extra year to the disposition time by tardiness in filing papers. Over a century ago in Great Britain, we are told, the *Edinburgh Review* complained that there is "scarcely a moment of delay which is not contrived to minister either to the ease or the profit of lawyers, if not to both." Echoes of that accusation are heard in amplified volume today. It is said that at times it suits the purpose of a lawyer to have delay—either because it assures him of an inventory of work ahead or because he can manipulate it for tactical advantage. Perhaps both points were in the mind of the defense lawyer who complained that "plaintiffs' lawyers stack up suits like airplanes and bring them in when they're clear." [9]

The bad habit is not one-sided. Defense counsel have been known to indulge their self interest by use of a different form of delay—postpon-

---

[7] Rosenberg and Sovern, *Delay and the Dynamics of Personal Injury Litigation,* 59 Colum. L. Rev. 1115, 1121-1124 (1959).

[8] Conard, Morgan, Pratt, Voltz, and Bombaugh, *Automobile Accident Costs and Payments* (1964).

[9] Banks, *The Crisis in the Courts,* 64 Fortune 86, 93 (1961).

ing settlement until the case reaches a trial courtroom. For instance, *Dispatch and Delay* reported:

> . . . There is evidence that a significantly large number of cases in Allegheny County are settled only after a jury is sworn in order to allow the attorney to collect his fee for a "day" in court. . . .

When one lawyer ask for a continuance, his adversary usually goes along in deference to what the late Chief Justice Vanderbilt of New Jersey called "the prevailing custom of professional courtesy of lawyers toward each other." Even if the court is prepared to refuse to play the game of suiting its trial schedule to the convenience or tactics of counsel, it may have trouble forcing the issue. If one of the trial attorneys points out that he has a prior commitment to trial in another case in another court, the difficulty goes beyond tactics or ease of counsel. That exposes the most serious reason of all for lawyer delay—the heavy concentration of trial work in a tight coterie of litigation specialists. Simultaneous demands for trial assignments frequently arise and courts tend to accept the plea of a conflicting trial engagement as a good ground for continuance. Then, as Professor Harry Kalven, Jr. has pointed out, "if the granting of the continuances causes gaps in the trial schedule, . . . the concentration of the bar will have a genuine impact on delay." On the other hand, if the court's capacity to try cases is not diminished by the adjournment, its sole effect is to delay the adjourned case. Waiting time for other cases is not increased, and may even be reduced.[10]

A backlash of too narrow a trial bar may be interference with pre-trial conferences. Overloaded trial specialists sometimes disregard court rules requiring that counsel who will conduct the trial shall appear at the pre-trial conference; they send junior associates instead. This allegedly has a "killing effect" on achieving the aims of the pre-trial procedure. Yet, says Chief Justice Joseph Weintraub of the New Jersey Supreme Court, to insist that the trial lawyers themselves attend the pre-trial conference would "tie up the trial time in other counties." [11] Rather than permit that to happen, many courts look the other way when the trial lawyers absent themselves from pre-trial conferences.

Eliminating delay that serves the lawyer's purposes will be difficult, considering how strong are their attachments to it. Professor Alfred Conard has offered a pessimistic appraisal of the problem in one of its aspects:

> Even if it were possible to elect enough judges, build enough courtrooms, and draft enough jurors to cut down the trial backlog, a part of the problem

[10] Zeisel, *Delay by the Parties and Delay by the Courts*, 15 Jour. Leg. Ed. 27, 33 (1962).
[11] Rosenberg, *The Pretrial Conference and Effective Justice* 87 (1964). [hereinafter cited *The Pretrial Conference*].

would remain uncorrected. Lawyers would still threaten to hold out until trial as a bargaining device when they think the nerves or resources of the opponent are unequal to their own. . . .[12]

It is important to understand that to the extent that delay is not attributable to court system failures but to dilatory lawyers, the corrective measures must be different. An analogue from the daily life of subway riders may elucidate.

Suppose that at rush travel hours people must wait their turn to board subway trains because there are more passengers on the platforms than the trains can accommodate. To spare the passengers lengthy waiting, it is theoretically possible to add more trains, lengthen platforms, or even increase tracks. But if one reason that delays arise is that the passengers are slow about moving into the trains, or across the platforms, or if they hold open the doors for latecomers, the mere abolition of system delay will not solve the passenger-caused delays.

There are many suggestions for steps to get rid of lawyers' delay, as well as dozens of plans, "cures," and "remedies" for court-system delay. I propose to examine some of the major suggestions, after a brief analysis of the dynamics of the problem.

Delayed Trials: of "Causes" and "Remedies"

Trials are few, settlements are legion. Despite that fact, there are good reasons for paying concentrated attention to the tried cases. First, the small percentage of suits that reach trial absorb the bulk of the court's chief resource, the time of its judges. Furthermore, the rate of flow of cases requiring trial sets the pace for the mass of others that terminate short of a full hearing. Trial delay is the main key to over-all court system sluggishness. What accounts for it?

Or is that question beside the point? We have been told on high authority that it is "an error in perspective to look for the causes of delay" because they are likely to be shrouded in the mists of the past, because the search for causes leads to blaming and accusing, and because, in any event, the burning question is not how the delay came to be but how to get rid of it. I agree entirely that we need to identify current correctives much more urgently than ancient scapegoats. Still, to understand the wherefores seems essential if we want to do more than merely paper over the problems on a temporary basis. The forces that make for delay, whatever they are, ebb and flow constantly in any court. To get any measure of control of the problem requires that we have as good an idea as possible of what the forces are and what amplifies or modulates them.

[12] Conard, *The Economic Treatment of Automobile Injuries*, 63 Mich. L. Rev. 279, 315 (1964).

Moreover, I find it awkward to try to come to close quarters with the problem without thinking of causes and consequences in at least the sense of learning whether some factors do correlate in predictable ways with more trial delay. If so, there is no need to quibble about whether we call them causes or correlatives.

Analysis must turn first to personal injury cases, which, besides being juridically bland and prone to require a jury, are so numerous and so likely to get an underallocation of court resources that they are nearly always the focus of the trouble in courts seriously in arrears in disposing of their work. It is clear that if the intake of these cases were shut off, the workload of many jammed courts would shrivel to insignificance. With sharply cut loads, the courts presumably would soon get and remain current in dispatching their dockets. In giving main attention to negligence suits, one need not forget that other classes of litigation may also suffer delay, as Pope Paul has reminded us.

The dynamics—or perhaps the word should be statics—of the subject are by now well recognized. In oversimplified terms, delay is the product of too much court business for too few judges, creating an imbalance in their work-time relationship. More precisely, systemic delay occurs when the demand made by a group of cases for courtroom processing exceeds the supply of court resources, namely, judge time, available to process them. A remedy that works is one that restores equilibrium by favorably adjusting the balance.

Every measure to relieve system delay can be classified according to its impact on the supply-demand situation. The classification process at times is arbitrary because some devices may both reduce demand and increase supply. For example, a measure which detours cases to non-judicial tribunals, as Pennsylvania's compulsory arbitration procedure does, can be classified either as a supply-side aid because it provides added personnel to conduct hearings or as a demand-reducer because it supposedly deflects cases from courtrooms. In the discussion that follows the choice of label depends upon whether the direct objective of the procedure is keeping cases out of the court process (thereby curbing demand) or enlarging the court's supply of available judicial time to handle suits that come into the court.

DECREASING THE DEMAND FOR COURT PROCESSING

It would be tedious to examine all the suggestions and proposals being advanced to keep cases out of the courts. Most of them are directed at personal injury cases and more particularly at those caused by automobiles, since in most courts these cases account for about two-thirds of the tort suits. Some of them propose attacking the deep roots of the problem

—the high volume of motor accident injuries—by training drivers in safe habits, requiring improved safety appliances, enforcing traffic laws more sternly, and the like. The proposals of interest here, however, are the ones which apply after the accident has happened. They either work directly by closing the courthouse to certain types of cases or indirectly by reducing the incentive to sue.

Among the *direct barriers* to the influx, the most dramatic are laws that strip the courts of competence over specified categories of cases, as occurred nearly half a century ago when workmen's comensation statutes removed employment injuries from the courts in most states. The famous Columbia Plan of 1932 and a group of newer proposals would similarly exclude most automobile injuries, thus eliminating their heavy demands for judge time. In the common law world, only the province of Saskatchewan has so far adopted an automobile injury compensation plan; not as a measure to relieve delay, but on substantive grounds.[13]

Examples of *indirect barriers* to court litigation are the countless rules which compress or cut off liability for negligently caused bodily injuries. Their effect on court calendars is often purely incidental to their objective of changing rights and duties. Some of the rules are judge-made, such as those allowing the defense of contributory negligence and assumption of risk, while others are legislative creations, such as the guest statutes requiring automobile passengers to prove more than simple negligence to recover against the host.

Several of the recently advanced alternatives to the present way of compensating auto victims will presumably keep accident claims from the courts by sharply reducing the monetary rewards of suit as a deliberate, not an incidental, measure to relieve overworked courts. For instance, there are plans which would abolish damage awards for pain and suffering, and prevent duplicated recoveries for an injury,[14] precisely so injured persons would have less reason to bring suit.

Other indirect obstacles to marginal damage suits are the perennial proposals to raise by large amounts the cost of filing a suit. Still others would limit the use of the contingent fee in order to discourage suits by plaintiffs who feel they have "nothing to lose, so why not sue?"

Inducing Settlements without Suit. Measures to induce settlement of injury suits range from basic revisions of the substantive law, thereby changing people's rights and duties, to minor alterations of the proce-

[13] The operation of the Saskatchewan plan is now under close field study by Dr. John F. Adams and his associates under a grant from the Walter E. Meyer Research Institute of Law, Inc.

[14] See, e.g., Keeton and O'Connell, *Basic Protection—A Proposal for Improving Automobile Claims Systems,* 78 Harv. L. Rev. 329, 363 (1964). See also Conard, Morgan, Pratt, Voltz, and Bombaugh, *op. cit, supra* n.8; Keeton and O'Connell, *A Basic Protection Insurance Act for Claims of Traffic Victims,* 2 Harv. J. Leg. 41, 42 (1965).

dures by which lawsuits are conducted. Only a handful of the widely used ones will be touched upon.

Frequently the proposals try to facilitate settlements by increasing the parties' certainty regarding whether the defendant is liable to the plaintiff. Comparative negligence rules are in that category. Instead of completely barring a recovery if the plaintiff's own fault contributed to the injury, the amount of his recovery is pared in proportion to his culpability. In theory this should warn plaintiffs not to expect maximum awards and defendants not to resist to the end in hope of total victory. The result should be to narrow the gap in their expectations and make compromise easier. Empirical studies show that the theory corresponds to the fact to some degree, but not completely. A Columbia Project survey of "before and after" experience in 1957 with the then-new Arkansas comparative negligence statute showed that while the changed rule probably increased before-trial settlements, it also tended to increase the frequency of suits, producing a standoff in respect to gain and loss in cutting the courts' burdens in personal injury cases.[15]

A vigorously urged measure to induce defendants to settle more rapidly and more often is to award interest from the time an injury is sustained instead of from the time the victim gets a judgment. The argument is that insurance companies, which at present have the use of money without interest for as long as they can avoid paying it out, would have an incentive to settle and stop the accrual of interest. In *Delay in the Court,* Zeisel, Kalven, and Buchholz do a superb job of demolishing the theory on which the proposal proceeds, by demonstrating that the interest would in effect become merely another item for the parties to bargain about.

The presence of insurance is a recurring focus of proposals to induce pre-suit settlement of motor accident cases. One plan would provide coverage to a traffic victim without regard to fault as under existing medical payment and collision coverages. Another would borrow English practices of loss-sharing, halving, and "knock-for-knock" arrangements by which each party in a two-car collision in effect trades coverage with the other and looks to his own carrier for reparation. A recent field study, *Who Sues in New York City?,* proposes a simplified scheme of claims processing by insurance companies to avoid suits.

By far the most ambitious and imaginative insurance plan for handling automobile injury claims is the recently developed "basic protection" concept advanced by Professors Robert F. Keeton and Jeffrey O'Connell.[16] Its core idea is to cover actual economic losses up to $10,000

---

[15] Rosenberg, *Comparative Negligence in Arkansas: A "Before and After" Survey,* 13 Ark. L. Rev. 89, 102 (1959); reprinted in 36 N.Y. Bar Journal 393
[16] Keeton & O'Connell, *op. cit. supra* n.14.

without allowing duplicate reparation and without regard to fault, while preserving the present tort system for larger claims. In its main features the basic protection proposal might be described as providing abundance without redundance.

Of the other settlement-inducing schemes, mention should be made of the proposal to copy the English practice of awarding the winning party not merely trivial court costs, but the fees of his attorney, as a charge against the loser. A more restrained suggestion is to allow a party to recover legal fees only in flagrant circumstances, such as unreasonable refusal of his offer to settle at a named figure.

ENLARGING AVAILABLE JUDICIAL RESOURCES

On the supply side of the courts' time-work equation, there are again both direct and indirect approaches. First and foremost of the *direct* additives is to expand personnel resources by creating new judgeships. But as the Chief Justice of the United States has said: "We cannot expect our real strength to flow merely from expanding the judiciary, . . . our strength must come mainly from improved methods." Other approaches are to utilize overage judges for full or limited service, and allow the transfer of judges from the underworked courts to the undermanned ones. There have even been proposals to expand the judges' work time by opening court earlier and closing it later, scheduling night sessions and cutting down on the number of holidays the judges observe —especially as the weekend nears. Into the same category falls the plan which many members of the bar regard as Satan's own, the scheduling of trial sessions during the summer.

Indirect measures to improve the supply picture concentrate on shortening by various means the time required to dispose of a given load of cases. They try to achieve this by reducing judicial work in before-trial stages, by eliminating or shortening trials, and by avoiding lost time from gaps in the flow of cases into trial courtrooms. One way to do all three things is to create auxiliary adjudicative services which function within the courts but do not call upon the judges for work. A vivid example is the plan sketched by Dean Leon Green in his book, *Traffic Victims*. Automobile cases would enter the court as now, but once inside, "masters" would hear them and make an award, subject to review by a judge on request of a party. Except for that occasional review task, judges would be spared all pre-trial and trial work in automobile cases. Since, in addition, the procedure would obviously cut out all possibility of time loss to the judges from interrupted work flow, it would indirectly augment the supply of court time in all three ways.

Similar objectives underlie the Massachusetts auditor and Pennsylvania arbitration plans, with two variations. In both procedures the cases remain in normal court channels until referral to auditors or arbitrators; and in both plans the parties are accorded the right to insist on a full court retrial if they are dissatisfied with the arbitrators' or auditors' findings. Below, each of the plans receives fuller consideration. At this point I propose to survey rather summarily other devices to save court time.

Sparing the Judges Pre-trial Work. Many states believe that auxiliary court personnel acting in limited judicial capacities can effectively relieve judges of pre-trial work. Many judges find this a congenial prospect, for they look on most aspects of the pre-trial processing of cases as too humdrum for their talents and conceive of trial work as their destiny. The best known example of a quasi-judicial functionary who takes over the pre-trial procedures is the English Supreme Court master. Shortly after issue is joined in a civil action, the master assumes complete responsibility and, in an order called a "summons for directions," maps in detail the required course of the proceedings up to the trial. His rulings are seldom appealed, almost never reversed. The judges of the Supreme Court as a result have little to do with pre-trial work and can devote their efforts to trials.

Two United States District Courts have for several years utilized "pre-trial examiners" on a more limited basis to relieve judges of the burden of conducting pre-trial conferences. Unlike the English masters, the examiners do not supplant the judge in ruling on pre-trial motions. Their function is more to conciliate or mediate than to adjudicate.

Conserving Trial Time for the Judges. A growing list of rules of "procedure" (regulating how lawsuits are to be conducted) aims to assure that even if disputes do persist to the point of suit, and even if they do enter the court process and absorb a little judicial attention in pre-trial stages, they will soon be deflected; or compromised short of trial; or at worst that the trials will be abbreviated.

Most of the "deflecting" procedures are designed to channel cases from the busier courts to the less congested ones. Almost everywhere this means shunting cases from major-jurisdiction courts to those with lower limits. In personal injury suits the channelling procedures are particularly necessary because plaintiffs have a strong tendency to enter suits in the higher-stake courts where, their attorneys believe, the same case is worth more money.[17] As a countermeasure the rules in some states permit the higher courts to transfer the undersize cases they de-

[17] A questionnaire sample by the Columbia Project at a meeting of the New York Plaintiff Trial Lawyers Association on January 24, 1959 disclosed that more than 95 per cent of the attorneys were of the opinion that the same case is worth more in a higher than in a lower court.

tect to lesser courts. Another device penalizes the practice of suing in a higher court than necessary by denying recovery of usual court costs to a plaintiff who recovers less than a lower court could have awarded. Since the penalty can attach only to cases that have gone to judgment, since relatively few cases last to that point, and since the amount of costs is usually trivial, the penalty does not work effectively. In New York, at least, another approach is to use delay itself as a penalty by placing undersize cases upon an unmoving list where they will languish, without assignment to trial, for years unless the plaintiff will scale down his demand and consent to transfer the case to a lesser court. In New York City the bar has come to refer to such dead-storage lists as a "never-never" calendar.

A second deflection method is to shunt cases to deputized adjudicators outside the court, either with or without the parties' consent. Outstanding examples of the non-consent procedure are the Massachusetts auditor and Pennsylvania arbitrator plans, both of which preserve to the litigants the option to return the case to the courts if they are sufficiently dissatisfied with the determination made to meet the conditions imposed for returning to court.

Numerous procedural devices aim at inducing settlements during the litigation. Prominent among these are broad pre-trial discovery and the practice of requiring formal pre-trial conferences. Discovery, because it increases mutual knowledge of the evidence in the case, is widely believed to be efficacious to increase the frequency of settlement. Recent findings from a nation-wide survey of federal court discovery do not bear out that assumption. Pre-trial conference procedures were adopted in many places for the purpose of avoiding trials, on the theory that a confrontation between the lawyers and judge in advance of trial would result in many negotiated compromises. Intensive research by means of a controlled official experiment in New Jersey has established that pre-trial conferences in negligence cases did not have any marked tendency to get cases settled. Furthermore, they did not observably shorten trials.[18]

One of the best conceived measures to induce compromises during personal injury suits is the practice of calling upon impartial medical experts when it appears that there will be a fierce battle between the litigants over the extent and duration of the plaintiff's injuries. The theory is that it narrows the gap between the positions of the litigants and their partisan expert witnesses to obtain the views of an eminent doctor who is neutral. This in turn may facilitate settlement or at least compress the trial.

Introduced in New York in 1952, the plan has spread to other states

---

[18] *The Pretrial Conference*, 46. See text, pp. 2-18 to 2-21.

and to some of the federal districts. In New York the Academy of Medicine and the New York County Medical Society have created a panel
of experts who are specialists in various fields of medicine, including
psychiatry and neurology. When a Supreme Court judge in his discretion believes that it would be of "material aid" to a just decision,
after consulting counsel he calls upon an appropriate specialist to examine the plaintiff and report his findings to the court. The litigants
have access to the report.

There is evidence that the settlement rate improves with use of impartial experts, but they are relatively infrequently used.

Shortening Trials. Some devices to shorten trials do so by eliminating
issues, particularly the question of fault. Others encourage or compel a
different form of trial—nonjury rather than jury, on the correct assumption that it takes substantially longer to try the same case before
a jury than before a judge alone. The most drastic measure of all is
outright abolition of the jury trial in civil actions.[19] In lieu of the
jury either a judge alone, a panel of judges, or various panels composed
of judges, lawyers, doctors, and laymen are suggested.

Less drastic proposals look toward inducing voluntary waivers of the
right to a jury trial in personal injury cases, for instance by creating a
panel of "attractive" judges known to be neither "plaintiff-minded" nor
"defendant-minded." One judge of the panel would be selected by lot
and the case would be tried before him without a jury. Other measures
seek to encourage waivers by setting a high jury fee or by deliberately
restricting the number of jury parts, so that cases bound for jury trials
experience long lines and long delay, while nonjury cases are heard
promptly.[20]

The French provide us with an interesting example of procedures
directly designed to condense the amount of proof which will be produced at the trial. Prima-facie effect is accorded to police reports (*procès
verbaux*) in automobile accident cases, to discourage introduction of
evidence on points covered by the reports.[21] The intention is apparently similar in Massachusetts, where the auditors' reports carry
prima facie weight at trial. Other trial time savers range from reforms

[19] See, e.g., Desmond, *Juries in Civil Cases—Yes or No,* 36 N.Y.S. Bar Jour. 104 (1964);
Peck, *Modernizing Trial Practice, The Economic Benefits,* 6 Buffalo L. Rev. 14, 20
(1956). See also *Jury Trial on Trial: A Symposium,* 28 N.Y.S. B. Bull. 322 (1956).

[20] In the New York County Supreme Court, delay is concentrated on the personal
injury jury calendar, while the other trial calendars are kept up to date. See *Delay in
the Court,* 7.

[21] See, e.g., Garraud, "L'utilisation, a titre de preuve, dans un procès civil, de pièces
et documents tirés d'une information pénal," *Semaine Juridique,* Part I, 317 (1943);
Ruellan, *Des Procès-Verbaux,* Doctoral Thesis, Rennes (1921).

in the rules of evidence to more active control by the judge of interrogation of witnesses, to streamlined methods for selecting the jury.

Avoiding Calendar Breakdowns. Finally, there is a battery of devices designed to conserve judge time by avoiding wasteful gaps in the flow of court work. Calendar breakdowns may occur because of dilatory tactics, unreadiness, or overcommitment by the lawyers, as I have already noted. Antidotes include the "certificate of readiness," which requires the attorney to certify that he is fully ready for trial before his case is listed; and rules limiting the number of continuances he may request and the number of cases he may place on the list at the same time.[22] A variety of rules aim at preventing oversaturation of trial attorneys and firms, the one in Cleveland's Common Pleas Court being notable in requiring that a firm with two hundred pending cases be ready for trial concurrently in two courtrooms, with three hundred cases in three courtrooms, and so on.

To avoid calendar gaps because of last minute settlements, the traditional measure is to overload the trial list so that, come what may, the judge will not be left without cases poised for trial.[23] This generates unreadiness on the part of the lawyers far down on the list, for they do not anticipate being reached and therefore do not make final preparations for trial. If the prior cases unexpectedly drop off the calendar, the overloading device is then to some extent self-defeating.

The responsibility for assuring a steady work flow in the court's operations is generally considered to be a function of calendaring. Both individual assignment and central-calendaring systems have been described as the more efficient, the former because judicial time is not wasted by having several judges review the same case before it is disposed of, the latter, because it avoids the possibility of some judges having little or no work while others are overburdened.[24] Some multi-judge courts combine the systems by operating generally on a central calendar, but assigning certain protracted and complicated cases to a single judge for processing.

[22] See General Rules, D.D.C., R.145 (d), discussed in Hart, *The Operation of the Master Calendar System in the United States District Court for the District of Columbia,* 29 F.R.D. 191, 265 (1962).

[23] See, e.g., Brennan, *Proceedings of the Attorney General's Conference on Court Congestion and Delay in Litigation,* 83 (1956); Ellenbogen, *Justice Delayed,* 14 U. Pitt. L. Rev. 1, 3 (1952); *Dispatch and Delay,* 78.

[24] See Chandler, *The Direction of Administration of Trial Courts,* 21 F.R.D. 65, 68 (1957); *Proceedings of the Attorney General's Conference on Court Congestion and Delay in Litigation,* 15, remarks of Delmar Karlen, citing Judge Vanderbilt (June 16, 17 (1958). For a general discussion of the advantages and disadvantages of both calendaring systems, see Carter, Effective Calendar Control—Objectives and Methods, 29 F.R.D. 191, 237-241 (1961).

It seems beyond argument that modern managerial methods are badly needed in busy courts to achieve a constant, efficient flow of work to the trial courtrooms. There are fortunately signs that the use of system engineering and professional managerial talent is increasing steeply.[25]

Four Major Delay Antidotes Appraised

Of the suggested remedies for court delay which have been frequently and seriously urged, four are evaluated here: 1) the split-trial procedure, 2) the pre-trial conference, 3) compulsory arbitration of small claims, and 4) hearings before auditors. Each of these procedures has been tried out in one or more courts and has come under systematic investigation by "outside" observers, unconnected with the court system which adopted it. Each procedure is used in personal injury suits and is designed primarily to spare courts the heavy outlay of time required for the trial of large volumes of these cases. At one time or another each of these procedures has been touted as a sure-fire cure for courts suffering from backlogged and delayed calendars.

Apart from the appointment of more judges, the measure most often urged as the ultimate solution is abolition of the right to a jury trial in civil suits. Many judges, lawyers, and citizens regard this proposal for a "final solution" to the delay problem as almost in a class with Hitler's final solution. The proposal has not yet been put into effect in any state of the Union. The English experience with virtual, but not total, abolition is, in my judgment, largely irrelevant because English laws and institutions are different in ways which bear importantly on the problem.[26]

SPLIT TRIALS

A relatively new time saver prescribed for delayed courts is the "split trial," a procedure designed to take advantage of the known fact that in personal injury trials juries being in verdicts of no liability about 40 per cent of the time. This device commands special attention because it has been carefully studied in practice by a leading authority and afterward hailed as "a uniquely powerful delay remedy" and "by far

---

[25] Arthur D. Little, Inc., *Congestion and Delay in the Court, A Preliminary Report to the Greater Philadelphia Movement* (July 1961).

[26] The English do not permit the contingent fee; "contributory negligence" is applied universally in negligence cases with the result that damages are apportioned according to fault; the bar is extremely small and close-knit by American standards; and insurance practices are different in major respects. Of transcendent importance, judges are few in number, essentially nonpolitical and enjoy the confidence of the bar to an extent not generally true in the United States.

the most forceful remedy for court congestion" of all those recently devised or revived.[27]

In an ordinary unified personal injury trial, a verdict for the defendant implies that in the jurors' deliberations they never had to reach the question of how much money to award the plaintiff, hence all the damage evidence they heard and saw was wasted on them. A split trial in theory avoids this waste in two categories of trials: in the 40 per cent or so of the hearings in which the defendant is let off; and in some fraction of the other 60 per cent because, when confronted in those cases with a verdict of liability, the defendant will come to terms and settle on the damage issue. In either event, so the theory runs, the court will enjoy the substantial time saving of avoiding damage proof.

Professor Hans Zeisel prophesied early in 1960 that separating the liability and damage issues in negligence trials would save at least 20 per cent of the court's trial time.[28] His prediction was reported to be confirmed by his and an associate's findings after close study of the splitting procedure at work in the United States District Court for the Northern District of Illinois for the two year period (1960-61) after it had been introduced on the court's own initiative. By a variety of converging statistical approaches the study arrived at the conclusion that in personal injury trials a net of about 20 per cent of the trial time was in fact saved.

This is not the place to analyze in detail Zeisel's ingenious research methods or his conclusions. Suffice it to say that a careful review of the report embodying the data from the research on the splitting procedure is persuasive that:

1) Splitting personal injury trials on a selective, not routine, basis in the District Court for Northern Illinois did apparently result in some saving of court time compared with what would have been expected as time costs under normal unified trial procedures.[29]

2) The amount of the saving from route installment trials should be estimated—if warrant is sought in the data—at substantially less than 20 per cent of the time absorbed by the regular method of trial.

[27] Zeisel and Callahan, *Split Trials and Time Saving: A Statistical Analysis*, 76 Harv. L. Rev. 1606, n.2 (1963); Zeisel, *Splitting Liability and Damage Issue Saves 20% of the Court's Time*, A.B.A. Section of Insurance, Negligence and Compensation Law 356 (1963).

[28] Zeisel, *The Jury and the Court Delay*, 328 Annals 46, 52 (1960).

[29] Of 186 personal injury jury trials during the survey period, the judges ordered installments trials in 69, or 37 per cent. The reasons for splitting or not are unknown, but it presumably was "purposeful." Zeisel and Callahan, *op. cit. supra* n.27 at 1611-1612; 1616-1619.

3) Whatever the amount of the saving, the splitting procedure has a pro-nounced substantive backlash.

The last point is not dealt with directly in the Zeisel report, which did, however, frankly recognize that there are questions concerning "the possible effect of separation on the substance of the jury verdicts" and that these should be "included in an over-all appraisal of the rule." The authors said they had postponed the matter for discussion in a later report, conditioned on developing significant data.

Even with no additional data, any plaintiffs in routine personal injury cases who read the figures appearing in the Zeisel report ought to re-gard splitting as a headache. Beyond any doubt, the separated trial procedure introduces loaded changes into the process by which the jury deliberates. No one can calculate precisely what differences it makes for the result of a particular case, to blindfold the jury to the damage evidence when it determines liability, but there can be no question from the Chicago data that, as an actuarial matter, two-stage trials produce more verdicts for defendants than unified trials would have produced in the same group of cases.

Under the normal integrated procedures, as Zeisel, Kalven, and Buchholz report in *Delay in the Court,* "in some 40 per cent of all personal injury suits tried to completion, there is a verdict for de-fendant." As earlier indicated, that is a widely observed norm in many courts and it is true in the Chicago court for the regularly tried suits, which produced non-liability verdicts in 42 per cent of the cases which were tried to completion.[30] We might have expected a similar rate of defense records in the remainder of the cases, but for the separated trials the figure rocketed to 79 per cent. A comparison of the percentages gives some sense of the distortion in results that may ensue when merely "procedural" changes are introduced for efficiency's sake with-out regard to their substantive impact. Professor Jack B. Weinstein's warning seems most apt:

> . . . The bifurcation rule . . . has within it potentialities for a major change in the relative position of plaintiffs and defendants in negligence cases and the rule cannot be appraised merely by procedural efficiency tests which might be appropriate for other proposed procedures.

Juries, as Kalven has told us, in fixing the amount of damages to award, "may simply fuse the liability and damage issues." A similar fusion may take place when they determine liability. Converting the

---

[30] Zeisel and Callahan, *op. cit. supra* n. 27 at 1617, Table 6. In New Jersey and New York City samples of personal injury verdicts showed that almost exactly 40 per cent were returned for defendants. *The Pretrial Conference,* 60, 148 (n.24).

process to fission by compelling a split verdict alters not only the size of the end reaction, but also its quality. A competent law-making body might deliberately determine that such a change is desirable, either to discourage compromise verdicts that may unduly favor plaintiffs, or to expedite trials, or for both purposes. As long as the legislature were aware of the substantive consequences of adopting the splitting procedure as a routine technique, its action would be prima facie defensible. Definitely not defensible, however, is an accidental or heedless tampering with the adjudicative process in a way likely to distort the outcome in large groups of cases. It is even worse when the courts do the tampering (as they did in Chicago by installing the splitting procedure), for they are not the most appropriate bodies to weigh the complex values involved in shifting the substantive balance against one class or another of litigants in an area so saturated with insurance considerations.

In all, it is uncertain that a *routinely* applied splitting procedure would save substantial court time. It is manifest that it risks appreciable distortion of substantive rights as an unlooked-for side effect. As a cure for delay it ought to be regarded as too heroic for use, at least until a way is found to test and evaluate its effect upon the outcome of the trial.

THE PRE-TRIAL CONFERENCE

In 1959, *Ten Cures for Court Congestion* named the pre-trial conference "Cure One," and it is at the top of many other lists of remedies. In 1960, it was described as "the salvation of the administration of justice in the twentieth century." [31] Equally distinguished authorities stressed the tendency of "pre-trial" to improve the ensuing trial by eliminating surprise, sharpening issues, and increasing the litigants' mutual knowledge of the case. This was the official view in New Jersey, the first state to make pre-trial compulsory in nearly all categories of civil suit.

Pre-trial's dynamics in its usual form are simple. When a case is well on its way to trial, the court calls the lawyers to a formal conference, in an effort to round the case into shape and improve its presentation at trial. It is claimed that even if settlement is not a deliberate objective of the pre-trial conference, settlement will often result from the trial-shaping activities. Pre-trial also allegedly saves court time by shortening any trials that do take place, in part by inducing jury waivers. The time thus saved may then be spread by the judges to other cases, with the end result a quickened dispatch of court business.

[31] Wright, *The Pretrial Conference, Seminar on Practice and Procedure,* 28 F.R.D. 37, 141, 157 (1960).

Not all lawyers would agree with these claims. Many have criticized pre-trial as a waste of time, particularly in personal injury cases. They contend that the issues are routinely simple and that neither efficiency goals nor improved trials are realized by pre-trial conferences.

In 1959, when the state bar launched a serious effort to cut out pre-trial in accident cases, Chief Justice Joseph Weintraub of New Jersey asked the Columbia Project to make a study of the effects of the mandatory system in those cases. There resulted the first official controlled experiment in the administration of civil court processes. A major purpose was to determine whether the pre-trial conference did in fact substantially reduce the court time required to handle personal injury suits.

As part of the experiment the Supreme Court suspended the rule requiring that all personal injury cases go through a pre-trial conference. In seven test counties, for six months starting January 4, 1960, every other case was given a pre-trial, and the alternate ones were not unless one or both lawyers requested a conference. Thus the second group of cases served as a statistical "control" group. During the next six months, a total of 3,000 cases were processed under the alternating plan. By 1962 they had run their courses, either settlement or reaching trial. Through detailed follow-up, a mass of information was obtained from the judges, lawyers, and clerks concerned with the test cases, and the facts were assembled, tabulated by electronic computers, and analyzed.

Three main sets of findings emerged. They may for brevity be expressed as a loss, a gain, and a difference, all attributable to the impact of the pre-trial conference when used across-the-board instead of under the experimental setup.

1) The loss was in efficiency. It developed that the universal pre-trial program absorbed appreciable quantities of judge time; that the settlement rate (76 per cent) was no higher than for the group of cases used as a statistical control; that trials were not shorter; and that juries were not waived frequently. The conclusion reached was that if New Jersey abandoned the compulsory pre-trial requirement in all personal injury cases and went over to the reduced basis used during the experiment, there would be a saving of roughly five per cent of available judges' time in the "law divisions" of the court, or approximately the work of two judges a year.

2) The gain was in improving the quality of the trial process in a portion of the pre-trial cases that reached trial courtrooms. According to the Columbia research team, the evidence was that pre-trial improved the process by promoting lawyer preparedness, enhancing clear presentation of the theories of the cases at trial, and curbing the frequency

with which tactical surprise or deficiencies in the evidence were noted.

3) The difference observed was in the outcome of the cases in the two groups created by the test. Average amounts recovered were noticeably higher in the group of cases which had all been through a pre-trial conference than in the control group. An irony of the finding is that it was mainly defendants (by two to one) who chose to have a pre-trial conference when none had been ordered by the court. It appears that a major result of their choice was to increase the amount of money which they had to pay in the 92 per cent of the cases wherein the plaintiff realized a recovery.

Of course, it is the first of the findings that bears directly upon the question of trial delay. Contrary to the beliefs of many eminent judges and lawyers, pre-trial conferences, when used routinely in personal injury cases, are not the answer to court delay. While they do tend to improve the litigation process, they also show evidence of changing the results by increasing plaintiffs' recoveries. The Columbia report concludes that although under some circumstances it may be useful to employ pre-trial conferences for settlement purposes, it makes more sense to use them to improve trials. This requires that they be applied selectively to types of cases in which there is a high potential yield, instead of indiscriminately and across-the-board. To perfect criteria for selecting appropriate cases, the court authorities "should incorporate means of obtaining needed knowledge through experience" and should introduce "on a limited, temporary basis built-in procedures for testing and auditing the program in operation." Similar tests, with appropriate controls, might establish means of selecting trial-bound cases. Then these could be processed in the way best calculated to minimize the drain on court time, while preserving the other values which the judicial process seeks to advance.

Influenced by the Columbia Project's findings, the New Jersey Supreme Court in September 1964 modified the state's pre-trial-conference rule by making pre-trial optional in automobile accident cases. In Missouri, in February 1965, the circuit court in Kansas City became the first to install data-collection procedures to test the feasibility of predicting which civil cases will reach trial, upon the basis of the Columbia Project's recommendations.

COMPULSORY ARBITRATION OF SMALL CLAIMS

This remedy dates from 1952, when a Pennsylvania statute authorized each county at its option to adopt by court rule a plan for compulsory arbitration of suits claiming no more than $1,000. Two-thirds of the counties adopted the program, some with the aim merely of easing the handling of minor suits, others to combat delay. In 1958, arbitration was made obligatory for suits up to $2,000 in the Philadelphia Municipal Court, which has a jurisdictional ceiling of $5,000.

A way had to be found to square the compulsory-arbitration program with the state constitutions' guarantee of trial by jury in suits at law for money damages. This was done by outflanking the problem. A dissatisfied party was permitted to return to court after going through arbitration, provided he paid a prescribed fee.

Thus the routine in Philadelphia is as follows: Within ten days after the pleadings are filed, the suit is referred to a panel of three lawyers, chosen by a court official from a list of several thousand volunteer attorneys. The arbitration hearing goes forward to an award, and if either party desires to "appeal" to court and obtain a new trial he has the right to do so upon paying the county the fees of the arbitrators, which were fixed at $85 for all three. Even if the appealing party wins in the court trial—usually before a jury and with never a mention of the preceding arbitration—he does not recoup the fees.

For Philadelphia the chief purpose of the plan was to reduce court delay for larger cases in the Municipal Court by sidetracking smaller ones to the auxiliary arbitration tribunal. Did it work, as its promoters enthusiastically assert?

A Columbia Project investigation of the Philadelphia experience covering its first twenty-two months found that the arbitration system had these results: 1) it permitted disposition of the arbitrated small cases more quickly and conveniently than by normal court proceedings, 2) it apparently spared the municipal court between 2,500 and 4,000 trials in small cases, 3) nearly three arbitration hearings were required for each trial that was saved, and 4) quite possibly about one-third of the litigants came out differently before arbitrators than they would have before a jury; juries reversed arbitrators' findings in 32 per cent of the negligence cases, usually by overturning awards for plaintiffs.

The Columbia team also concluded that the reason arbitration was effective in permanently deflecting so many cases from the court was that the typical award was for only a few hundred dollars, and neither side saw advantage in risking the $85 fee required to appeal for a new trial. There is no evidence that the scheme would work in larger cases, where the cost of returning to court either would not be out of proportion to the possible yield or would have to be set so high that it might be struck down on state constitutional grounds as an indirect prohibition of trial by jury.

No other state has adopted the Pennsylvania plan, apparently because the use of attorneys' time at bargain rates to subsidize court operations is not favored and because of misgivings as to the utility and soundness of the whole idea. In Pennsylvania itself, the legislature has declined to extend the procedure to larger claims, perhaps because it regards arbitration as "second class" justice.

It seems quite clear that for a variety of reasons going to both its wisdom and efficacy, compulsory arbitration à la Pennsylvania, though it may work in lesser courts, does not warrant adoption as an antidote for delay in major courts.

THE AUDITOR PROCEDURE

This plan is a revival of an old procedure, but with a modern accent: curbing delay by sending suits—permanently, if possible—away from the court channels they have entered, to save the time of judges. Auditors, who are akin to referees, were authorized in Massachusetts as far back as 1817 in accounting cases. However, they had been seldom used until 1935, when motor vehicle tort suits in great volume clogged the Superior Court dockets. During World War II, rationing of gasoline dried up automobile accidents and suits about them. The auditor system fell into disuse. But by 1956 trial delay had climbed to forty-eight months in one county, and the Commonwealth revived auditor references as part of a package program to speed up court dispositions.

Under this procedure Superior Court judges in their discretion send actions on their dockets to one of the eighty court-appointed auditors for hearing and report. An auditor serves about half-time in that capacity and continues to practice law the remainder of the time, but may not take motor vehicle accident cases. At a hearing he receives evidence and then renders a written report setting out the facts he has found and the legal rulings he has made. Either party may ask for a revision of the auditor's award or for a retrial in court, provided the reference was stipulated to be nonfinal. On retrial the auditors' findings are primafacie evidence and can be read to the jury. Unlike the Pennsylvania arbitration plan, the auditor procedure does not impose a cost penalty for a litigant who returns to court for a complete new hearing. Furthermore, it is used in large cases—usually, automobile-injury suits.

A Columbia Project study, based on an analysis of court records and a moderate volume of especially gathered data, found that 12 per cent of the cases heard by auditors returned to the courts for trial. Of the cases that went through retrial, about two out of five resulted in a reversal or modification of the auditor's decision. The researchers concluded that there was a marked rate of disagreement between auditors and juries in determining liability and damages, with the auditors tending to let off defendants more frequently than juries would have.

At an apparent direct expense to the public of about $90,000 a year in Suffolk County (Boston), auditors reduced the courts' work burden by the equivalent of one to two judges for each of the four years surveyed. In that period there was a dramatic drop in trial delay in the Suffolk court, but it seemed to the researchers that the auditors were a factor of limited importance in that drop.

A statistical analysis by Boston University investigators of Suffolk County's experience with auditor-heard cases in 1960-61 confirmed that referral of suits to auditors had not been effective in reducing burdens on Superior Court judges.[32] Apparently the Chief Justice of the Superior Court reached the same conclusion. In 1964 he recommended repeal of the statute under whose provisions auditors were authorized.

The two studied efforts to determine by statistical analysis the impact of auditor references on court workloads underline a difficult problem of method. In the words of the Columbia report:

> Massachusetts' recent experience in using auditors to help roll back trial delay in civil courts points up one of the toughest riddles in the enigma of delayed justice, namely, how astonishingly hard it is to tell whether a given delay "remedy" has worked or failed in practice. To some extent the men who devise the remedies help deepen the riddle of what happened by failing to provide in advance for the data that will be needed to answer that question. Their understandable attitude is that when a court is suffering from excessive delay in disposing of backlogged cases, its concern must be radical improvement, not the whys and wherefores or mechanics of the solution. They usually adopt countermeasures in packages, not singly. Afterwards, if the package as a whole has worked well, it is frustrating to try to learn which measure did what.

The epilogue to this brief review of several of the most highly praised remedies in use is clear. Mechanisms for systematic evaluation are essential for reliable appraisals of the actual effects of particular relief measures. On the evidence to date no single measure has been shown completely efficacious to roll back delay; at best, it will take many procedures to move us substantially toward a solution.

Perspectives

In the past decade ideas and events have joined as never before to push the problem of lagging civil justice to the center of the stage. For years the idea had been gaining ground among judges that they have a responsibility for the administration of lawsuits as well as for their adjudication. As this conviction steadily took hold, they abandoned their traditional laissez-faire approach for a mood of activism in

[32] Spangenberg and Neuman, Auditing the Auditor System, 44 B.U.L. Rev. 271 (1964).

managing court processes. Just about then, trial delay in major centers reached proportions which were grave by any reasonable standards. Thus the time was psychologically ripe for the judges to move forcefully, and they did. They mounted energetic attacks on the delay problem, chiefly by adopting a variety of devices that they hopefully but unprophetically dubbed "cures" or "remedies."

Meanwhile, back at the universities, a widening circle of law teachers set out to get to the roots of the problem by harnessing the new instruments of social research which the behavior scientists had been improving. A loose partnership gradually arose, with judges and bar groups busily inventing antidotes for delay, and academic researchers busily evaluating them to determine whether they work.

Viewed as a whole, the campaign has gone forward with much vigor but with no real breakthrough. There has been a definite pattern to the activity. The sponsors of a new device trumpet it as a miracle remedy, manage to get it introduced and almost instantly pronounce it a lavish success. After a time, experience and careful research deflate the premature boasts and then something new is invented. Today it can be fairly said that there is no acceptable evidence that any remedy so far devised has been efficacious to any substantial extent. Only a few of the new measures have worked even to a modest extent, and some of them have been positively counter-productive on the efficiency scale. More important, many of them have had unsuspected side effects in changing the outcome of appreciable numbers of lawsuits.

A major lesson of this chronicle is that progress in coping with the old problem of court delay will have to come from marshaling relief measures in groups, not from a one-injection miracle cure. There is no such panacea.

In spite of the failure to produce delay-killers that are truly potent, there has been important progress. We know much more than we did ten years ago about methodology: which court records to keep, which tests to make, how to analyze the data, and how to assess the results. Apparently we have also learned at last to call in qualified professionls, including systems engineers, to deal with deficiencies in the mechanical and managerial aspects of the apparatus of justice. That is as it should be, for breakdowns in scheduling, bottlenecks in a sequential process, and failures in the flow of work are not uniquely problems of courts, judges, or lawyers.

THE SWEETER USES OF DELAY

Except that delay inflicts hardships sometimes bordering on tragedy for individual suitors, one would be tempted to say in summary that on balance delay owes us nothing. If it does not provoke irreparable damage to the courts, it may in the long run help strengthen them. The furor over delay has mobilized vast activities of great promise for improving the administration of justice. The first of the indirect blessings is that the stress on the courts' day-to-day functioning has helped move a significant sector of legal research from the library to the field. It "has, indeed, marked the beginning of scientific inquiry in the area of judicial administration." [33] Crisis language about delay has also caused foundation funds to flow more generously into this area of research than would have been conceivable without the clamor. In some states the panic has helped promote long overdue increases in judicial manpower and has even aided passage of programs for modernizing the courts' structure and administration. Those developments are so welcome that perhaps one ought not to be concerned that the reformers often were too glib in promising that the reforms would roll back delay.

The agitation over lagging civil justice has also led indirectly to a variety of intriguing insights, mainly in the form of various broad observations about the impact of law in action. One is that the contents of legal rules very often do not get through to those whose actions they are supposed to shape. A vivid example of this turned up in a survey in New York City of minor personal injury accidents. When victims were asked why they had pressed claims against the other driver notwithstanding the fact that they conceded their own contributory fault, most of them showed they had no knowledge that the law declares that their own lack of care, however slight, bars recovery under the doctrine of contributory negligence. Indeed, they registered amazement amounting to disbelief that the law contained such a rule.[34] The New Jersey pre-trial study showed that even judges are at times unaware of rules they are assumed to apply almost daily. Survey findings that certain rules of law are not getting home to those they are aimed at may help us put in better perspective the limits of at least some legal rules as instruments of social control.

A second benefit is to shed light on the question of whether there are basic dynamics at work in the litigation process by which one can explain and predict, within useful limits, the movement of civil cases through the courts. At least one insight of that sort has emerged from the research on delay, namely, the "size-durability" principle, which postulates that cases with large economic stakes are much more likely to persist to trial than cases of small size.[35] Awareness of this and similar

[33] Zeisel, *Delay by the Parties and Delay by the Courts,* 15 Jour. Legal Ed. 27 (1962).
[34] Hunting and Neuwirth, *Who Sues in New York City?,* 153-180 (1962).
[35] Rosenberg and Sovern, *Delay and the Dynamic of Personal Injury Litigation,* 59 Colum. L. Rev. 1115 (1959).

correlations permits the courts to apply pre-trial procedures to the cases on a selective rather than a blunderbuss basis, thus reducing the cost and increasing the effectiveness of the process.

Thirdly, the deeper we probe into the problem of efficiency in court processes, the more apparent it becomes that the vital neglected problem is the quality, not the speed, of the processes. We have been brought face to face with the issue of which attributes are, in the last analysis, essential to well conducted civil trials. In the words of a layman, "the hard facts of delayed justice have driven responsible judges to rethink their procedures and search avidly for better ways of getting justice done." [36] For the researcher the task is to attempt to devise yardsticks of trial quality that will approach scientific standards of objectively and generality.[37]

Finally, systematic inquiry into how procedural devices function in practice has disclosed time and again that their chief effect is not so much to change the speed of the flow of cases through the courts as to change their results.

The huge energies poured into the campaign against court delay would not have been worthwhile if the gains had been limited to the dubious remedies that have resulted. Fortunately, the by-products have been substantial and promising. Building on the insights that have accumulated, we can go forward with improved research methods, exploring and, in proper circumstances, experimenting to deepen our understanding of how the law functions. It seems safe to predict that court delay will be only one of the targets in the work that stretches ahead.

COSTS AND GUIDING PRINCIPLES

Offsetting its paradoxical benefits for the administration of justice, the counterattack on trial delay has involved heavy costs—more than merely in money and effort. A serious debit has been the loss of a sense of proportion by many well-intentioned custodians of civil justice. Many of their cures for delay are much worse than the disease itself. One legislative solution is to hold up judges' salary checks, thus "fighting delays in judging with delays in paying." Some require the judges to use speed-up tactics based upon unseemly haggling and pressuring the parties to reach settlements. Sometimes the expediting techniques deliberately

---

[36] Banks, "The Crisis in the Courts," *Fortune*, Vol. 64, No. 86 (1961), 190.

[37] Measures of trial quality utilized by the Columbia University Project for Effective Justice in the pre-trial conference experiment in New Jersey were: 1) how well the case was presented under general standards of legal disputation; 2) incidence of gaps or excesses in the evidence; 3) avoidance of testimony by unnecessary witnesses; and 4) absence of maneuvering or surprise. *The Pretrial Conference*, 32.

circumvent guarantees found in constitutional or statutory provisions, with the result that the court looks devious or hypocritical. Lastly, there is the fact already mentioned that, although the expediting techniques often make sharp differences for which side wins, their promoters act unconcerned about substantive results so long as they think the lines of cases are melting away more rapidly.

In sum, among the costs of the obsession with speedier justice has been an erosion of the integrity of the judicial process from the viewpoint of the litigants and lawyers, some of whom have the impression that the courts regard their cases as merely counters in a numbers game. Slow justice is bad, but speedy injustice is not an admissible substitute. Some of the measures that have been adopted would be wrong even if they worked. Antidotes for delay must meet certain minimum tests of principle, among which are the following:

First, the measure should not often or materially warp the results of the litigation process for the parties; or, if it does, the probability of changed results should be known and acceptable as a price for added efficiency.

Second, the measure ought to operate simply as an administrative matter and inexpensively as a financial matter, in comparison to the saving that it produces. All relevant costs, both to the litigants and to the public at large, should be included in the balance.

Third, the remedy should not involve the custodians of justice in subterfuge or hypocrisy. That is, it should not do by indirection what the courts are unable or unwilling to do directly.

Finally, the remedy should not breed disrespect for the courts by giving the public an unsatisfactory impression of their fairness or good faith.

Prospects

The prospects are better than the record of meager concrete accomplishment might suggest. To start with, we now have gotten a more realistic view of what a formidable problem confronts us. False hopes of quick cures have given way to realization that steady efforts on many fronts are needed. We have a new and advancing methodology for research, not alone into problems of court efficiency, but into how to improve in basic ways the quality of the processes of justice.

We have learned humility. Ahead, the prospect is not for a sudden breakthrough that will permit all civil courts to dispense instant justice. We shall have to learn to live and cope with court delay as we must with pathology in other human processes. Dean Jefferson Fordham has put it well:

. . . The point . . . is not that it is bootless to try to do something about delay in legal action but that the disease is chronic and, as such, is not likely to respond to a facile ersatz specific. To pursue the metaphor—the affliction can be kept in bounds, but long experience and a fair appreciation of human nature do not inspire hope that a complete cure is in prospect.

The problem of delay may be old, but it is by no means obsolescent; it is complex, but not insoluble; it is stubborn, but not hopeless. In the past we have acted as if we could wage a blitzkrieg against it, but now we see that we must tool up for a long compaign of attrition. The tools we need are persistence, resolution, and a willingness to apply scientific methods of research.

Geoffrey C. Hazard, Jr.

3

After the Trial Court
—the Realities of Appellate Review

Appellate decisions, particularly those of the Supreme Court of the United States in constitutional cases, can be front-page news, but there are widespread public misapprehensions of the governing principles of appellate review of trial court decisions and of the functions of the appellate courts in the administration of civil and criminal justice. This chapter describes and analyzes the institutions and characteristics of appellate review in the United States, with particular emphasis on the problem of delay and the procedures which are or might be employed to keep the workload of the appellate courts within manageable bounds.

This discussion of the appellate courts and their work is related to and supplements the preceding analysis (Chapter Two) of trial court delays in civil suits. A claimant who has had to wait a year or more to get his case to trial, and then faces further postponement of reparation awaiting the outcome of his opponent's appeal, may well ask, with Saint Joan, "How long, O Lord, how long?" The present chapter is similarly related to the discussion in Chapter Four of the realities of criminal justice in the United States. Appeals from criminal convictions are freely available in our legal system. To what extent, if at all, does the right of appeal in criminal cases provide insurance against the dangers of injustice that may accompany today's procedures of mass-production judicial enforcement of the criminal law?

GEOFFREY C. HAZARD, JR., *the author of this chapter, is Administrator of the American Bar Foundation (the independent research affiliate of the American Bar Association) and is also a professor of law at the University of Chicago. Before moving to Chicago in 1964, he was for several years a professor of law at the University of California at Berkeley. He is*

the author (with David W. Louisell) of Cases on Pleading and Procedure: State and Federal *(1962), and his other published writings include
articles on civil practice and procedure and court reform.*

In recent years, concern about the overcrowded condition of
court dockets has focused on the trial courts, and particularly the trial
courts of general jurisdiction. Indeed, as trial court backlogs have extended into years, and as awareness has increased that the largest single
type of trial court business is the personal injury suit, "delay in court"
has become almost entirely identified with the problem of delay in automobile accident cases. A more recent anxiety has been generated by
contemplation of the consequences anticipated when *Gideon vs. Wain-
right* becomes a trial-court fact of life rather than a Supreme Court mandate. This case, decided by the Court in 1963, held that indigent felony
defendants (and indigents constitute at least half of all felony defendants)
are entitled to the assistance of counsel despite their inability to pay counsel fees themselves. It is foreseen, and rightly, that if there is any substantial increase in the number of criminal cases actually brought to trial,
which may be one consequence of Gideon's broad-scale implementation,
the already badly swamped trial courts of general jurisdiction will slowly
submerge in a sea of cases. And in viewing the system as a whole I should
say that the flood of litigation in the trial courts presents far more difficulties—in terms of rendition of justice, the administration of judicial business, and the limits of public financial support for the judicial establishment—than the increase of appellate litigation.

Nevertheless, attention to the problem of appeals is well deserved.
Although the number of appeals in any jurisdiction of the United States,
or in the nation as a whole, is dwarfed by the number of trial court
proceedings, appeals are of special strategic importance. This is true not
only generally but in relation to the problem of delay in the administration of justice. Appeals are conspicuously visible and comparatively few
in number, so that individual cases become identified. The Caryl Chessman case is the most notorious but surely not the only example that
comes to mind;[1] litigation like Chessman's, which went on for twelve
years, makes the interested public aware in a direct sense of how long
litigation may drag on. In contrast, the image of delay in the trial court
is of a slow moving but undifferentiated mass of proceedings.

[1] See note, *The Caryl Chessman Case: A Legal Analysis,* Minnesota Law Review 44
(1960) p. 941. In a 1960 study of capital cases, Donald M. McIntyre of the American
Bar Foundation concluded that the modal elapsed time between sentence and execu-
tion—most of it spent in post-trial review of the cases—was seven to twelve months,
and not infrequently ran to thirty-six months. Capital cases are of course atypical, but
for that reason they clearly test the system.

It is not surprising, therefore, that one of the first questions an interested member of the public might ask about the courts, and indeed did
ask on the occasion of the planning of this book is:

Why is American justice so often stalled in the appellate courts, both in
criminal cases (as in the Chessman case) and in urgent civil matters?

This is not a naive question. The same issue was posed by Justice
Cardozo when he suggested many years ago that something like 90 per
cent of cases appealed were destined to be decided only one way, which
is also to say that many of those cases ought not to have been appealed
at all.[2] Appellate courts in particular jurisdictions periodically become
swamped with an unmanageable volume of cases, with resulting great
delay in the hearing and disposition of the controversies appealed to
them. This kind of congestion occurred in the Oregon Supreme Court
a number of years ago for example, and is presently the situation in the
Court of Appeals for the Fifth Circuit in the federal system. Hence, the
question is an altogether fitting one.

It is, however, also a complex one. Trying to "do something" about
curbing the volume of appeals, or about the delay in bringing particular
appealed cases to final resolution, requires fair consideration of the fact
that litigation is a complex process serving complex ends. Simplistic
solutions free of drawbacks are unlikely to be forthcoming. To appreciate
why this is so requires an appreciation of the process of appellate litigation itself. Since understanding the process is anterior to reforming it,
I shall speak mostly of the problems that have to be taken into account
in approaching the problems of delay rather than of the various devices
that have been propounded to solve them.

The difficulty in establishing an appellate judicial system that will dispose of its cases with satisfactory speed is nothing less than the difficulty of
establishing a system of appellate courts that will achieve in satisfactory
measure the whole range of competing objectives we would like the courts
to achieve. Putting the point somewhat differently, it seems to me that
the main reason why appellate courts, considered as a system, work at an
agonizingly slow pace is because they are expected to perform an agonizingly difficult complex of jobs. My theme throughout will be that the
conduct and administration of appellate litigation is simply a special
instance of the conduct and administration of litigation generally, so that
the strengths, the weaknesses, the aspirations, and the dilemmas encountered in the appellate courts correspond, in a numerically small but
dramatically large way, to those of the courts in general.

[2] Cardozo, *The Growth of the Law* (1924) p. 60; cf. Llewellyn, *The Common Law
Tradition* (1960), pp. 19-61.

The Organization and Procedure of Appellate Courts

ORGANIZATION

As we have seen in Milton Green's essay, the basic unit of our judicial system is the trial court of general jurisdiction. This is primarily a court of first instance, where litigation proceedings are commenced, issues formulated, proofs taken, and judgment rendered, but it also functions as an appellate court for cases of lesser importance, such as misdemeanor criminal matters and civil matters of lesser consequence. In short, the court of general jurisdiction is, in most states, not only the forum for the *trial* of important civil and criminal matters, but also the court of *appeal* from municipal courts, Justice-of-the-Peace courts, magistrates courts, and other trial courts of "limited jurisdiction."

This arrangement is predicated on the assumption that cases of such minor consequence as to be heard, in the first instance, in courts of limited jurisdiction are also the ones in which it is unlikely that there will be extended appeals, if indeed an appeal at all. The purpose of the arrangement, therefore, is to afford an easily accessible and reasonably inexpensive method of obtaining appellate review of the decisions of minor courts. Advantageous as this arrangement is as a general matter, it results in the fact that cases of formally minor importance which happen to involve great issues of substantive law and policy may have to go through an additional tier of courts in working their way up to the highest appellate courts for authoritative decision. There have been major constitutional cases that were tried initially in a justice court or police court because they involved "petty offenses," thereafter appealed to the local circuit court or county court, and ultimately appealed to the highest appellate court, even to the Supreme Court of the United States.[3]

With the important qualification just noted, the trial court of general jurisdiction—the superior court, circuit court, or whatever its name—is the place of origin of litigation. It is from the decisions of this court that appeals proceed to the appellate courts, that is to the courts whose *sole* business it is to determine appeals.

In most of the populous states, and in the federal system, the appellate courts are aligned in two tiers above the trial courts. Immediately above the trial courts of general jurisdiction is a level of intermediate appellate courts to which appeals from the trial court of general jurisdiction are ordinarily taken. The intermediate appellate court in the federal system

[3] See, e.g., *Thomson v. Louisville,* 362 U.S. 199 (1960); *Tumey v. Ohio,* 273 U.S. 510 (1927).

is known as the Court of Appeals, in New York as the Appellate Division of the Supreme Court, in California as the District Court of Appeal, and in Illinois simply as the Appellate Court.

Speaking generally, the intermediate appellate courts have jurisdiction of appeals coming up from trial courts located in designated geographical areas. In the federal system, these areas consist of groups of states. For example, the United States Court of Appeals for the Second Circuit, sitting in New York City, hears appeals from federal District Courts located in the states of New York, Connecticut, and Vermont. In state court systems, the area constituting the intermediate appellate court's territorial jurisdiction consists of a group of counties; in Illinois, for example, the Appellate Court for the First District hears appeals from Cook County; the remaining counties of the state are organized into separate districts, each with its appellate court.

Intermediate appellate courts consist of three or more judges. Almost uniformly, the judges sit in panels of three to hear a case. In some jurisdictions, by law or custom, the panels are fixed, so that the same three judges sit together regularly; in other jurisdictions, for example in the federal system, the panels are constituted *ad hoc* and change from case to case. The use of panels permits appellate courts to adhere to the American tradition that an appellate court is a collegial tribunal, and at the same time—by increasing the number of panels—permits expansion of the courts' productive capacity. Another solution to the problem of increasing the capacity of appellate courts is to redivide their geographical jurisdiction and create additional appellate court units. Over the long range of history, both processes have occurred in the federal system and in the more populous states. Thus, in the federal system the number of circuits has increased from five to the present eleven; in California, the number of District Courts of Appeal has increased since 1945 from three to the present five. In the main, however, the tendency has been and probably will continue to be to increase the number of judges, and so the number of available panels on existing intermediate appellate courts, rather than to create new courts by subdividing districts.

Most of the states, the less heavily populated ones, do not have an intermediate appellate court. The judicial structure in these states consists of a tier of minor courts of limited jurisdiction at the bottom, a tier of trial courts of general jurisdiction, and a single appellate court, typically known as the Supreme Court of the state. In states that have intermediate appellate courts, these courts constitute an additional tier in the system, immediately above which is the state's highest appellate court. In the federal system, of course, the highest court is the Supreme Court of the United States, which not only is the apex of the federal court system but also has authority to review state court decisions involving questions of federal law, notably questions concerning the Constitution of the United States.

The Supreme Court of the United States consists of nine members. The highest appellate courts of most of the states consist of seven members, though some have five, and one, curiously enough, has eight. In the federal system, and in states having an intermediate appellate court system, the highest appellate court almost invariably hears all cases *en banc,* i.e., sitting together. In states without intermediate appellate courts but with enough trial court litigation to generate a large volume of appellate litigation, the practice has developed of having the one appellate court sit in divisions. Typically, in a seven-man court, a division will consist of the chief justice and three associate justices, so that the chief justice sits in all cases. This method of dividing the appellate bench permits it to increase its productive capacity to some extent, since any particular decision then must pass muster among four men rather than seven. However, important cases are reserved for *en banc* hearing, and a certain amount of time and effort has to be spent in coordinating the work of the divisions. The increment in efficiency is therefore a modest one at best. The use of supreme-court divisions is in practice a state's last alternative before it takes the expensive and complicating step of creating an intermediate appellate court system.

Each appellate court, whether the highest court of a jurisdiction or an intermediate appellate tribunal, has a staff of supporting personnel. The clerk of the court is the chief executive officer for routine operations. Under his supervision are management of the docket, dealings with attorneys in connection with preparation of papers and other routine procedural matters, the distribution and publication of opinions, and the like. The clerk usually is legally trained and has a supporting staff appropriate to the duties and workload of his office.

In most states and in the United States courts, each appellate judge is provided with a law clerk. Sometimes law clerks are long-term employees, some of whom develop considerable independent skill and capacity while others become hacks. In other jurisdictions (and this seems to be the trend) the law clerks are graduates fresh from law school who stood at the top of their classes. The custom of using recent graduates as law clerks, which has occasioned some rather excited criticism on occasion, provides the judges with bright, energetic assistants. It also provides a method of communication between the legal academic world, which supplies the clerks, and the appellate bench, which employs them.

Perhaps the most conspicuous fact about the appellate judicial establishment is its small size and inexpensive cost, compared to the executive establishment and the increasingly formidable legislative branch. The executive, including administrative agencies, is a burgeoning bureaucracy that has become almost unwieldly in size and complexity in the federal

system and the larger states. Similarly, legislative organization has frag-
mented into legions of standing committees, subcommittees, *ad hoc*
committees, and interim committees, each staffed by technical assistants.
In contrast, the appellate judicial establishment remains comparatively
simple, and most of its work is done "by hand," as it were, the direct
mental and emotional product of the responsible public official himself.
Delegation of function, ghost writing, and the like are minimal.

It is worth stressing this tradition, because it is a limiting factor on the
productive capacity of the judiciary. It is not difficult to imagine ways
in which the appellate system could be reshaped to handle the present
volume of appeals at a much higher rate of speed, or to handle a much
greater volume of appeals at the present rate of speed. But it is difficult
to imagine how one could organize a judicial establishment that would
have this kind of productive capacity and at the same time retain the
intimate personal responsibility, even institutional quaintness, that is
characteristic of the appellate judicial process as it exists today.

The attempt to dispose of the volume of business which appellate
courts are *presently* called upon to entertain has resulted in a proliferation of intermediate appellate courts, an avalanche of published judicial
opinions, and perhaps a dilution of the quality of individual opinions.
The welter of judicial voices may be muting what is identified as the
voice of justice: the stated opinions on questions of major legal importance propounded by the highest law officers of the political sovereign.
And it must be added, too, that many appellate courts, including the
United States Supreme Court, show a tendency to assume wider- and
wider-ranging responsibility for questions of general social and political
interest. In doing so, they perhaps have failed to perceive that as the
volume of cases received goes up, the character of the judicial organization changes subtly but unmistakably, and the character of the judicial
establishment thereby changes also. This kind of institutional consequence is one of the major complications that follow from having a great
many appeals, whether or not one has "too many" appeals.

BASIC PRINCIPLES OF APPELLATE REVIEW

Before coming to a description of appellate procedure itself, it may be
helpful to identify three underlying principles on which procedure in
appeal is predicated. These premises are only occasionally stated by the
courts, but they would be immediately recognized everywhere. They not
only constitute formal rules of the appellate procedure system but also
determine the system's general structure.

Party Initiative. An appeal, like other phases of American litigation,
proceeds by initiative and counter-initiative of the parties. Generally

speaking, neither the trial judge nor the judges of the appellate court can instigate appellate review of a particular case or a particular question. Trial courts are sometimes authorized to refer questions of apparent importance to an appellate court on their own initiative. Even where this is so—and it is not a prevalent device—in practice a trial judge will not refer such a question unless one of the parties has asked him to. There is no American jurisdiction in which an appellate court has authority, without being requested to act, to call up a case, or a question in a case, for hearing before it.

Not only is the occasion of an appeal within the option of the parties, but so also is the subject matter of the appeal—the questions sought to be reviewed, the arguments, and the supporting record of the proceedings. This party monopoly of initiative is, to be sure, subject to important qualifications. Once an appellate court gets a case, it has a good deal of latitude in how it will treat the issues for decision. The appellate court can find issues that the parties did not, can ignore issues that the parties presented, and can range between these extremes in limitless variations. Further, the court has authority to permit, and indeed invite, the use of techniques which transform the case from that presented by the parties. It can direct the parties to file additional briefs on issues the court believes to be important; it can remand the case for the taking of further evidence in the trial court if the evidence presented by the parties fails to disclose factual aspects of the case in which the court is interested; and it can permit or solicit the filing of *amicus curiae* briefs, that is, arguments by persons who are not parties to the suit and who speak, as the old term describes it, as "friends of the court."

These devices, if used artfully, could go a long way to give an appellate court much fuller control over the kinds of questions it considers and the posture, in terms of arguments and evidence, in which they will be considered. But it is only in the Supreme Court of the United States that extensive use is made of these control techniques, and, even in that tribunal, their use is the rare exception rather than the rule. Hence, although account must be taken of the possibility that an appellate court could exercise a wide degree of control over the character of the cases it will decide, the fact remains, as a general proposition, that this control is exercised by the parties.

The fact that the parties to a lawsuit control the cases that will be brought to an appellate court has important consequences regarding the "mix" of the cases at the appellate level. For one thing, cases that, individually, involve relatively small amounts of money rarely reach the appellate courts, even though they may involve issues of law which, in the aggregate, are of great significance. For example, questions concerning the scope of coverage of the Social Security Act, matters of procedure

and substance in "petty" crimes, matters touching the employment relations of hourly-wage earners, and the like are rarely brought before an
appellate court. This is perhaps less true today than in the past. In a
growing range of cases, government agencies—such as the Department
of Labor—are authorized to prosecute, and take up on appeal, cases that
are of general interest and significance, even though individually incon-
sequential. Similarly, private action groups, such as the NAACP, have fi-
nanced and supported appeals in cases of an individually petty nature in
which important principles of law are involved. But the fact that small
cases can reach the appellate courts only through the propulsion of organizational litigation, as distinct from individual initiative, has its own consequences. These kinds of cases come to be thought of and decided in very
general terms, rather than on a case-to-case basis. This may indeed be desirable, but it is different from the way ordinary appeals are handled. And
organizational litigation is still comparatively exceptional.

Another consequence of party initiative is that parties who have fre-
quent occasions to be in litigation, and have strong vested interests in
the rules of law produced by the appellate courts, can exercise special
leverage to determine how a certain kind of question will come before
an appellate court. Thus, a government agency concerned with the
enforcement of a disputed statute can stall certain cases in the trial courts
and push others, so that the ones that "look good" will reach the appeal
stage first. Corporations with broad-ranging interests can do the same
thing, although their range of initiative is more restricted. At its most
sophisticated level, this kind of party manipulation of the timing, and
occasion, of appeal on important questions of law can become a fine art,
as former Solicitor General Robert Stern has explained.[4]

The general point to be kept in mind is that the judicial branch, in
contrast to the legislature and the executive, is to an important extent
in a dependent relation as concerns the type, timing, and posture of the
decisions it is called on to make. It is likewise in a dependent relation
in respect to the volume of cases it must consider and dispose of.

Appeal from Final Judgment Only. The second general premise underlying appellate procedures is expressed in what is known as the "final
judgment rule." No case may be appealed, nor may any question within
a case be sent up for appellate disposition, before the case as a whole has
been presented, considered, and disposed of in the trial court. Even
though the parties agree that resolution of a particular issue of law is
of crucial importance in the litigation between them, that issue of law,
ordinarily, may not be presented to an appellate court for authoritative
resolution in advance of the case itself. The case itself must be decided

[4] See Stern, *The Commerce Clause and the National Economy, 1933-1946,* Harvard
Law Review 59 (1946), pp. 645, 883.

first and fully in the trial court, and final judgment rendered in that court. This is so, again speaking generally, whether or not the crucial issue is presented at the threshold of a suit or at some other early stage of the proceedings in the trial court.

There are significant exceptions to the "final judgment" principle, and it seems safe to say that the variety and frequency of the exceptions to it will continue to increase, as seems to have occurred in the past quarter century. Procedures exist whereby certain questions may be referred by the trial court to an appellate court for determination as a predicate for further trial-court proceedings. There are methods by which a party in some circumstances can frame an issue at the threshold stage of the litigation in such a way that an appellate court's determination can be secured before the trial of the case. But these procedures for interlocutory appellate review, as it is called, are exceptional. The generalization holds: an appeal may not be taken until the trial court has reached a disposition which, in all formal respects, is final and determinative of all the legal and factual issues in the case.

The "finality" rule is, of course, justified on the ground that it prevents seriatim appeals and thereby in some measure restricts the number of appeals. It is supposed that if interlocutory appeals were available, there would be many more appeals, resulting in yet greater delays than are entailed in the present system. Possibly this is true, but the policy support- ing the finality rule carries a price. In a case in which there is a crucial legal issue, much wasted time and effort may be consumed in the trial court while the parties proceed without authoritative appellate resolution of what everybody understands to be the case's central point.

Particularly because the processes of preparation and proof at the trial- court level are often extremely expensive, the finality rule has been sub- ject to increasing qualification in recent years. There is a tension between the objective of preventing delay by keeping down the volume of appeals, on the one hand, and the objective of expediting important cases by per- mitting interlocutory appeal, on the other. The tension between these two objectives is exacerbated by the fact of party autonomy. Party au- tonomy permits abuse of the appellate process—either by procrastination in trial, so that an appeal may ultimately be so expensive as to be almost fruitless, or, if an interlocutory appeal is allowed, by frivolous and repet- itive resort to the appellate courts. This tension illustrates the difficulties involved in trying to work out an institutional structure and a procedural system that will satisfactorily accommodate the complex objectives of an appellate system. We shall see more of these tensions presently.

The Requirement of Timely Presentation. The third premise on which our appellate procedural rules are built is, in a sense, a corollary to the first two. This principle may be called that of timely presentation: no

contention of law or fact may be made on appeal unless it was made in
the trial court at the first appropriate opportunity. For example, if it is
contended on appeal that the trial court should have received or ex-
cluded certain evidence, or that it should have considered or ignored
certain legal propositions, an appellate court, as a general rule, will not
consider the contention unless it was advanced seasonably in the trial
court. This "timely presentation" rule is, in part, an aspect of the principle of party autonomy, the idea being that party initiative carries with
it a party's responsibility to see that his contentions are advanced at the
appropriate time and in the appropriate manner. The party who fails to
avail himself of that opportunity will not be heard to complain on appeal.
The rule also is an aspect of the principle of finality, for, until the trial
court disposition is compete, there is no sure way of assessing the time-
liness of a point made on appeal; the appeal may indeed be premature.

The practical impact of the rule of timely presentation is to preclude
the parties from having second thoughts. Litigation thus can be thought
of as a process in which the parties must systematically put up or shut up.
In this respect, judicial procedure is at variance with legislative procedures. In the legislative process, bicameralism, successive readings, the
committee system, and the like are designed to require, not merely permit,
second and third and fourth thoughts. In this respect, judicial procedure
is also at variance with administrative or bureaucratic procedures, which
characteristically involve internal review procedures designed to identify
and eliminate missteps before a committing decision is made.

The principle of timely presentation obviously has a sharp cutting
edge, but it is not easy to see all its ramifications. Some seem fairly clear.
It probably results in a good number of appeals that would be unnecessary if a more deliberate and relaxed pace were permitted in trial court
litigation. Many appeals seem to be little more than desperate efforts
to salvage blunders committed in the trial court through haste, inad-
vertence, indecision, impetuosity, incompetence, or accident. While there
are remedies that can be sought in the trial court to retrieve such blunders,
the fact that the trial courts themselves apply the principle of timely presentation, coupled with the fact that they are under heavy pressure to clear
their dockets, means that efforts to obtain relief at the trial-court stage
have only modest chances of success. And in seeking relief in the trial
court the attorney for a party must frequently acknowledge that he has
blundered, while his posture on appeal is that the blunder was committed
by the trial judge.

On the other side of the coin, the principle of timely presentation is a
handy weapon, in some courts altogether too handy a weapon, with
which to frustrate the presentation of cogent but unwelcome contentions
on appeal. An appellate court, for example, can say to a party who com-

plains that improper evidence was received at the trial that he did not object to the evidence when it was *offered* (as distinct from when it was actually received), or that he should have anticipated the presentation of the evidence and made his objection known at an earlier stage. These techniques may not be frequently indulged in, but there is no question that they are employed more than occasionally. And functionally they may be an indispensable counterweight to party initiative; if a court strongly wishes not to have to decide a particular issue thrust upon it by a party, it can avoid doing so by finding some procedural irregularity in the way the contention was presented in the trial court. Relying on the principle of timely presentation, the appellate court can thus dismiss the issue and avoid deciding it.

MECHANICS OF APPELLATE PROCEDURE

With this general background, the procedural mechanics of appeal can be stated rather shortly.

An appeal is initiated by the loser in the court below, loser in the sense that he did not obtain an award of the judgment he sought. A plaintiff may appeal if he obtained nothing at all or if he obtained less than he sought. A defendant may appeal if anything was awarded against him. But no appeal may be taken on the ground that the *reasons* offered by the trial court were inappropriate. If the litigant got the kind of judicial remedy he was seeking, he is not entitled to appeal even though the reasons offered by the trial court to justify his victory were, from the litigant's point of view, unimportant, irrelevant, or even ridiculous. This is an important point to notice, for it brings home the fact that *trial* courts are not principally responsible for articulating rules of law as much as for the granting or denial of legal remedies in particular cases. It also means that no procedural avenue exists for appellate review of a case that presents interesting or important questions of general legal interest unless, in the course of the presentation of those questions, the party who is interested in taking the appeal has suffered an adverse award of judgment.

The appellant, generally speaking, has the responsibility for seeing that the record of the proceedings in the trial court is assembled and presented to the appellate court for its consideration. The steps in preparing the record vary from state to state, but schematically they are these:

1. The loser in the trial court files a notice of appeal, a simple but formal statement that an appeal is being taken.
2. The appellant, as he has now become, instructs the clerk of the

trial court to prepare copies of what the appellant considers the important papers that were filed in the trial court as the action proceeded. These
are prepared for transmission to the appellate court. It will be noticed
that the judicial establishment itself, acting through its clerk, does not
have control over what papers will go up to the appellate court. While
it is true, as we have seen, that the appellate court has procedures to
bring up additional portions of the record, the fact remains that the
principle of party initiative gives the parties primary authority over the
make-up of the official file that will be presented to the appellate court.
(This is not so absurd as it may sound. In many law suits a great deal
of the material filed in the trial court has no bearing on any given appeal.
The parties can perform, and properly should perform, an important
function of winnowing out irrelevant documents.) In any event, the
appellant and the "respondent" (the opposing party in the appeal) between them designate and counter-designate the materials that will be
submitted to the appellate tribunal.

3. The appellant requests a transcript of the stenographic notes of the
oral proceedings in the trial court, if such a report was kept. In trial
courts of general jurisdiction, normally all oral proceedings in open court
—arguments to the court, presentation of proofs (including testimony of
the witnesses) and related motions and other activities—are contem-
poraneously reported by a stenographic reporter. But the stenographer's
notes ordinarily are not transcribed except for special purposes, a principal one of which is an appeal. Upon direction of the appellant, the
court reporter transcribes his notes into a typescript showing what was
done at the trial court, at least what the reporter has recorded as having
been done.

In this connection, it should be pointed out that it is not customary
to have a court reporter in trial courts of limited jurisdiction, chiefly
because transcripts of such proceedings are rarely needed and court
reporters are very expensive. This absence of an accurate transcript of
the oral proceedings in minor courts often complicates the appeal of
individually petty cases involving major principles of law. This was
typically true, for example, of the sit-in cases in the South and has been
true of misdemeanor cases involving issues of constitutional law that
have arisen in other parts of the country. (The tension between
the demand for inexpensive trial court proceedings and the needs of
effective appellate review is personified by the court reporter: having one
costs too much, not having one may prevent the reversal of injustice.)

4. The excerpts from the trial court file, together with the transcript
of the stenographic report of the oral proceedings at trial, constitute the
"record" on appeal. In most state courts the record is transmitted to the
appellate court in typescript form. (In the federal system it is printed,

and this involves some additional time and considerable additional expense.) The parties then submit their arguments, based on the record. Under the principle of timely presentation, they are not permitted, as it is said, to "go outside the record." No contentions can be made on appeal unless the argument involved was presented at the proper time in the trial court and unless the record shows that any evidence necessary to establish the contention was presented in the trial court. On appeal the parties cannot offer additional evidence to supplement the record, nor, as a general matter, introduce any assertion not made in the trial court. Appellate litigation is, in the very strictest sense, review rather than fresh consideration of the case.

The appellant's argument is presented in a written brief, typically printed, copies of which are made available to every judge participating in the case. After the appellant has submitted his brief, the resondent, to whom the record and the appellant's brief are made available, prepares his counterargument, also in the form of a brief.

5. When the record and the briefs have been submitted, the case is in proper form for hearing, "at issue," as it is called. At this point, the initiative in the proceedings passes to the court, and the clerk assigns a date for oral argument of the case. Normally, oral argument is comparatively short. In some courts, including the Supreme Court in the United States, each side is typically allowed one hour. In many state supreme courts, and in most intermediate appellate courts, the parties may be allowed only one half-hour each. It is obvious, therefore, that the burden of argument must be carried in the written brief, the oral argument being used chiefly for clarification and rebuttal.

6. The internal procedure of appellate courts for handling appeals varies, but the following system is generally thought to be the best and is widely followed:

(a) Once the appeal is "at issue," the case is assigned to a particular judge for review and preparation of a preliminary memorandum. This memorandum summarizes the case, outlines the parties' major contentions and indicates what are thought to be the most difficult issues. It is circulated among the other judges to facilitate their reading of the briefs and record and their other preparations for oral argument.

(b) Oral argument consists in part of a presentation by the parties and in part of questions asked by the judges. Most well-run appellate courts use oral argument as the occasion for probing the weaknesses, the ramifications, and the implications of the parties' contentions. At its best, oral argument is something like a contentious seminar.

(c) After oral argument, the court has a private conference on the case, in the course of which a preliminary consensus of views is developed. Discussion will be long or short depending on the rapidity with which general agreement is reached and the vociferousness of any dissident judges. When a result is arrived at to the satisfaction of a majority of the court, one judge from the majority is assigned to prepare an opinion. When drafted, the opinion is circulated among all the judges for criticism and emendation. This process, too, may be swift or prolonged, depending on the rapidity and firmness with which agreement is reached among the judges. In cases of great difficulty, the court may request reargument, either to give itself more time to think about the case or in the hope that reargument may develop perceptions the court was unable to realize on its own.

7. If an appeal is taken initially to an intermediate appellate court, there is a possibility of further appeal. After the intermediate appellate court has rendered its judgment, the person who is then the loser (this may be the original appellant or it may be the original respondent) may, under certain circumstances, take a further appeal. Generally speaking, an appeal is not allowed from an intermediate appellate court except for specified good reason. Such reasons include, typically, the following: that there was a division of opinion in the intermediate appellate court; that there is a conflict of legal opinion between the particular intermediate appellate court and some other parallel intermediate appellate court; that a question of law or special novelty or difficulty is presented; or that one or more judges of the intermediate appellate court has indicated that further appeal should be allowed. It is, of course, the very purpose of a three-tier judicial system to empower the intermediate appellate courts to dispose of routine appeals and so reserve the strength and capacity of the highest appellate court for the cases of special moment. Existing limitations on appeal from intermediate appellate courts reflect this purpose.

The foregoing description of the procedure on appeal holds generally both for the state and federal court systems. A word has to be added, however, about appeals from state courts to the Supreme Court of the United States. In general, litigation commenced in a state trial court must be appealed through the appellate courts of that state; resort may not be had to the federal District Courts or courts of appeals, even though questions of federal law are involved. It must be understood, too, that no appeal lies from the state appellate courts to the Supreme Court of the United States in the vast majority of cases. An appeal may be taken from a state court to the Supreme Court of the United States only if the case presents a question of federal law, that is, a question arising under the Constitution of the United States or involving some issue of federal statutory or decisional law. Even in cases involving federal-law questions, it is only in rare situations that an appeal can be taken directly to the United

State Supreme Court from a state trial court or intermediate appellate court. The appellant must first proceed through the state's appellate system, and it is only when he has "exhausted" his remedies of appeal within the state court system that he may take his point of federal law to the Supreme Court of the United States. Widespread lack of awareness of these limitations on United States Supreme Court review of the decisions of state appellate courts accounts perhaps for a corresponding public underestimation of the importance of state appellate tribunals as the courts of last resort for most cases, even cases of great magnitude and importance.

The requirement of "exhaustion" of state appellate possibilities before proceeding to the United States Supreme Court may seem complex and dilatory. In some cases, it manifestly is, especially where a federal constitutional issue of great moment is presented from the outset. The rule, however, is but a combination of two firmly established principles which themselves are hardly assailable. The first of these is the rule of trial court finality, to which we have already referred; efforts to obtain vindication of an asserted legal right must be made in the trial court first, and only thereafter in an appeal. In parallel fashion, remedies must be sought in the state court system as a whole before resort is made to the federal judiciary.

Secondly, the rule of exhaustion of state appellate remedies is an aspect of American federalism, in which the powers of government repose in the states except to the extent specifically granted to the national government. It is true, of course, that in the almost two hundred years of the Republic, the powers exercised by the federal government have rapidly expanded and, in an economic sense, the United States has become a unitary community. But it has not become such in a political sense, and it is still not in a legal sense. The Constitution remains an instrument that delegates limited powers to the federal government. The judicial corollary of this principle is that the courts of the United States will supersede the judgments of the state courts only as a last resort. An additional modern justification for this policy is that it conserves the limited energy of the nation's highest court.

The Volume of Appellate Litigation

It is difficult to see any objection to a given volume of appeals, however large, unless it were perceived that the volume of appeals has some effect on the rapidity with which the appellate court system is able to dispose of the cases before it, or unless the sheer volume of cases has some qualitative impact on the appellate judicial process. It is conceivable that a *paucity* of appeals could have an adverse effect on the appellate judicial process by not giving the judges enough variety of things to think about. But in our time, the significant relation between volume of business and the quality of business done is almost always that rising volume adversely affects quality, or is thought to do so. An overflow of work manifests itself earliest and most clearly in the creation of a backlog. Only later on and less clearly does the increase in case volume manifest itself in the form of dilution of the craftsmanship of the job performed. And usually it is only the sense of lost craftsmanship that stimulates serious consideration of reform measures to abate the flow of cases. By this time the court's calendar is typically a long one.

There are no comprehensive statistics on the volume of appellate litigation in the United States. Some states, for reasons not altogether clear, seem to have experienced no significant increase in the number of appellate cases in their courts. The situation in what can be considered a rough cross-section of American jurisdictions appears in the table below.

CASES DOCKETED IN APPELLATE COURTS
Illustrative Jurisdictions

United States Supreme Court

Year	Number of Cases
1935-36	980
1940-41	973
1945-46	1315
1950-51	1181
1955-56	1640
1960-61	1940
1963-64	2371

Circuit Courts of Appeals

Year	Number of Cases
1944-45	2730
1949-50	2830
1954-55	3695
1959-60	3899
1962-63	5437

California Supreme Court and District Courts of Appeal

Year	Number of Cases
1949-50	1347
1954-55	1535
1959-60	1820
1961-62	2315

New York Court of Appeals and Appellate Division, Supreme Court

Year	Number of Cases
1954-55	2888
1959-60	2684
1962-63	3703

Wisconsin Supreme Court

Year	Number of Cases
1956-57	250
1958-59	255
1960-61	235
1962-63	229

"DELAY"

We all wish that the process of appellate litigation were less time-consuming than it is. The question remains whether we are willing to sacrifice in some degree the competing objectives—fullness of hearing, extensiveness of review—realization of which stands in the way of saving time. That question is implicit in all of what follows.

The total workload of an appellate court, as of a trial court, is determined by the number of cases that have to be handled, multiplied by the average amount of work that has to be performed in connection with each case. The distribution of the workload is determined by the number of working units available—judges or panels of judges. The time required to process the work as a whole is determined by these three factors.

It is possible to change the rate of speed at which judicial work is processed by varying the number of cases to be handled, the average amount of work done on each case, or the number of judges available for the total task, or by varying all three. Several not-so-obvious points follow from this proposition. Unless the number of cases is reduced or the number of judges increased, the time required to carry the workload cannot be reduced, unless the work is done differently. Judicial work could be done differently by eliminating or reducing certain of its steps, or by being done more intensively, that is, with fewer diversions during the working day and from day to day. This means that to speed up the process of appellate litigation, one or more of the following measures would be necessary:

1. Some cases previously cognizable in the courts might be turned away. Unless this is to be done in an arbitrary or whimsical fashion, the rules of jurisdiction of the particular appellate court will have to be revised by legislative act. This tends to excite opposition and so becomes politically unpalatable for the legislature. Further, unless a particular type of controversy is ameliorated by some change in the substantive rules applicable to it, closing the door of an overburdened court may have the effect of channeling the controversies elsewhere. For example, if appeal

is cut off, proceedings in the trial court may become more elaborate and time-consuming.

2. Certain steps in the appellate process might be eliminated or reduced. It is difficult, and in some instances constitutionally impossible, to make changes of this sort. Established procedures achieve a sanctity akin to or even identified with Due Process of Law. To tinker with settled procedural rights or opportunities, such as the generally accorded right to at least one appeal, is, in the best of circumstances, a matter of some delicacy and in some circumstances politically impossible. Moreover, efforts to eliminate or reduce some steps in the adjudicative process often are vitiated in large part by the resultant complication of other steps in the process. The pressure is simply transferred to some other point in the system. Be this as it may, the search for ways of reducing the incidents and complexity of the appellate process, without impairing important procedural rights or opportunities, remains the most attractive and most heavily traveled road toward speeding up appellate adjudication.

3. The number of judges can be increased. This solution has been adopted, in varying extent, in practically every jurisdiction having a "delay" problem at any level of its judicial hierarchy. A variant of this solution is to create new courts, most notably by the insertion of a layer of intermediate appellate courts between the trial courts of general jurisdiction and the highest appellate court. This solution, however, is comparatively expensive, both in direct cost and in the incidental costs that are incurred whenever a system is made more complex. And increasing the number of judges has the consequence of diffusing responsibility for the performance of the judicial function and so may impair the integrity of the judiciary as an agency of government.

4. The judges might produce more work in a given period, by spending longer or more intensive working hours, or both. Alternatively, better judges might be employed, judges who could produce more work in any given time interval than the present average. There are serious limitations to this remedy, quite apart from the fact that it is not easy to superintend the work of judges without intruding on their independence, or, for that matter, to superintend judges at all. Judging is not chopping wood. Being an effective judge requires a more diverse range of intellectual activity than being doggedly attentive to cases immediately at hand. Nevertheless, it is possible to exert general pressure on judges to induce them to be as hard-working as can reasonably be expected of them. The most effective specific measure seems to be the compilation and dissemination of performance statistics, which establish comparative norms of performance and thus excite pride as an antidote for sloth.

The solution of the "delay" problem, if it is to be found by speeding up the process, has to be worked out in terms of the foregoing components. There is no magic way of overcoming delay in a traffic bottle-neck or a production line—or in the appellate courts. Demands for the elimination of "technicalities," "formalisms," "obstructive tactics" and the like are simply loaded calls for the reduction or elimination of particular steps in the adjudication process. A technicality is simply "any unanswerable point raised by the other side" [5]; the only way to eliminate a technicality is to reformulate or repeal the rule on which it is predicated.

One other solution to the "delay" problem—and emphatically it *is* a solution—is to reduce the level of our expectations for the appellate system. Indeed, if it is impossible to make the appellate judicial system produce at a faster rate, within the limits imposed by the other expectations we have for it—full hearing and just result—complaints about "delay" are simply childish.

The question is whether changes can be made in the present system of appeals that will result in its producing outcomes at a higher rate of speed, but without entailing unacceptable sacrifices in the realization of other objectives. To the extent that the adoption of such changes would still fall short of our expectations for the system's speediness, the question is whether we are ready to be more realistic in our hopes. If both questions are answered affirmatively, the problem of "delay" will be on its way to solution.

Eliminating "Too Many Appeals"

If the foregoing analysis of the determinants of work flow through the appellate courts is correct, any effort to relieve an excessive volume of appellate litigation must take the form of manipulating one or more of those determining factors. The precise question is what combination of manipulative efforts will produce the desired result, while at the same time preserving, to the maximum degree possible, the desirable present characteristics of the appellate system. For it is impossible to preserve all the characteristics—and *a fortiori* all the desirable characteristics—of the present system and at the same time alter the system so that it operates differently. This is perhaps an obvious point, but it is often lost sight of in the rhetoric of procedural law reform.

We may begin by excluding the idea that we will assume a more relaxed attitude toward "delay." Given the tempo of modern society, it seems unlikely that the community would indulge a lowered rate of productive speed in the appellate system. A decisional process materially slower than the tempo of the events with respect to which it is supposed

[5] Sloss, *M. C. Sloss and the California Supreme Court*, 46 California Law Review 715, 726 note 24 (1958).

to be decisive, is destined before long to become irrelevant. (The importance of this point is in no way diminished by the fact that procrastination in adjudication is a frequently used and frequently useful strategy. It is one thing to put off decision until tomorrow as a matter of expediency; it is quite another thing to put a decision off until tomorrow because it is impossible to get at it today.) If appellate litigation is not geared in tempo to the times, the times will simply pass it by. No one who values the judicial function wants to pay that price for refusing to change the present system.

I would think it profitless to suppose that any great improvement in the *speed* of the appellate process can be found by recruiting better judges or, except within very narrow limits, by inducing incumbent judges to work longer or more intensively. Of course, I do not disfavor efforts to improve the quality of judges; my point is simply that intensive reform effort in this direction is unlikely to improve the case capacity of the appellate bench.

In the first place, staffing judicial office, whether by appointment, by election or by a combination of both, is subject to wide play of chance and to a correspondingly high degree of blunders. There seems to be no method of selecting, and assessing the competency of, judges that would be politically acceptable and, at the same time, result in the appointment of judges systematically better than those chosen in the past. Perhaps the general improvement in the competency of the legal profession as a whole, which I believe is taking place, will have an equal if not greater effect in this direction.

In the second place any qualitative improvement in judicial personnel is likely to be offset by other factors. One is the increasing difficulty of the average case that finds its way into contemporary appellate litigation. Today the average case in the highest appellate court of any state is far more complicated and has more ramifications than the average case of half a century ago. These complexities and ramifications take time and energy to unravel. Then, too, the qualities that we would hope to find in "better" appellate judges—greater circumspection, greater technical proficiency, greater social wisdom—are not necessarily qualities that lead to the production of a greater number of decisions. On the contrary, something might even be said for *reducing* the quality of judges if all we want to do is increase their quantitative production. To carry it to absurdity, we might simply appoint country Justices of the Peace and equip them with dice.

I think it also necessary to reject an increase in the number of appellate judges as a long range solution. Obviously some efforts can be made in this direction. Thus all states that now have a two-tier system of courts could introduce an intermediate appellate court system without complicating their judicial establishments beyond what has been found tolerable in the more populous states. Some increase could be made in the number of intermediate appellate courts, and in the number of judges now sitting on present intermediate appellate courts. But the danger lies not far ahead that proliferation of the number of intermediate appellate courts and intermediate-appellate-court judges will have serious consequences for the integrity of the judicial establishment.

This is not a phantom fear. It is a known fact, for example, that a committee ceases to be effective as such when it becomes enlarged beyond a certain point, and this is also true of a legislative body, as attested by accepted limitations on the size of Congress and the state legislatures. The same intrinsic limitations of scale are found in business and public administration and, indeed, are the subject of a management subscience. It seems to me that the same is true of the judicial establishment. The federal system is already confronted by this dilemma. Some of the circuits, notably the Fifth Circuit, are badly overburdened, but proposals to add new judges, or to divide the Fifth Circuit in two, are regarded as involving a dilution and division that would seriously if not morbidly weaken the federal judiciary in the Southern states.[6]

The crisis in the Fifth Circuit is an extreme example, to be sure, but it is unique only in the manifest nature of its extremity. The Appellate Divisions of the Supreme Court in New York ceased long ago to write extended thoughtful opinions, except on rare occasions, and have become what they are in name, virtually a branch of the trial court rather than an intermediate tribunal for plenary review. I do not mean to suggest that this is an unwise institutional arrangement; it may be that just such an approach will have to be adopted elsewhere. The point is that the Appellate Division, though it handles a great deal of business, does not perform its work with the same thoroughness as intermediate appellate courts in other jurisdictions.

In California an effort has been made to maintain the full function of the intermediate appellate courts. To sustain this burden, the number of intermediate appellate courts has been increased from three to five, and there has been an even greater increase in the number of judges sitting on those courts. To push the California development a few steps further, suppose that there were ten or fifteen intermediate appellate courts in that state ten years hence. In such circumstances, what were once authoritative appellate tribunals, subject to occasional review by the Supreme Court of California, would have been converted into a judicial Tower of Babel. The proliferation of utterances could divest any one of these courts of significant authority.

[6] See Wright, *The Overloaded Fifth Circuit: A Crisis in Judicial Administration,* 42 Texas Law Review 949 (1964).

It will therefore be simply impossible, in the forseeable future, to solve the problem of "too many appeals" by increasing the number of judges. It would, I think, be even more disagreeable to consider the possibility of inserting an additional tier of courts in the judicial systems of the larger states and the federal union: the idea of a four-tier system of courts is surely repugnant even to those who believe, as I do, that thorough scrutiny is a hallmark of justice.

The lines of practical solution are therefore reduced to two: 1) some cases now cognizable in the appellate courts will have to be turned away, or 2) certain steps in the process of hearing an appeal will have to be eliminated or reduced. Turning to the second of these alternatives, I am afraid that only very limited gains can be made in this direction if the basic purposes of an appeal are to be preserved. These purposes are the review of the trial proceedings in a case with an eye to its fairness and conformity to established principles of substantive law, and a consideration, with a view to possible reformulation, of the legal rules that ought to be applied in it and other similar situations. If we were willing to reduce sharply the intensity of review for regularity, or to reduce sharply the scope of judicial rule creativity, we could sharply reduce the procedural complexities of the appellate process. This would certainly reduce the amount of work involved in any particular appeal, but it would also reduce the prospective value of any appeal. By hypothesis there would be less that an appellate court could do to rectify procedural or substantive unfairness in the court below. This reduction in the value of an appeal would no doubt, in turn, reduce the future number of appeals.

Choosing this course, however, would carry its price. It would require placing greater trust in trial judges and much greater reliance on legislative and administrative agencies to reconsider and regenerate the substantive principles of law. It might also entail accepting a slower rate of social change engineered through legal institutions. I would personally favor some development in all these directions, and I think it is bound to come, but there are political and practical limits to movement along these lines. The fact remains, therefore, that only marginal reductions can be made in the steps involved in the appellate process without sacrificing capabilities of the judicial establishment that we are not prepared to surrender.

The conclusion seems unavoidable that the greatest headway that can be made is in reducing the present volume of appeals, or at least leveling off their growth rate, by turning away some classes of cases which now reach the appellate courts. There appear to be three methods only by which this can be done: First, the categories of appealable cases can be narrowed. For example, appeal could be denied when the amount in controversy does not exceed, say, $3,000, or in a criminal case where only a fine but not imprisonment is imposed. For another example, appeal could be denied altogether in certain types of cases, such as automobile accident litigation. While these suggestions are more extreme than the limitations that exist under the rules obtaining in any state, limitations of logically similar structure do exist in most states and could be made to exist in all.

The principal difficulty of this approach is that the social and political significance of a legal issue may have, and often does have, no relation at all to the monetary or other intrinsic significance of the particular case in which it arises. This difficulty is so well understood that there is great reluctance to increase the rigor of existing formal limitations on appeal. Such additional limitations as have been imposed in recent years are of such minor significance as to have no material impact on the volume of appeals. Hence, this approach leads to a dead end.

A second method of limiting appeals is to require the approval of some member of the judiciary before a party is permitted to press an appeal. This may be done either by requiring that the trial judge certify that the case is of such significance that an appeal should be allowed, or by requiring that the would-be appellant submit a request to the appellate court for leave to appeal. The first method is characteristic English procedure, and it is a device of increasingly wide use in this country. So far, its use here has been limited largely to interlocutory appeals, but it is entirely possible and, I should think, desirable to extend it increasingly to appeals from final judgments.

The other device, requiring leave from the higher court before an appeal can be taken, is already in use between the middle and highest levels of most three-tier court systems in this country. In states without intermediate appellate courts, there is great resistance to this method of limiting appeals. The feeling at the bar is strongly that there ought to be one appeal as of right in every case, and this opinion is so widely shared by the general public that it can be taken as virtually a postulate of American legal procedure. Accordingly, we may not expect soon to see the development of discretionary appellate review in states with two-tier court systems. Some day, however—and not too long hence—the fact will have to be faced that, even in a three-tier system, there cannot be an appeal of right in all cases.

When this day comes, a third method of limiting appeals may find utility. This would be to alter the conditions of choice under which a litigant, dissatisfied in the trial court, exercises his initiative as to whether or not to appeal. The easiest and probably most effective way of altering these conditions is to make it more expensive to appeal *at the litigant's sole initiative*. In other words, one way to deter unmerited appeals is to raise the cost of taking an appeal. If it turns out that an appeal had real merit, the appellate court could be empowered to remit to the appellant the cost imposed on him for his appeal.

That some such approach is necessary seems not at all fanciful. Examples spring to mind in connection with the recent burgeoning of legal services being made available to indigent accused persons as the result of the Supreme Court's decision in *Gideon v. Wainwright.* The indigent criminal defendant has practically nothing to lose by appealing; he puts up none of the money. There is no good reason why, in these circumstances, indigent accused persons should not choose to litigate indefinitely, and some have shown themselves prone to do just that. It might be worth considering whether a rule should not be adopted that a convicted criminal offender runs the risk of having his sentence revised upward if his appeal is found to be without significant merit. I do not think it far-fetched to justify such a rule upon the principles of criminal correction.

With regard to civil litigation, there is surely justification for discouraging unmerited appeals by manipulation of the cost consequences of taking an appeal in a civil case. Some special provision would have to be made to ameliorate the cost consequences for the poor and those of modest means. I do not think such a manipulation of civil litigation costs is class legislation, in any proper sense, or otherwise objectionable as imposing one standard of justice for the rich and another for the poor. Litigation—certainly appellate litigation—is in any event sufficiently expensive to be the prerogative of the at least moderately well-to-do, or well-organized. It seems unlikely that they would suffer unduly if confronted with financial inducements not to appeal cases of only routine significance.

Edward L. Barrett, Jr.

4

Criminal Justice:
The Problem of Mass Production

During the past decade, criminal law and criminal procedure have become top-priority subjects in American legal scholarship and in the thought of the legal profession generally. The great Model Penal Code of the American Law Institute has been completed and provides a challenging standard for reappraisal and reform of the substantive criminal law. There is heightened professional and public concern about the growth of violent crime, particularly in the hothouse of the metropolis. The Supreme Court of the United States, in a series of widely discussed cases, has established far higher standards of fair play in the investigation and prosecution of criminal offenses; an effective right to counsel has been guaranteed to indigent accused persons, and new restrictions have been imposed by the Court on the use of searches, wiretapping, confessions, and prolonged interrogation by police officers and prosecutors. Each of these developments has contributed to bring about today's intense interest in the long neglected area of criminal law administration.

The emphasis of this chapter is on the realities of criminal justice in the lower trial courts. These "inferior" tribunals stand low in the judicial hierarchy, but it is there that the burdens of the law explosion are heaviest and the problems of judicial administration most challenging. In a decent legal system, justice is not an abstract concept in the books but an attribute of the law in action. One of law's great questions in our time is whether the quality of justice can be maintained in the conditions of mass-production enforcement of the criminal law.

EDWARD L. BARRETT, JR., now dean of the new law school of the University of California at Davis, was a professor of law at the University of California at Berkeley from 1946 to 1964. His principal fields of scholarly

*interest are constitutional law, criminal law, and criminology, and he has
been since 1960 Reporter to the Advisory Committee on Criminal Rules
of the Judicial Conference of the United States. His publications include*
The Tenney Committee (1951), *a significant study of state legislative
investigation, and* Cases and Materials on Constitutional Law *(with Paul
Bruton and John Honnold) (2nd edition, 1963).*

Theory and Reality in Criminal Law Administration

The dignity and worth of the individual in a free society are nowhere better seen and better protected than in the full-fledged criminal
proceeding in an American court. Here the individual and the government clash on relatively equal terms before an independent judge and
jury. The government has, it is true, the benefit of greater resources, of
its investigative agencies, of the general presumption of regularity of
official conduct. But the individual defendant is given by law many pro-
tections which go toward equalizing the contest. He may choose his own
lawyer. In many cases the defense lawyer, whether employed by him
or provided to him as an indigent, will be equal or superior in ability to
the prosecutor. The prosecutor has an unusual burden of proof—he must
establish not merely that it is more likely than not the defendant committed the crime, but rather that the evidence shows beyond a reasonable
doubt that the defendant did so. Many forms of evidence which might
most clearly show the guilt of the defendant cannot be used. Evidence
obtained by means determined to be illegal may not be introduced even
though it clearly demonstrates the defendant's guilt. A confession may
not be used unless it is shown to be truly voluntary—a result of the free
will of the defendant. Certain forms of communications are also privi-
leged. Thus what the defendant told his wife or his lawyer or, in some
instances, his priest or his doctor may not be used as evidence against
him.

The defendant need not himself take the stand in court unless he
wishes. The prosecutor must establish at least a prima facie case (evidence which if believed would be sufficient to justify a verdict of guilt)
before the defendant is obligated to come forward with evidence of any
kind and to decide whether to testify himself. In addition, the defendant
may, if he wishes, have the protection of trial before a jury. Twelve citizens from the community then have the final say as to his guilt or his
innocence, twelve citizens who represent not the government and its bureaucracy, but the conscience of the community.

In the trial, whether before court or jury, the focus is upon the defendant as an individual. He appears before a tribunal which decides

whether he has transgressed the law. If he is found guilty, the judge decides what punishment is appropriate to mete out to this individual under these particular circumstances. And after guilt has been determined the defendant may appeal his conviction to a higher court—even though (except in a state or two) the government may not appeal an acquittal. On the defendant's appeal, he may have many aspects of the legal side of the trial examined. If sufficient error is found the case will be reversed after which he must be released or a new trial held. The defendant may even be able to attack his conviction, after appellate review has been had or the time for appeal has run, in various collateral proceedings.

Such is the general image we have of the administration of criminal justice. But if one enters the courthouse in any sizeable city and walks from courtroom to courtroom, what does he see? One judge, in a single morning, is accepting pleas of guilty from and sentencing a hundred or more persons charged with drunkenness. Another judge is adjudicating traffic cases with an average time of no more than a minute per case. A third is disposing of a hundred or more other misdemeanor offenses in a morning, by granting delays, accepting pleas of guilty, and imposing sentences.

Wherever the visitor looks at the system, he finds great numbers of defendants being processed by harassed and overworked officials. Police have more cases than they can investigate. Prosecutors walk into courtrooms to try simple cases as they take their initial looks at the files. Defense lawyers appear having had no more than time for hasty conversations with their clients. Judges face long calendars with the certain knowledge that their calendars tomorrow and the next day will be, if anything, longer, and so there is no choice but to dispose of the cases.

Suddenly it becomes clear that for most defendants in the criminal process, there is scant regard for them as individuals. They are numbers on dockets, faceless ones to be processed and sent on their way. The gap between the theory and the reality is enormous.

Very little such observation of the administration of criminal justice in operation is required to reach the conclusion that it suffer from basic ills. More detailed knowledge is required, however, to appreciate the nature of the problems and the obstacles to their solution. One needs to know something of the agencies involved in administering criminal justice, of the principal steps in the processing of criminal cases, of the size of the workload borne by the system, of the methods by which large volumes of cases are handled. It is the purpose of this essay to describe the existing system and identify some of its problems. Such a description, it is hoped, will provide a background of information sufficient to challenge laymen

and lawyers to come together in the urgent task of devising solutions to
these pressing problems of law in contemporary society.

Perhaps the principal barrier to reform is that knowledge of the actual
workings of the system of criminal justice is not widespread in the community or even in the legal profession. The public generally tends to
have a Perry Mason image—clouded but not dispelled by personal contact with traffic courts. Law students read appellate opinions, which deal
in the main with serious crimes that were handled through traditional
procedures of trial and conviction. Lawyers generally, aside from the few
actually involved in criminal work, are almost as ill-informed as members
of the public.

No complete description of the criminal justice system as it actually
works is possible in a paper like this one.[1] First, it must be realized that
there is no *one* system. Each state has its own unique set of institutions
for the administration of criminal justice. Within each state there is such
decentralization that institutions and procedures will vary dramatically
from city to city and from rural areas to urban areas. The courts involved
will differ in name and in jurisdiction. Significant procedures may vary
not only from state to state and city to city but even from one year to
the next within the same city.

Second, relatively little statistical data is available. Many states do not
have centralized statistical agencies dealing with the administration of
criminal justice. Even in those states with the most adequate records, the
data are not complete. Limited law enforcement statistics and court statistics may be available, but data regarding the operation of prosecutors'
or public defenders' offices are seldom if ever collected on a state-wide
basis.

Third—and this is a point not to be lost sight of in discussions of
possible approaches to reform—the crucial steps in the operation of a
system of criminal justice are often not visible to the observer. Only a
person familiar with the system in any particular city can give a realistic
picture of how it actually works, of the manner in which decisions are
made, of the real system as opposed to the formal system portrayed in
the law books.

In view of these limitations, this paper will concentrate, in large part,
on describing the institutions, workloads, and procedures of criminal law
administration in a single state. California has been chosen as our
example for special study for four reasons: 1) relatively complete statis-

---

[1] A description of lower court procedures based on observations in a dozen or so
cities will be found in Note, *Metropolitan Criminal Courts of First Instance,* 70 Harvard
Law Review 320 (1956). Limited observations are also reported in Trebach, *The Rationing of Justice—Constitutional Rights and the Criminal Process* (Rutgers University
Press, 1964).

tical information is available for California[2]; 2) the California court structure is simple and easily described; 3) California, with its great urban areas, has all the problems that attend criminal law enforcement in metropolises; and 4) the author is most familiar with California. It is hoped that an appreciation of the problems of criminal justice as they appear within the framework of California institutions will enable the reader to understand the same problems as they confront the legal institutions of his own state.

A General View of the System

It is necessary at the outset to have a general view of the agencies involved in the administration of criminal justice and of the principal steps in processing criminal cases.

THE AGENCIES OF CRIMINAL JUSTICE

While they may have a variety of names, the following agencies appear, in one form or another, in every state of the United States:

Law-enforcement offices perform the basic functions of investigation of crime and apprehension of offenders. These offices are mostly local police forces, administratively responsible only to the government of the cities or towns in which they operate. County officers (usually termed sheriffs) perform similar functions outside cities and towns. A few state-wide agencies with limited jurisdiction, particularly for traffic-law enforcement, also exist. The diversity and number of law-enforcement agencies is illustrated by the situation in California where, in addition to fifty-seven sheriff's offices, there are 341 separate local police forces, the State Highway Patrol, and the State Bureau of Narcotics Enforcement. In 1963 city police forces in California ranged in size from Los Angeles, with 5,097 sworn personnel, to 55 forces with fewer than 5 men each on the rolls.

Prosecutors' offices have the basic responsibility for prosecuting criminal cases in court. These offices usually have county-wide responsibility, sometimes supplemented by city prosecutors with jurisdiction over minor offenses. In California each county has a district attorney, and in most areas of the state he is the only prosecuting officer. In some counties, how-

---

[2] Where not specifically indicated otherwise, the statistical data relating to California used in this paper are derived from the following sources: State of California Department of Justice, *Crime in California, 1963* and *Delinquency and Probation in California, 1963;* California Judicial Council, *Report of the Administrative Office of the California Courts, 1962-63.*

ever, the larger cities have separate city prosecutors with jurisdiction over all misdemeanors committed locally.

Public defenders' offices exist in many cities to provide legal assistance for defendants unable to hire private defense counsel. This function is performed in other cities by legal aid societies and similar voluntary agencies. In most parts of the country, individual lawyers appointed by the courts carry the defense burden for indigent accused persons. In California there are public defender offices in most of the larger counties, and a few cities have city public defenders' offices restricted in function to defending persons charged with misdemeanors in the municipal courts.

Courts of first instance, variously termed magistrates courts, justices courts, city courts, police courts, municipal courts, and criminal courts, have the major responsibility for the adjudication—perhaps the realistic word is "processing"—of criminal cases. All defendants make their initial appearances before such courts. The courts of first instance conduct preliminary hearings in felony cases and have jurisdiction to try and sentence offenders charged with less serious offenses, often including all misdemeanors.[3] In California, the magistrates court—in the larger metropolitan areas called the municipal court—has jurisdiction over all misdemeanors committed within the district it serves. (Municipal courts also have a civil jurisdiction—basically all civil actions in which $5,000 or less is involved.) In rural areas there are justices courts which perform essentially the same functions in criminal cases, except that they do not have jurisdiction to try misdemeanors for which the penalty can exceed six months in jail. In 1963, 72 municipal courts and 293 justice courts were in operation in California.

Courts of general jurisdiction, also known in the United States under a wide variety of names, have jurisdiction to accept pleas from persons charged with felonies and to try and, upon conviction, sentence them. In California these courts are called superior courts and have county-wide jurisdiction over all felony cases (as well as their basic jurisdiction in civil cases).

Juvenile courts, specialized courts to deal with juvenile offenders, exist almost everywhere in the United States, though the details of their jurisdiction and procedure will vary widely from state to state. In California all cases involving persons under the age of 18 are handled by a juvenile court, which operates as a special department of the superior court.

---

[3] Crimes are usually divided by statute into two classes: *felony* and *misdemeanor.* Felonies include the most serious offenses—typically those for which the penalty may exceed imprisonment for a year or in which the penalty may be imprisonment in a state prison. All other crimes are referred to as *misdemeanors.* Sometimes the least serious misdemeanors are referred to as petty offenses or summary offenses. In this paper the term *felony* will be used to refer to the more serious offenses and the term *misdemeanor* to refer to the less serious ones.

Probation offices perform two primary functions. They conduct pre-sentence investigations to assist the trial courts in arriving at the appropriate sentence, at least in more serious cases. They also supervise the many convicted offenders who are released to the community for a probationary period in lieu of imprisonment. Each of California's 58 counties has a probation office with county-wide jurisdiction.

THE STEPS IN THE CRIMINAL LAW PROCESS

The following are the principal steps involved in the processing of criminal cases. With variations of detail, these steps can be found in any community in the country.

Pre-arrest Investigation. The process usually starts with an investigation, undertaken to determine whether a crime has been committed and by whom. The major burden of investigation is borne by the police agencies. In the United States, there is relatively little private investigation of crime, and the courts play a very minor role at this stage. The prosecuting attorney may have a role, however, in stimulating and even guiding police investigation, and it is common for him to assume the burden of investigating certain types of offenses, particularly offenses involving fraud.

The Decision to Charge. The second step is that of determining whether there is sufficient evidence against a person to justify bringing him before a court and formally charging him with a crime. This decision is made in a variety of ways depending upon the kind of case.

In some cases, the first action taken (other than pre-arrest investigation) will be the filing of a complaint in court charging a person with an offense. This complaint may be filed by a private citizen, a prosecuting officer, or a policeman. In some jurisdictions, the prosecuting officer will decide whether there is sufficient justification to file a complaint and will screen requests for complaints made by private citizens or by the police.

In other jurisdictions the prosecuting officer may not be involved until after the complaint has been filed. Once the complaint is filed, the judge, perhaps after questioning the complainant but more often in practice on the basis of the paper itself, will issue a warrant of arrest or a summons to bring the defendant into court to answer the complaint.

In other cases, most commonly those involving traffic and parking offenses, the process will begin by a police officer serving a citation (a "ticket" or a "summons") upon a person, notifying him of the offense with which he is charged and the time and place for him to appear in court. A copy of the citation may be filed in court to serve as a complaint. The person charged must appear or (in minor offenses where permitted) deposit and forfeit bail.

Where police officers actually observe persons committing offenses, the process begins with arrest on the spot. The normal procedure then is for the officer to take the person to the police station, whereupon a complaint is filed and the person brought before the court as soon as possible. In many places the arrested person will be given an opportunity, shortly after his arrest, to go free on posting bail in lieu of staying in custody until his initial court appearance.

An important group of cases are those in which arrests are made by an officer on the basis of reasonable cause to believe that a felony has been committed. In such cases an arrest will often be a step in the process of determining whether there is sufficient basis to charge a suspected person with the crime. He may be taken to a police station, "booked" into jail, interrogated, placed in a line-up, and so forth. After the investigation the police may release him or file (or request the filing of) a formal complaint in court. After the complaint is filed the person is brought before the court.

Another but not common group of cases are those which begin with the presentation of evidence to a grand jury. If the grand jury *indicts*, that is, decides there is sufficient evidence to justify trying the defendant, a warrant or summons is issued to bring him before the court to answer the charge.

The Procedures in Court. The major involvement of court time in criminal cases comes after the filing of the complaint. Again it is useful to divide the cases into categories.

In terms of sheer numbers, by far the largest group of cases is that of minor traffic offenses (particularly parking) in which the defendant is given a citation with the option to post bail ("Mail in the two dollars") and forfeit it in lieu of appearing personally in court. Unless the defendant seeks a trial of his case, the whole process is handled administratively in the court clerk's office without involving the time of the judges.

Persons charged with other misdemeanors normally must appear before a magistrate. At the initial appearance the judge advises the defendant of his rights, sets bail, and, in some jurisdictions, sees that he has a lawyer if he wants one. The defendant may then either plead or seek additional time in which to decide how to plead. If he pleads not guilty, the case may be either tried on the spot or set down for trial at a future date. In many jurisdictions, the magistrate before whom this initial appearance is made also has authority to try and sentence persons charged with misdemeanors. In other jurisdictions the more serious misdemeanors must be sent to a higher court for trial. Usually, also, misdemeanors can be tried on the basis of the complaint filed with the magistrate. In some states, however, there must be an indictment by a grand jury before more serious misdemeanors can be tried.

If a defendant is charged with a felony the procedure is quite different. The person arrested on a felony charge is brought before a magistrate or, if he has been summoned or released on bail after arrest, he appears before the magistrate. At that first appearance it is the magistrate's duty to advise the defendant of his legal rights, to make certain that he is represented by counsel if he wishes it, and to set the date for a *preliminary hearing*. At this hearing, which also takes place before the magistrate, the prosecuting attorney is required to bring in sufficient evidence to persuade the court that there is probable cause to believe that the defendant committed the crime and hence should be held for trial. In a preliminary hearing, the defendant (or his attorney) may cross-examine prosecution witnesses and, if he wishes, present evidence on his own behalf. Normally, however, only prosecution witnesses are heard, and the burden imposed upon the prosecution at this stage is not large.

Here, for the first time, the court (magistrate) can play a significant role in screening out cases in which there is not sufficient evidence against the accused to justify a trial. How much of a role the court plays in fact will depend upon the extent to which the prosecutor has screened the cases to be presented. If the prosecutor has a very high standard of proof that has to be met before he will authorize the filing of a complaint and the holding of a hearing, the magistrate screens out few cases. If the prosecutor sends many more doubtful cases to this point in the criminal process, the magistrate then screens out a large volume of cases at the preliminary hearing. If the magistrate decides that there is not sufficient evidence to justify trying the defendant, he is discharged from custody. If the magistrate decides that there is sufficient evidence to hold the felony defendant for trial, he is then held for appearance before the court of general criminal jurisdiction for pleading and trial.

In some states and in the federal system, the preliminary hearing in a felony case must be followed by a grand jury *indictment*. In many other states, the preliminary hearing is sufficient, and if the magistrate orders the defendant held for trial, the prosecuting officer then files a formal *information* in the trial court, which becomes the basis for the proceeding in that court.

Whether the felony prosecution is instituted by information or by grand jury indictment, the next step is that the defendant appears before the trial court of general jurisdiction for formal *arraignment*. At this arraignment, he pleads guilty or not guilty. If he pleads guilty, the defendant is sentenced by the court, either then or at a future time. Many courts delay actual sentencing in a case long enough to permit the preparation of an advisory pre-sentence report by the probation office. If the defendant pleads not guilty, his case is set for trial before a jury or, if he waives jury trial, for trial before the judge without a jury.

The Workload of the System

In what volume are cases processed by our system of criminal justice? How heavy is the caseload of the courts and other agencies involved in the system? The magnitude of the task will be illustrated here by presenting some of the data at hand for California. Both state-wide statistics and statistics referring to particular courts or other agencies will be used, as available. It is to be kept in mind that the California situation is not special and unusual but offers a fair and not untypical example of the contemporary situation of criminal-law administration everywhere in the United States, particularly in states with one or more great metropolitan areas. Substitute New York or Chicago for Los Angeles—or Philadelphia or Detroit for San Francisco—and the problems, at least quantitatively, would be virtually the same.

The reader is warned at the outset that this section of the paper is, at times, unrelievedly statistical. This heavy use of statistics is justified and necessary, in the author's judgment, to drive home the most important point that any commentator can make about contemporary criminal justice in the United States. The crisis in criminal law administration is a quantitative crisis. The enormous gap, already referred to, between theory and reality in the administration of our criminal law has come about chiefly because of quantitative pressures on the system. Few people, including lawyers, have any notion of the size of the workload that must be carried by our courts, prosecutors, and other agencies of criminal justice. Only the figures, one statistic piled on another, can tell the story of mass-production criminal justice.

THE POLICE

Almost the total intake of the system of criminal justice comes as the result of action by the police. They issue the citations, serve the summonses and warrants, and make the arrests that result in bringing persons before courts on criminal charges.

There is little reliable data available as to the total amount of crime committed or, for that matter, as to the total number of cases investigated by police. Statistics published by the Federal Bureau of Investigation[4]

⁴ *Uniform Crime Reports—1963,* p. 47. For a general discussion of statistics on criminality and their limitations, see Sellin, *Crime and Delinquency in the United States: An Over-All View,* 339 The Annals of the American Academy of Political and Social Science (January 1962) 11.

show the numbers of seven serious offenses—murder, forcible rape, robbery, aggravated assault, burglary, larceny over $50, and auto theft—which are reported to police. Two million, two hundred and fifty-nine thousand and eighty-one such offenses were reported during 1963 in the United States. Statistics as to other crimes are much less reliable because of the difficulty of knowing how many crimes are committed but not reported to or discovered by the police. It is also difficult to know the volume of cases investigated, because reliable data begin to appear only when persons have been arrested and taken to police stations or jails where records are made. Much screening goes on prior to this point, however. Many persons suspected of crime are not arrested because investigation either dissipates the suspicion or fails to produce enough evidence to provide reasonable grounds for arrest.

Total recorded arrests do, however, reflect with reasonable accuracy the great number of persons formally brought into the system of administration of criminal justice because investigation has provided a fairly substantial basis for suspecting them of violation of the criminal laws. The FBI data show that during 1963 there were 4,437,786 arrests reported by 3,988 police agencies covering areas totalling 127 million in population.[5] In California alone during 1963 there were 98,535 adult felony arrests and 595,992 adult misdemeanor arrests. In addition there were 244,312 arrests of juveniles for delinquent or criminal activities.

A glimpse of the magnitude and variety of police work can be obtained from the following list of "highlights of Department activity for 1963" contained in the 1963 Annual Report of the Los Angeles Police Department:

> Investigated 183,299 crimes
> Investigated 55,658 traffic accidents
> Made 171,252 adult arrests
> Made 24,663 juvenile arrests
> Cited 1,550,773 traffic violations
> Processed 200,763 misdemeanor warrants
> Made 10,726 drunk driving arrests
> Located 4,654 missing children
> Transmitted 4,628,472 radio messages
> Responded to 2,425,205 calls for service
> Traveled 28,981,060 miles in providing police service
> Conducted 15,363 Police Commission investigations

Almost all adults arrested on misdemeanor charges have complaints filed against them in court. Many of those arrested on felony charges,

---

[5] *Uniform Crime Reports—1963*, p. 104.

however, are released without the filing of formal charges in court. During 1963, in California, 27,704—or 28.1 per cent—of the 98,535 adult felony arrests were disposed of by releases without the filing of complaints. During the same period, 54 per cent of all juveniles arrested were released by the police without referral to probation departments or courts for further processing.

This screening at the police level, which is usually the result of actions by both police and prosecutors, is of great significance to the system. Felony cases, as we have seen, impose a substantially greater burden on the courts at every level. Screening at the police stage serves particularly to reduce the number of preliminary hearings which must be held by magistrates.

THE PROSECUTION

General statistical data are not available concerning the operations and workload of prosecutors' offices. In metropolitan California counties, the prosecutors perform a wide variety of tasks. Perhaps the best way to give a picture of the total operation of such offices and the magnitude of their caseloads is to describe a single office. The following description is taken from the 1963-64 report of the District Attorney of San Francisco.

The prosecutor screens those cases in which arrests for felonies have been made without a warrant. (In San Francisco, such arrests are called "suspicion arrests.") "Procedurally, in such matters, the facts of the case are reviewed with witnesses and the Police Inspector assigned to the case, and thereafter a decision is reached whether the matter will be heard in court as a felony, be reduced to a misdemeanor, or be discharged. Such decision is based upon the law applicable to the facts, as well as the consideration of the weight of the evidence available." Suspicion arrests in San Francisco numbered 7,186 in the reported fiscal year. Of these the prosecutor refused to issue a complaint in 48 per cent of the cases, ordered complaints filed charging misdemeanors in 13 per cent, and authorized continuance of felony prosecutions in 39 per cent.

The next step in a felony prosecution is, of course, the preliminary hearing in the municipal court. During 1963-64 the San Francisco prosecutor presented 3,770 cases to the municipal court for preliminary hearings. Of these the municipal court held 44 per cent for trial in the superior court, dismissed 30 per cent, and ordered 15 per cent reduced to misdemeanors.

The prosecutor's office conducts the prosecution of misdemeanor offenses within the municipal court. A total of 59,577 such cases were handled in San Francisco during the year. Most were disposed of as guilty pleas.

The prosecutor receives many requests from private citizens and government agencies for the issuance of complaints charging persons with crime. To determine whether the request is groundless, or whether the dispute can be settled by agreement of the offending party to keep the peace or obey the law, the prosecutor issues citations to appear in his office where an informal hearing is conducted by a deputy. The great majority of these hearings result in settling the dispute without filing a complaint in court. During the 1963-64 year in San Francisco, 4,670 citations were issued and 3,970 citation hearings held.

A significant part of the workload of the prosecutor's office is the handling of felony cases in the superior court. This work divides itself into appearing on the question of sentence in cases where there is a guilty plea and conducting trials where a not-guilty plea is entered. During 1963-64, 1,903 defendants appeared before the superior court in San Francisco on felony charges and 1,710 felony cases were finally disposed of; 1,339 persons were convicted on pleas of guilty or nolo contendere. Only 371 went to trial, of whom 305 were convicted and 66 acquitted. Eight deputies were regularly assigned to three superior courts for the conduct of felony cases.

The prosecutor's office is also responsible for the presentation of matters to the grand jury. During 1963-64 there were 242 indictments returned involving 371 defendants. Nine hundred sixty-three witnesses were called to testify before the grand jury.

An appellate department of the superior court hears appeals from municipal court decisions in criminal cases. About 40 appeals were taken to this court during the year, and the prosecutor handled the preparation of briefs and the arguments for the state in those cases.

The San Francisco prosecutor's office has a Psychopathic Division with the following duties:

1. Investigation of alleged mentally ill and intemperate persons, as well as those addicted to narcotics or habit-forming drugs.

2. When indicated, the initiation and processing through the Superior Court of petitions of mental illness, intemperance, and the addictions mentioned. One thousand seven hundred four petitions—893 mentally ill, 774 intemperance, and 37 drugs—were prosecuted before the court with the result that 1,517 persons were committed, 123 discharged, and 61 placed on probation.

3. Preparation and trial of cases arising from demands for jury trials by committed persons. During 1963-64 there were 21 such jury trials held.

California law imposes on the prosecutor the duty to investigate cases where Aid to Needy Children funds have been granted and to explore the suitability of prosecution as a means of securing support for the children concerned. Under this law all applicants for welfare under the Aid to Needy Children program must be referred to the prosecutor at the point at which they request such aid. During the year the office closed over 1,700 such cases. In addition it established paternity and got 256 men to sign paternity statements obligating them to provide child support.

The prosecutor has a Bureau of Family Relations which

> investigates all criminal complaints involving family problems. This includes family units, common-law relationships and "casual" situations. Such complaints cover Failure to Provide cases, Assault and Battery, Disturbing the Peace, Malicious Mischief, Threats Against Life, Threats of Bodily Harm, Mental Illness, Alcoholism, and other miscellaneous domestic difficulties. Interviews and citation hearings conducted by the Bureau of Family Relations often eliminate the necessity of a criminal warrant. At informal hearings, the facts are ascertained and appropriate remedial action is taken where possible. This procedure saves court costs, lessens congestion of already over-crowded court calendars and eliminates additional police work in arrests and reports.

During the year the bureau issued 2,092 citations and conducted 1,523 hearings.

The magnitude of the operation of prosecutors' offices is also indicated by the figures for the District Attorney of the County of Los Angeles. Despite the fact that this office does not handle misdemeanor prosecutions in the city of Los Angeles and certain other cities in the county, it had during 1962-63 a staff of 546 (with 180 lawyers) and a budget of just over $4,800,000. During the same year the City Attorney of Los Angeles processed 1,371,246 reports of arrests and traffic investigations and actually tried 17,690 misdemeanor cases.

THE DEFENSE OF INDIGENTS

The defense of criminal cases, like prosecution and judging, also becomes a mass-production operation. In California, publicly provided defense services are available to persons charged either with felonies or with misdemeanors. In most metropolitan areas of the state these services are furnished by public defender offices.

Some notion of the dimensions of the defense burden can be seen in the figures from Los Angeles. In the city of Los Angeles legal representation for indigent persons is provided in misdemeanor cases by a city public defender office. The report of this office for 1963-64 shows that a staff composed of the public defender, ten deputy public defenders, and three clerical workers handled the following volume of work during the year:

Misdemeanors

ARRAIGNMENTS (124,060)

Arraignments on Intoxication Charges 56,714
Miscellaneous Arraignments 67,346

OTHER COURT HEARINGS BEFORE TRIAL (4,009)

Dismissals 910
Changes of Plea 3,099

TRIALS (3,222)

Guilty 1,973
Not Guilty and Dismissed 1,249

PROCEEDINGS AFTER FINDING OF GUILTY (6,758)

Hearings on Probation and Sentence 4,183
Miscellaneous Appearances for Modification of
   Sentence, etc. 2,575
                                TOTAL   138,049

Legal Advice to Indigents

OFFICE CONSULTANTS

Civil 13,610
Misdemeanors 10,760
                                TOTAL   24,370
                                      + 138,049
                    GRAND TOTAL   162,419

A County Public Defender's Office handles all felony cases within the county of Los Angeles, but no misdemeanor cases. The report of the office for 1961-63 shows that it had an annual budget of $1 million and a staff of 91 (including 66 lawyers and ten investigators). In addition to handling straight felony cases beginning with the preliminary hearings, the office represents persons in proceedings for revocation of probation, sanity hearings (including sexual-psychopath hearings and civil insanity proceedings), juvenile court cases, and proceedings against narcotics addicts under the Narcotic Rehabilitation Act. During 1962-63 the office received 30,382 new cases, each case representing the total services provided to a single defendant in one action.

A little of the operating flavor of the work of the public defender's office in the superior courts that handle felony cases can be gained from the following excerpt from a letter written by a deputy public defender in the Los Angeles County office:

> There is one criminal master calendar department[6] in the Superior Court in downtown Los Angeles and 18 criminal trial departments. In the master calendar department we have four deputy public defenders who each ordinarily appear every fourth court day and handle all the matters on that day. In the trial departments, there are generally some three to four new cases on each trial court calendar every day. Most trial departments have three deputy district attorneys. The Public Defender has two trial deputies in some departments and one trial deputy in other departments. Generally speaking, our office assigns approximately four cases per week to each trial deputy, and, of course, this figure is flexible.

THE MAGISTRATES COURTS

Despite the preliminary screening done at the police and prosecution level, the magistrates courts have an enormous caseload. During fiscal 1962-63 there were 4 million non-parking filings in criminal cases in the municipal and justice courts of California. Parking filings added almost another $4 1/2 million cases. That this load is not unique to California is shown by the 1963 report of the Criminal Court of the City of New York listing 3,374,365 "arraignments," of which 2,156,670 involved parking offenses.

Felony Cases. A sizeable segment of the business of the magistrates courts consists, as we have seen, of handling the preliminary stages of the prosecution of persons arrested on charges of commission of felonies or other serious crimes over which the magistrate does not have trial jurisdiction. The handling of preliminary hearings takes a substantial amount of the time of the magistrates courts. During 1962-63, 45,424 felony complaints were filed in the municipal courts in California, and these courts disposed of 38,626 such cases. Over 63 per cent (24,549) of the cases were contested and involved actual hearings. The time required for preliminary hearings is suggested by the fact that in the Los Angeles Municipal Court it takes four judges, with some assistance from a fifth, to average ten preliminary hearings per court day. In San Francisco, four judges devote their time to preliminary hearings. They handled 3,770 during the year ending June 30, 1964.

---

[6] In courts with several judges, cases may all be assigned for appearance before a single judge who will then assign cases for trial to the judges who are available. This administrative device is known as a master calendar system. The master calendar judge may also handle the guilty plea cases and various preliminary motions in contested cases.

Parking and Traffic. It has been pointed out that the automobile is a chief cause of the workload and delay on the civil side of our court systems. The automobile plays a similar role in criminal cases. In a recent study for the California Judicial Council, the following statement was made:

> The influence of the automobile on the courts has been a continuing concern of the Judicial Council. Personal injury cases involving autos present a huge burden for the superior court. . . . Similarly, the municipal and justice courts have been swamped by a huge load of criminal traffic matters. During the 1961-62 fiscal year, there were 7,157,730 cases filed in the municipal courts in California. Of this number 6,213,550, or 87 per cent, were misdemeanor traffic violations, 3,604,037 of these were for illegal parking, and 2,609,513 were other traffic violations. In the same fiscal year, 84 per cent of the justice court filings were misdemeanor traffic cases. . . . The importance of these cases is measured by the two-fold responsibility they present to the courts, first to make a substantial contribution to traffic safety, and second, to help inculcate respect for the law in the multitude of the people who are involved.[7]

The volume of traffic cases continues to grow. In California during the year ending June 1963 there were 7,763,660 filings in the justices and municipal courts—a ratio of approximately one filing for each 2.3 of California's 18 million people. Similar volume exists elsewhere. In New York City during the year 1963, the report of the Criminal Court shows 2,962,415 arraignments on traffic offenses—a ratio of one arraignment for each 2.6 of New York's approximately 7,800,000 persons.

How is this enormous volume of traffic cases processed? How can the criminal law and the courts cope with such volume? Fortunately, most of the cases involve parking offenses, and the system of citation and bail forfeiture results in the disposition of nearly all such cases without contest or judicial appearance. Parking cases do, however, pose a substantial burden on the system apart from that of processing by the clerk. A great deal of police time is spent handing out parking tickets, and in trying to apprehend persons who ignore parking tickets and neither deposit bail nor appear in court. During 1963, the San Francisco municipal court issued 119,226 warrants in parking cases, which the police had to serve. A substantial burden is imposed on the courts by contested parking citations, even though they are a small percentage of the total. In the California municipal courts during 1962-63, fewer than 4,000 of more than 3,600,000 parking filings disposed of were contested. This is a contest

[7] Judicial Council of California, *19th Biennial Report to the Governor and the Legislature, 1963,* p. 96. For a detailed description of traffic cases in California, see Note, *California Traffic-Law Administration,* 12 Stanford Law Review 388 (1960).

rate of only one-tenth of 1 per cent, but, since the total number of California's contested criminal cases of all kinds was about 108,000 that year, contests in parking cases represented almost 4 per cent of all contested cases. If the rate of contested parking tickets were to rise from one-tenth of 1 per cent to 1 per cent, parking contests would represent one-third of the total volume of contested criminal matters. The 1963 report of the Criminal Court of New York City shows a substantial number of contested parking cases in that city. Of the 1,304,654 parking dispositions, 2,144 were the result of findings of guilt after trial.

A much greater burden is imposed upon the courts by non-parking traffic offenses. During 1962-63, there were 2,745,304 non-parking traffic filings in the California municipal courts, and 2,649,043 such cases were disposed of during the year. Fortunately, as shown by the California Judicial Council study,[8] many of these cases can be handled expeditiously:

> In order to process the huge number of traffic violations, California has evolved a system by which most are disposed of through bail forfeitures. Normally, a bail deposit is used to insure defendant's presence at the trial, but in traffic cases the law gives the judge discretion to forfeit bail and consider the case closed. . . .
>
> Generally, the courts require personal appearance for the more serious violations, but the courts and judges disagree as to what cases are serious enough to merit this treatment. For example, some courts do not require defendants to appear in cases involving accidents, had-been-drinking, speed contests, or failure-to-appear.

Even though most traffic filings are disposed of by bail forfeiture, a large number survive for court appearance. Most of these are merely appearances to plead guilty and receive sentence. A substantial number, however, are contested and result in trial. In the California municipal courts during the 1962-63 fiscal year, 58,816 traffic cases were disposed of after trial; 4,030 juries were involved. Statistics are similar in New York City; the 1963 report of the Criminal Court shows that 13,136 traffic cases other than parking were disposed of after trial.

What all of this means to the conduct of a single court may be illustrated by the statistics for the metropolitan portion of the Municipal Court, Los Angeles Judicial District.[9] During August 1964, 12,258 arraignments were held on traffic charges, i.e., there were that many traffic cases in which persons were required to appear in court. It took the time of two and one-half judges to handle these initial appearances. Six hundred

---

[8] Judicial Council of California, *19th Biennial Report, 1963,* 97, 100.
[9] Statistics given in the text here and at later points concerning the Municipal Court, Los Angeles Judicial District are taken from a letter to the author from the clerk's office of that court.

twenty-three traffic cases went on trial during the month, and this required the time of one judge to conduct the master calendar assigning cases for trial), five judges to conduct jury trials, and two judges to conduct trials by the court without a jury. The relative impact of the cases which go to trial, instead of being disposed of on guilty pleas on arraignment, is suggested by the fact that, in this court, judges handling arraignments disposed of an average of 4,900 cases each per month while those handling trials averaged 79. A 5 per cent increase in the number of traffic cases contested and sent to trial in the Los Angeles court would double the volume of trials in such cases and require the time of seven additional judges for this purpose alone.

Drunkenness. Much of the time of the agencies of criminal justice is given over to handling intoxicated persons. Statistical data are difficult to use here on any comparative basis, because of wide variations in procedures. In some jurisdictions, drunks may be picked up, held until sober, and then released, without arrests being recorded or prosecutions instituted. In other jurisdictions, all drunks picked up will be arrested, booked, and charged in court. Between these extremes every variation exists.

A few figures will show the magnitude of the drunkenness problem. FBI statistics report that in 3,988 reporting agencies there were 1,514,-680 arrests for drunkenness during 1963,[10] just over a third of the total number of arrests reported for all offenses. In the city of Los Angeles that year, 80,805 of a total of 195,915 arrests were for drunkenness, and in San Francisco 26,229 of a total of 46,205 adult arrests. These arrest figures do not, of course, represent a similar number of different individuals. Repetitive arrests for drunkenness are common. It has been estimated that only 40,000 different persons were involved in about 100,000 drunkenness arrests in Los Angeles during 1959.[11]

The burden imposed on the courts in handling these cases is heavy. In San Francisco one judge from the municipal court sits each court day in the early morning at the city prison. During 1963 he handled 24,379 drunkenness cases. In Los Angeles, the burden is even greater with a special court handling as many as 60,000 to 80,000 cases a year.

Other Misdemeanors. Once traffic and drunkenness offenses are eliminated, the volume of cases dealt with by the magistrates court is less massive. Many of these cases, however, call for far less routine treatment, and significant numbers of them are contested.

Two sets of figures give a fair notion of the burden in these cases. In San Francisco, three judges of the municipal court disposed of 10,556

---

[10] *Uniform Crime Reports—1963*, p. 104.
[11] Taylor, "Los Angeles' Cure for Drunks," *The Saturday Evening Post* (April 23, 1960), p. 32.

misdemeanor cases during 1963. (These figures do not include drunken
driven and other misdemeanors closely associated with that offense.) in
the metropolitan portion of the municipal court in Los Angeles, eight
judges devote their full time to misdemeanor cases other than traffic and
drunkenness. One judge in this court handles arraignments and preliminary appearances numbering as high as 30,000 per year. Seven judges
are needed to handle the cases set for trial. Approximately 70 cases are
set for trial each day, of which 35 actually are tried. The seven trial
divisions held 123 jury trials and 415 court trials during the month of
August 1964 alone.

THE COURTS OF GENERAL JURISDICTION

For the trial courts of general jurisdiction, criminal business is not
the major portion of the load. In California during 1962-63, filings in
criminal, juvenile, and *haveas corpus* cases constituted less than a quarter of the total filings in the superior courts.

During that year the superior courts disposed of 32,949 felony cases,
of which 9,348 were contested. Two thousand six hundred and seventy-
seven juries were sworn in felony cases. In addition the superior courts
disposed of 44,331 juvenile petitions, of which 2,681 were contested, and
765 petitions for writs of *habeas corpus,* 299 of which involved hearings.
In Los Angeles County during 1963 the breakdown was as follows:[12]
15,185 felony cases were filed and 14,725 disposed of; 9,134 were disposed
of on pleas of guilty, 963 after jury trial, and 4,628 after trial before the
court. The average was about 233 trials per year for each of the 24 judges
sitting in the criminal departments, in addition to the judicial burden
of sentencing in more than 9,000 cases where guilty pleas were entered.
In addition, five full-time and two part-time judges sat in juvenile court,
assisted by eleven full-time referees and 18 juvenile traffic hearing officers.

THE JUVENILE COURTS

In California all cases involving juveniles under the age of eighteen
must (and cases involving those between eighteen and twenty-one may)
be referred to the juvenile court, which is presided over by a judge of
the superior court. All cases in which juveniles are arrested for criminal
offenses, major or minor, are within the jurisdiction of this court, along
with cases of juveniles sought to be made wards of court because of delinquent tendencies.

There is a very elaborate procedure in these matters, with a variety of

[12] The statistics in the text were taken from Los Angeles Superior Court, *Executive Officer's Report 1962-63.*

agencies and institutions, all supervised by the juvenile court judges. Police, often organized into specialized juvenile squads, normally initiate the process. Juvenile probation officers have authority to decide on temporary detention, and they carry the responsibility of preparing and presenting cases in the juvenile court as well as general supervision of persons who have been made wards of the court. Referees and hearing officers (for traffic cases) assist the juvenile courts in dealing with minor offenses.

A huge part of criminal conduct is reflected in juvenile court. In California during 1963, 59 per cent of all arrests for auto theft, and 45 per cent of all arrests for burglary involved juveniles. That year the police made 95,716 arrests of juveniles for law violations, in addition to 148,596 for "delinquent tendencies." Forty-one per cent of these cases were closed at the police level by reprimand or similar action. Fifty-four per cent were referred to the probation office for further processing. Probation departments received 79,302 referrals of juveniles charged with delinquency, and these resulted in the filing of 33,401 petitions in court and 24,597 declarations of wardship. Traffic matters bulked large in this context, too: 203,238 juvenile traffic cases were disposed of by hearing officers or referees without official court appearance, and another 1,448 were disposed of by the juvenile courts themselves.

PROBATION DEPARTMENTS

A major share in the administration of criminal justice is borne in California by county probation departments. Their workload falls into three main categories: preparation of presentence reports, supervision of adult probationers, and processing of juvenile offenders.

In California, every person convicted of a felony must be referred to the probation department for preparation of a pre-sentence report to aid the judge in arriving at a conclusion regarding sentencing. During 1963, 27,222 referrals were made for pre-sentence reports in felony cases and reports were prepared and filed in 24,591 cases. While pre-sentence reports are not required in misdemeanor cases, they are often used. Complete data are not available, but statistics from 26 counties, not including the three large counties of Los Angeles, San Francisco, and San Diego, show 13,764 probation referrals in misdemeanor cases.

Even more significant is the workload of probation departments in relation to the supervision of persons released on probation after conviction of a criminal offense. At the end of 1963, about 72,000 adult probationers were under active supervision in California. In addition to this burden, probation departments were exercising some form of supervision over more than 40,500 juvenile delinquency cases.

DELAY IN CRIMINAL CASES—BAIL OR JAIL

In most states, criminal litigation, unlike civil, is not characterized by long periods of delay between the initiation of court proceedings and final disposition. Constitutional guarantees, of "speedy trial," and statutory time limits require relatively speedy handling. In California, for example, defendants in misdemeanor cases must be brought to trial within 30 days after arrest, unless they consent to a delay, and defendants in felony cases within 60 days after the filing of the indictment or information.

The performance of the courts in disposing of felony cases is quite good. During 1963 in California, the median time from the filing of the indictment or information in a case to its final disposition (sentencing) was 50 days for all defendants. For those who pleaded guilty, the median time was 27 days, about 22 days of which were spent, after plea and prior to sentence, awaiting the probation office pre-sentence report. For those who were tried by court or jury, the median time was about 85 days. The figures suggest that even for cases going to trial (and including cases in which defendants consented to delay), about 80 per cent were finally disposed of within six months after the defendant's arrest.

Prompt as these time intervals may seem to one who has been reading about delay in civil cases, they do present serious problems to the extent that they involve holding accused persons in custody. Here the problem of delay assumes an entirely different aspect. Human liberty is sacrificed when the delay constitutes even one night in jail. The implications of holding a man in jail for several months before it is even determined whether he is guilty are, of course, tremendous.

The major problem in the criminal area is not one of reducing the time in which cases are disposed of by the courts. In fact, with respect to minor offenses, it may be that more judicial time should be allotted and fewer cases be disposed of in mass-production guilty-plea proceedings. Instead, the problem is the quite separate one of reducing the necessity for holding defendants in custody while their cases are being processed in the courts. This matter is now receiving a great amount of national attention, and many experimental projects are currently under way. No attempt can be made here to do more than state the nature of the problem.

In May 1964, the Attorney General of the United States convened a National Conference on Bail and Criminal Justice in Washington, D.C. In a paper prepared for that conference Daniel Freed and Patricia Wald described the bail problem as follows:

> Each year, the freedom of hundreds of thousands of persons charged with crime hinges upon their ability to raise the money necessary for bail. Those

who go free on bail are released not because they are innocent but because they can buy their liberty. The balance are detained not because they are guilty but because they are poor. Though the accused be harmless, and has a home, family, and job which make it likely that—if released—he would show up for trial, he may still be held. Conversely, the habitual offender who may be dangerous to the safety of the community may gain his release.[13]

The magnitude of the problem of bail was underlined by the figures from New York City, reported to the National Conference by Presiding Justice Bernard Botein of the Appellate Division of the New York Supreme Court: 58,000 persons—almost 13,000 of them adolescents—were confined to prison that year, awaiting the disposition of charges pending against them. These were not short stays in prison but averaged 28 days for the adults and 32 days for the adolescents. "Tragic and irretrievable," said Justice Botein, "is the damage done the community through ruination of members of the family and the family unit itself, the debasement of human dignity and moral values, and the disillusionment with the processes of American justice."

It is not possible here to discuss the many problems concerned with bail and the experimental programs now under way, in different parts of the country, seeking to devise better ways to facilitate the release of arrested persons pending trial of the criminal charges against them. It is strongly urged by critics of the existing bail system that a defendant's release from custody pending trial should not depend, as now, on his ability to put up bail or pay a bail bondsman's premium, but on all the factors that make it likely, or unlikely, that he will return to face in court the charges against him. It is entirely possible, as the critics contend, that the present bail system may be operating to detain many poor persons unnecessarily and, at the same time, working to turn dangerous professional criminals loose on the community.

Processing the Workload

How does the American system of criminal justice operate to make possible the processing of this enormous volume of cases? What are the procedures which have been devised to deal with the mass production problem?

Three basic assumptions underlie the system. *First,* only persons as to whom there is a relatively high probability of guilt will be brought before the courts. Preliminary screening by police and prosecutors will eliminate doubtful cases. *Second,* the overwhelming majority (at least three-quarters over-all) of all persons brought to the courts will plead guilty and not

[13] Freed and Wald, *Bail in the United States* (1964).

involve courts, prosecutors, and defenders in the time and expense of contested cases. *Third,* persons charged with minor offenses will be processed in volume, with a minimum of judicial time spent in disposing of each individual case.

PRELIMINARY SCREENING

Generally in California, as elsewhere, the prosecuting attorney performs the function of regulating the volume of cases (other than routine traffic offenses, drunkenness, and the like) which get to the courts. He is faced with a variety of problems. His own staff is short and can handle only a certain number of cases. The courts look to him to keep their volume within bounds. Constitutional and statutory time limits prevent him and the courts from building a backlog of untried cases. He cannot afford to have a larger volume of contested cases than his staff and the courts can handle within the time available.

How does the prosecutor operate? Through his complaint-issuing function he puts pressure on the police to bring forward only cases in which the evidence of guilt is substantial.[14] This function is performed primarily with respect to felonies which, if contested, involve the greatest amount of time to handle. During a two-year period (1961-63), the District Attorney of Los Angeles County issued 43,852 complaints in felony cases while rejecting 34,067 requests for complaints. In misdemeanor cases he issued 145,431 complaints while rejecting only 8,045 requests. During 1962-63 the City Attorney of Los Angeles, as the result of arrest and traffic investigation reports from the police, issued 138,912 complaints and refused 7,939.

Another use of the complaint-issuing function arises in connection with citation hearings, resulting from requests for the issuance of complaints by private citizens or regulatory agencies. Instead of initiating a criminal prosecution when a report of violation is made, the prosecutor may set a hearing in his office to determine whether or not a complaint should be filed in court. Particularly where regulatory offenses are involved and future compliance is the most important issue, these hearings serve to dispose of the cases without the necessity of involving the courts. During the year 1963-64, over 4,500 such citations were issued and more than 3,900 citation hearings actually held by the San Francisco district attorney's office. Even larger volumes are reported from Los Angeles, where the city attorney held more than 12,000 "laymen hearings" for similar purposes and, in the course of the year, actually refused to issue complaints on more than 18,000 requests from private citizens.

[14] See generally Miller and Tiffany, *Prosecutor Dominance of the Warrant Decisions: A Study of Current Practices,* 1964 Washington University Law Review 1.

THE PLEA OF GUILTY

The importance of the plea of guilty in our system of mass production criminal justice can be quickly illustrated. In 1963 in California, *65.8 per cent* of all felony cases were disposed of on pleas of guilty. During the 1963-64 fiscal year in the municipal courts, over three-fourths of all non-traffic misdemeanor cases were disposed of by pleas of guilty involving arraignment in court. A few such misdemeanors and three-fourths of all non-parking traffic offenses were disposed of by bail forfeitures without court appearance.

In felony and serious misdemeanor cases pleas of guilty may be the result of settlements negotiated by the prosecutor and defense attorney. Because the pressures of the system make prosecuting attorneys and judges responsive to proposals which will result in pleas of guilty, a practice akin to the out-of-court settlement in civil cases has arisen. At its best, this system is superior to that of trials. A good defense lawyer can present helpful information concerning his client and his problems which may lead to the working out of a more rational disposition than would be possible through trial of the case. A recent handbook designed to introduce lawyers to the problems of defending criminal cases has this to say about the process:

> Certainly an important part of representing any defendant in a criminal matter is discussing the case with the prosecutor. There is nothing illegal or unethical about such a practice. Very often the defense attorney will be able to present to the district attorney sufficient facts to induce the district attorney to reduce the charges against the client and in many instances dismiss them.[15]

Sometimes, however, the volume pressures can result in grave abuses. A deputy district attorney in a large eastern city wrote recently to the author:

> Volume pressures make statutory limits on sentence largely of academic interest. Our volume here is such that in more than 95 per cent of our felony cases a lesser plea is taken that has little resemblance to the crime charged. Then, because the defendant admitted his crime by his plea of guilty, the sentencing court is likely to give him a further break and not even inflict a sentence that approaches the maximum for the lesser plea.

Abuses of the system are even more likely with respect to minor offenses. Superior Court Judge Nutter has described the problem in the Los Angeles municipal court:

> The "repeaters" or their advisers are well versed in the calendar problems of the arraignment courts and are often able, because of the pressure of

[15] California Continuing Education of the Bar, *California Criminal Law Practice*, 57 (1964).

physical conditions, to induce the deputy city attorney to accept a reduced plea. There seems to be a presumption among "repeaters" that in return for a plea of guilty in the arraignment or master calendar court, the sentence will be within a certain range, and lighter than in the trial court. This expectation is founded upon the understanding of a simple fact. *An increase in not guilty pleas of only 5 per cent in the arraignment courts and the master calendar courts would result in a flooding of the trial courts and a breakdown of the entire system* [EMPHASIS ADDED]. . . . In many occasions, the "repeater's" knowledge of the arraignment system enables him to obtain a sentence of less severity than the first offender.[16]

The total dependence of the system on the routine guilty plea is dramatized by the occasional situation in which large numbers of defendants do not follow the normal pattern. One such situation occurred in 1964 in San Francisco when more than 400 civil rights demonstrators were arrested as the result of conduct including sit-ins in private business establishments. Many of the demonstrators were arrested on three or four different occasions, on charges ranging from disturbing the peace and trespass to unlawful assembly and failure to disperse. In his Annual Report for 1963-64, the District Attorney reported the episode as follows:

Attorneys for the defendants made many motions to dismiss, and other preliminary motions; then refused to waive time for trial, and demanded jury trials. The trials actually began on April 15, and concluded in August. During this period of time, all municipal courts were diverted to handle only criminal cases. In addition to the regular criminal calendars, nine courts were trying civil rights jury trials each day. The defendants were being tried in groups of fifteen in order to expedite the trials. The staff of the District Attorney was taxed to the extent that almost every deputy was assigned a trial.

The ultimate result of these trials is as follows:

Number of defendants		404
Guilty	200	
Nolo Contendere	85	
Total convicted		285
Not guilty	36	
Dismissed	10	
Total released		46
Referred to Juvenile		14
Jury disagreed		59

[16] Nutter, *The Quality of Justice in Misdemeanor Arraignment Courts,* 53 Journal of Criminal Law, Criminology and Police Science 215, 217 (1962). The quotations in the text are reprinted by special permission from the Journal of Criminal Law, Criminology and Police Science, Copyright © 1962 by the Northwestern University School of Law, Vol. 53, No. 2.

It is, indeed, a basic assumption of mass-production criminal justice that the overwhelming majority of persons charged will plead guilty. Volume processing would otherwise be impossible, as the above episode clearly demonstrates.

VOLUME PROCESSING BY COURTS

For the cases taken to the courts there are many techniques for handling volume. Much of the problem exists in the magistrates courts and is described below. However, even at the level of superior court trial of a contested felony case, short-cut methods have been introduced. In California, for example, many cases are tried by the superior court on the transcript of the preliminary hearing held in the lower court. The superior court, with the concurrence of the defendant, decides the merits of the case on the basis of the information present in the transcript. This device saves the court time involved in hearing the witnesses again, and is extensively used. In California as a whole during 1963, there were in felony cases 2,373 jury trials, 3,306 court trials, and 2,885 superior-court trials on transcripts. Some indications of the pressures of volume towards the most expeditious method of disposing of cases can be gained by contrasting the figures for Los Angeles County and those for the 35 least populous counties in California. In Los Angeles during 1963 in felony cases there were 976 jury trials, 2,789 court trials and 2,521 superior-court trials on transcript. In the 35 small counties, by contrast, there were 233 jury trials, 46 court trials and only 38 trials on transcript. Thus jury trials, the most time consuming, constituted just over 16 per cent of the total trials in the superior court of Los Angeles County and just over 73 per cent in the least populous counties.

In magistrates courts, a basic element of the process is that time is made for the handling of contested cases by using a small number of judges to dispose of the guilty plea cases in large volume, with but little individual attention to the persons coming before them. This can be seen from the following table which shows the distribution of the workload in the criminal department of the metropolitan branches of the Municipal Court, Los Angeles Judicial District during the month of August 1964:[17]

Preliminary Hearings (Master Calendar plus 4 divisions)

(Hearings held, pleas, and other dispositions)

August 1964—669

Plus hearings, Fugitive Complaints

August 1964—746

[17] See note 9, *supra*.

One judge handles the Master Calendar Division, conducts the arraignments, assigns cases to divisions for preliminary hearings, and hears all motions.

Misdemeanors

> (Arraignment Division—1 Judge)
>> August 1964—2,516

> *Intoxication*

> (Arraignment Division—1 Judge)
>> August 1964—4,630

Traffic

> (Arraignments—2½ Judges)
>> August 1964—12,258

Felony Preliminary Hearings

> Four judges are regularly assigned, and in addition the judge presiding in the Master Calendar Division hears preliminaries when necessary. The judges average 10 preliminaries each day.

Trial Divisions

> *Misdemeanor including intoxication*

> Six trial divisions plus the Master Calendar Division. All pleas, motions, and so on are heard in the Master Calendar. Approximately 70 cases are set for trial each day, of which 35 will go to trial.

>> August 1964—123 Jury trials
>> 415 Court trials

> *Traffic*

> Jury trials—1 Master Calendar and 5 trial divisions. Approximately 50 trials set each day of which 20 will go to trial.

> Court trials—2 Divisions

>> August 1964—623 trials

A few comments on the table may be of interest. Initial appearances, preliminary hearings, and motions involving persons charged with felonies occupied the time of one-quarter of the judges, even though relatively few felony charges were involved. In misdemeanor cases, including traffic and intoxication, there were 19,404 arraignments and 1,161 trials. Although probably 80 per cent of the arraignments resulted in pleas of guilty followed by sentence, only four and one-half judges were used to handle arraignments, while 15 judges were assigned to the small percentage of contested cases. For between 80 and 90 per cent of all persons brought before the municipal court during that month, then, the only contact with the judicial process was in courtrooms where individual judges were handling case volumes ranging from 2,500 to 4,500 per month.

An impression of what happens in courts like this can best be conveyed by letting the judges who operate them speak for themselves. Superior Judge Ralph W. Nutter has written of the system in Los Angeles where, as a municipal judge, he had presided over the misdemeanor arraignment court:[18]

> In Divisions 50, 58, and 59, defendants are informed of their constitutional rights in crowds ranging in size from 100 to 300 defendants. In Divisions 58 and 59, there are no seats available for the defendants, and they are crowded into a small space between the counsel table and the courtroom seats, in conditions similar to those of New Yorkers crowded in a subway during the rush hour. . . .
>
> To facilitate the arraignment process, bailiffs are obliged to line up the defendants in long lines, blocking up the aisles of the courtroom. As the names of individual defendants are called off, each defendant moves up in the line, shepherded ahead by the bailiffs. . . . By the time the defendant appears before the judge, frequently his only objective is to get out of the courtroom as fast as possible. . . . Under such conditions, it is possible that defendants plead guilty without adequate knowledge of the charges against them. . . . A plea of guilty under such circumstances does not create respect for the law enforcement process. It certainly does not create a climate for the education of the defendants.

Another former magistrate, Superior Judge Robert Clifton, presided over the intoxication arraignment court in Los Angeles for many years. He became deeply interested in the problem of how vast numbers of cases might be handled in ways that would help reduce the burden of alcoholism on the community, and he accomplished a great deal in devising methods for individualizing the treatment of offenders while still handling enormous volume. Here is a portion of his description of the procedures in his court (which "processed" 200 to 250 persons per day, with occasional days running as high as 400):[19]

> If the defendant pleads guilty (some 95 per cent or more do plead guilty) the judge immediately fixes the fine or sentence, or in a few cases continues

[18] Nutter, *supra* note 16, 215-216.
[19] From a speech given to the Health and Hospital Committee of the Los Angeles Chamber of Commerce in 1958.

the case to get a report from the probation officer. The judge may summarily, or later upon getting a report, put the defendant on probation and suspend the imposition of all or part of the sentence or fine, or suspend the imposition of any sentence and place the defendant upon probation upon reasonable terms and conditions. . . .

You say, "How can one judge handle 60,000 cases a year—250 a day?" "What do you do with them?" Well, first we have the "make sheet," a teletyped report from the Police Record and Identification Bureau, showing the date of arrest, the date of the last previous arrest for intoxication, the number of such arrests in the past six months, and the total intoxication arrests, plus a summary of the defendant's other arrests. . . . Then we have the defendant himself, and at a glance you can have some information as to whether he is in good shape or a physical wreck or on the verge of d.t.'s; whether he is well dressed or in rags, etc. . . . All this, the make sheet, the officer's arrest report and a glance at the defendant, give a world of information before he opens his mouth. Then, if he wishes, the defendant may make a statement of matters which might affect the sentence, and in addition, of course, the court may ask questions concerning his employment, family, what steps he has taken about alcoholism, etc.

Judge Clifton went on to describe in detail the various types of dispositions made in the cases. First offenders usually had their cases dismissed. Persons with records showing a number of arrests in recent weeks or months might be told that they have a very serious problem and put on summary probation, with the condition that they attend three meetings of Alcoholics Anonymous within 30 days. Others might be directed to a rehabilitation clinic to work out an out-patient treatment which the court would require be carried out as a condition of probation. Drunks who came off "Skid Row" might receive sentences of up to 120 days, to be spent at a rehabilitation center specially devised for such persons, who might otherwise spend most of their time in jail because of repetitive arrests.

Judge Clifton's description is eloquent testimony of the pressures imposed by mass production criminal justice on a thoughtful and conscientious magistrate. In a recent letter to the author, he made these further comments:

When you have a large number of defendants to handle, it is easy to develop techniques which could be criticized, such as: upon a defendant entering a plea of guilty, the judge could easily snap out "30 days" or some other disposition of the case and immediately call the next defendant's name while the last defendant was being hustled off, instead of asking the defendant, after his plea, about the offense. If the defendant were asked why he stole something or did something or other, and he made an explanation, this would slow down the procedure, because the next man, of course, would do the same thing, and the court in each case would have to listen to lengthy explanations beside the plea. Where there are here a large number of cases to handle, it is easy to develop a technique of quick sentences to avoid explanations. . . .

In courts where there are large numbers of cases, it is seldom that probation reports are obtained, That is, the judges sentence the prisoners without probation reports. Let me give you an example of that. I can recall very well one of our judges stating that in every drunk driving case he got a probation report. This procedure could be literally impossible in our drunk driving courts where I sat some ten years ago, when we had 65 arraignments on Monday, 50 on Tuesday, and 35 on the other days of the week. The probation officer wouldn't have time to handle many cases excepting drunk driving cases if we asked for probation reports in all cases.

These are the volume-processing techniques forced on our lower court magistrates by mass production criminal justice.

Problems Created by Mass-Production Justice

CAUSES DISRESPECT FOR LAW

The most significant fault in our present system of criminal justice is that in those areas where it comes in contact with the average citizen, as opposed to the working criminal or the depraved person, its performance is poorest. Mass-production techniques in traffic courts and misdemeanor arraignment courts are apt to create disrespect for law and the judicial process. Scant regard for human dignity and the worth of the individual can be evidenced where judges face daily calendars in the hundreds.

The automobile has made nearly every citizen a law violator or a potential law violator. Persons from every walk of life come into contact with police and courts as a result of traffic offenses. These experiences can create attitudes which undermine the foundation of our legal system. How can we expect respect for the law, and cooperation in its enforcement from citizens generally, when their personal involvement with courts is in mass-production settings where even individual explanations by defendants must be discouraged in order to clear up overcrowded calendars?

PREVENTS PROCEDURAL REFORM

Problems of volume make the institution of many desired reforms in criminal procedure difficult, if not impossible. In fact, the imperatives of

long calendars are causing ever greater disparities between the procedural
standards established by constitutions and statutes and those actually
applied in the courts. The problems can best be illustrated by considering current developments regarding the use of warrants, interrogation
and confessions, and the right of counsel.

WARRANTS

The formal law with respect to the use of warrants for arrests and
searches puts primary responsibility on the criminal-court magistrate for
supervision of the investigatory stage of criminal procedure, that is, for
determining the circumstances under which searches and arrests may be
made by the police. The Supreme Court of the United States has recently said that there is a constitutional preference for obtaining a judicial warrant as a prerequisite for making an arrest because "the arrest
warrant procedure serves to insure that the deliberate, impartial judgment of a judicial officer will be interposed between the citizen and the
police, to assess the weight and credibility of the information which the
complaining officer adduces as probable cause." [20] Only last year, in re-
versing a state conviction for a gambling offense on the ground that the
arrest and consequent search were unlawful because they were not based
on probable cause, the Court declared: "An arrest without a warrant by-
passes the safeguards provided by an objective predetermination of probable cause, and substitutes instead the far less reliable procedure of an
after-the-event justification for the arrest or search, too likely to be
subtly influenced by the familiar shortcomings of hindsight judgment." [21]
The Court has stated even stricter rules concerning police searches:
"Thus, evidence of criminal action may not, save in very limited and
closely confined situations, be seized without a judicially issued search
warrant." [22]

Not only has the Supreme Court indicated its preference for the use
of warrant proceedings, but it has held that the magistrate must do sig-
nificantly more than merely sign a document presented to him by the
police or the prosecutor. In a warrant proceeding, "the Commissioner
must judge for himself the persuasiveness of the facts relied on by a
complaining officer to show probable cause. He should not accept without question the complainant's mere conclusion that the person whose
arrest is sought has committed a crime." [23] More recently, in a 1964 case
reviewing the action of a local magistrate in issuing a warrant on the

[20] *Wong Sun v. United States,* 371 U.S. 471, 481 (1963).
[21] *Beck v. Ohio* (U.S.) 85 S. Ct. 223, 228 (1964).
[22] *Frank v. Maryland,* 359 U.S. 360, 365 (1959).
[23] *Giordenello v. United States,* 357 U.S. 480, 486 (1958).

basis of a very general affidavit presented by a police officer, the Court emphasized this requirement: "Although the reviewing court will pay substantial deference to judicial determinations of probable cause, the court must still insist that the magistrate perform his 'neutral and detached' function and not serve merely as a rubber stamp for the police." [24]

In a related move, the Supreme Court has suggested that the law leaves little if any room for screening by police and prosecutors once an arrest has been made. As an aspect of its reluctance to sanction convictions based upon confessions secured by police interrogation (to be discussed below), the Court has indicated that when a person is arrested the duty of the arresting officer is to take him immediately before a magistrate rather than hold him for further investigation or for complaint-issuing proceedings in the prosecutor's office. In a line of decisions so far made applicable only to the federal courts (and not generally followed by state courts) the Court has rejected the use of confessions obtained during periods of post-arrest investigation.

> The scheme for initiating a federal prosecution is plainly defined. The police may not arrest upon mere suspicion but only on "probable cause." The next step in the proceedings is to arraign the arrested person before a judicial officer as quickly as possible so that he may be advised of his rights and so that the issue of probable cause may be promptly determined. The arrested person may, of course, be "booked" by the police. But he is not to be taken to police headquarters in order to carry out a process of inquiry that lends itself, even if not so designed, to eliciting damaging statements to support the arrest and ultimately his guilt.[25]

The quotation just given is from the Supreme Court's controversial and widely discussed 1957 decision in *Mallory v. United States,* which has been hailed by some commentators as a landmark for procedural regularity and criticized by others, particularly prosecutors, as imposing impossible strains on practical law enforcement.

Adjustment of existing law-enforcement procedures to meet the standards suggested by the Supreme Court in this area would throw an enormous additional burden on the magistrates. How can a magistrate be more than a "rubber stamp" in signing warrants unless he devotes at least some minutes in each case to reading the affidavits submitted to him in support of the request for a warrant, and inquiring into the background of the conclusions stated therein? And where is the judicial time going to be found to make such inquiries in the generality of cases? The

---

[24] *Aguilar v. Texas,* 378 U.S. 108, 111 (1964).
[25] *Mallory v. United States,* 354 U.S. 449, 454 (1957).

Los Angeles Municipal Court with annual filings of about 130,000 (excluding parking and traffic) *finds itself so pressed that in large areas of its caseload it averages but a minute per case in receiving pleas and imposing sentence.* How could it cope with the added burden that would be involved in the issuance of warrants to govern the approximately 200,000 arrests made per year in Los Angeles for offenses other than traffic? What would be the extra burden on police and prosecutors in preparing for warrant hearings on such a gigantic scale? And what would be the additional burden imposed on magistrates presiding over arraignments and preliminary hearings, if arrests were not followed by investigation and by prosecutor screening designed to weed out the more doubtful cases? [26]

INTERROGATION AND CONFESSIONS

Courts are evidencing increasing reluctance to sanction convictions based upon confessions obtained after police interrogation. The Supreme Court of the United States has set high standards which must be met by the prosecution before a confession may be used in a criminal trial.

> Is the confession the product of an essentially free and unconstrained choice by its maker? If it is, if he has willed to confess, it may be used against him. If it is not, if his will has been overborne and his capacity for self-determination critically impaired, the use of his confession offends due process.[27]

Furthermore, the Court has held explicitly that the probable truth of a confession is not determinative of its admissibility as evidence against the accused.

> It is now axiomatic that a defendant in a criminal case is deprived of due process of law if his conviction is founded, in whole or in part, upon an involuntary confession, without regard to the truth or falsity of the confession, . . . and even though there is ample evidence aside from the confession to support the conviction. . . . Equally clear is the defendant's constitutional right at some stage in the proceedings to object to the use of the confession and to have a fair hearing and a reliable determination on the issue of voluntariness, a determination uninfluenced by the falsity of the confession.[28]

The Court has also sought to reduce the use of confessions by reducing the opportunity for police interrogation. Hence in cases like *Mallory v.*

---

[26] For general discussions of the tensions between the law and the practice in this area, see Barrett, *Police Practices and the Law—From Arrest to Release or Charge,* 50 California Law Review 11 (1962); LaFave, *Detention for Investigation by the Police: An Analysis of Current Practices,* 1962 Washington University Law Quarterly 331.

[27] *Culombe v. Connecticut,* 367 U.S. 568, 602 (1961).

[28] *Jackson v. Denno,* 378 U.S. 368, 376 (1964).

United States, the Court has suggested that, once an arrest is made, police should take the arrested person to a magistrate without any substantial period of interrogation (or other investigation) while he is in custody. In a related development the Supreme Court last year held that under certain circumstances police may not interrogate a person in custody without permitting him to consult his lawyer. In this connection, the Court said:

> It is argued that if the right to counsel is afforded prior to indictment, the number of confessions obtained by the police will diminish significantly, because most confessions are obtained during the period between arrest and indictment, and "any lawyer worth his salt will tell the suspect in no uncertain terms to make no statement to the police under any circumstances." . . . This argument, of course, cuts two ways. The fact that many confessions are obtained during this period points up its critical nature as a "stage when legal aid and advice" are surely needed. . . . The right to counsel would indeed be hollow if it began at a period when few confessions were obtained. There is necessarily a direct relationship between the importance of a stage to the police in their quest for a confession and the criticalness of that stage to the accused in his need for legal advice. Our Constitution, unlike some others, strikes the balance in favor of the rights of the accused to be advised by his lawyer of his privilege against self-incrimination. We have learned the lesson of history, ancient and modern, that a system of criminal law enforcement which comes to depend on the "confession" will, in the long run, be less reliable and more subject to abuses than a system which depends on extrinsic evidence independently secured through skillful investigation.[29]

This judicial development runs afoul of the imperatives of law-enforcement volume processing at two basic points. At the police level the implications of attempting to secure for the large volume of felony cases processed (since interrogation and confessions are problems in the main only in felony cases) extrinsic evidence "through skillful investigation" are enormous. No one knows the magnitude of the resources that would have to be committed at the police stage to achieve a tolerable level of criminal law enforcement without the use of interrogation and confessions both as investigative tools and as providing evidence to induce pleas of guilty or secure convictions in court.

At the court level this development tends to challenge head-on the basic assumption upon which the mass production system depends—that most persons charged with crime will plead guilty. As the number of confessions is reduced, it is predictable that there will be a marked in-

---

[29] *Escobedo v. Illinois,* 378 U.S. 478, 488 (1964).

crease in the number of contested cases, and particularly of serious cases which involve substantial commitments of resources for trial. In California, where about 66 per cent of felony dispositions come after plea of guilty and only 26 per cent after trial, contests in an additional 10 per cent of the cases filed in the superior courts would require an increase on the order of 30 per cent in the numbers of judges, courtrooms, prosecutors, defense lawyers, and associated personnel now involved in the trial of felony cases. The strains this would add to an already overburdened system are manifest.

COUNSEL

Our constitutional ideal is that every person charged with crime should have the opportunity to be represented by counsel. In practice, only a very small percentage of the total number of persons who come before the courts and plead to charges of crime have such representation.

In felony cases where the volume is less and the consequences for the defendant graver, great strides are now being taken toward providing lawyers for all defendants unable to obtain their own. The Supreme Court[30] has held such representation to be a constitutional necessity at all vital court stages of a felony prosecution—essentially from preliminary hearing through trial and appeal—and legislatures and the legal profession are actively at work on the great task of devising means of providing lawyers for the estimated 150,000 felony defendants a year unable to hire their own.[31] It appears reasonably assured that ways and means will be found satisfactorily to discharge this constitutional obligation.

Volume creates far more difficult problems, however, when it comes to providing counsel to indigent accused persons in misdemeanor cases. California courts alone process annually nearly half a million charges of misdemeanors other than traffic. *It is probable that each year throughout the United States more than a million people who cannot afford counsel are charged with misdemeanors.* The cost in manpower and money of providing lawyers for all such persons would be astronomical.

An even more fundamental problem exists with respect to the availability of counsel to persons charged with minor offenses. The courts simply could not deal with their present enormous calendars of such cases if any substantial percentage of the defendants, indigent or not, were represented by counsel. Cases where lawyers appear for the persons charged cannot be disposed of at a rate of a minute or less. Lawyers will

<hr/>

[30] *Gideon v. Wainwright*, 372 U.S. 335 (1963). For a fascinating account of this case and the legal problems involved, see Lewis, *Gideon's Trumpet* (Random House, 1964).

[31] Silverstein, *Defense of the Poor in Criminal Cases in American State Courts—A Preliminary Summary* (American Bar Foundation, 1964).

insist upon speaking for their clients and upon a certain individualization of treatment. The system works now only because in the great bulk of cases defendants believe that it is not worthwhile to employ or seek the appointment of counsel.[32]

The Directions for Reform

What should be done about our system of administration of criminal justice? What are the directions for reform? What should be the concern of those not directly involved in the administration of the law? It is not the author's present purpose to discuss detailed answers, but a brief outline of the avenues which should be explored in seeking solutions is surely appropriate.

First, and this may be most important of all, society must begin to pay serious attention to the magistrates courts and other lower criminal courts, where criminal justice takes on its reality for many hundreds of thousands of people every year. We cannot afford not to be doing every-

---

[32] In the very recent case of *In Re Johnson,* 42 California Reporter 228 (California, 1965) the Supreme Court of California faced the question of whether an offender charged with five separate offenses of driving with a revoked license had waived his right to counsel which, the court said, is not limited in California to felony cases "but is equally guaranteed to persons charged with misdemeanors in a municipal or other inferior court." The magistrate had made a general statement at the beginning of the day's calendar to all defendants present telling them, among other things, of their rights to be represented by counsel. This statement was not repeated to the defendant when he pleaded guilty and a waiver of counsel was presumed from his failure to request counsel. The court found this procedure erroneous in the particular case, stating:

> We must recognize that the typically crowded arraignment calendars of our courts pose urgent problems in the administration of justice in California. . . . For example, probably the vast majority of citizens haled into court on traffic violations share the judge's interest in prompt disposition of their cases, feeling themselves sufficiently inconvenienced by having to make personal appearances in the first place. To require the judge to orally examine each such defendant at length for the purpose of determining his capability of defending himself would seem to be an idle and time-wasting ritual. . . .
>
> In the case at bar, however, additional considerations were present to distinguish it from the ordinary simple traffic offense. The trial court had apparently decided, within its discretion, to deal sternly with this repeated offender; for this reason his case was specially continued for sentencing until all other matters had been completed, whereupon the court recalled him before the bench and imposed five maximum and consecutive jail sentences totaling 900 days. Reduced to lay terminology, this amounted to nearly two-and-a-half years in jail. In view of the multiplicity and potential seriousness of the charges the court should have made a reasonable effort, before accepting petitioner's pleas of guilty, to determine whether he understood his predicament and was capable of representing himself effectively at all stages of the proceedings.

thing possible to improve the quality of justice dispensed in magistrates courts if law and order are to be maintained in our increasingly urbanized society. In law administration, as everywhere, lack of understanding and public indifference are the greatest enemies of reform. Until the existing procedures and pressing problems of the magistrates courts become generally known, it is unlikely that anything substantial will be done about them. Lawyers and judges and bar associations can view with alarm, as they have been doing for quite a while now, but they cannot solve the problems of mass-production law enforcement without general public interest and support. Community leaders and citizens generally must somehow be made to realize that the administration of the criminal law is of genuinely vital concern to everyone.

Second, we must be prepared to spend more public money to increase the amount of judicial time allotted to misdemeanor arraignment courts.[33] Even if no other reforms were undertaken, a vast improvement would be registered if we could double or treble the number of judges actually sitting in the lower criminal courts. Reduction of daily calendars to the point where individualized and humane treatment becomes possible is clearly a matter of first priority. This means that the budgets of the lower criminal courts in our great cities would have to be two or three times what they are today, but the investment would be relatively small, compared to the magnitude of other public expenditures, and it would pay real dividends in greater respect for the institutions of law enforcement that are basic to the stability and order of our society.

Third, we need to give careful consideration to ways and means of reducing the load carried by the criminal courts generally. If we are going to be able to afford a system of administration of criminal justice which even approximates our declared ideals, we must keep to a minimum the areas of human conduct that are regulated by the imposition of criminal sanctions.[34] Wherever possible, civil penalties, with simplified

[33] In a recent letter to the author Judge Robert Clifton makes the point as follows:

> For years I have suggested that we need more arraignment courts, and have said over and over again that those in charge of the administration of the judiciary have devoted too much time to the question of the trial of cases and keeping down the size of the trial calendars and not enough time to the question of the sentences—what to do with a person who has pleaded guilty. We are willing to allow a judge and a jury a full week to try a drunk-driving case (involving an heiress) on the theory that a person is entitled to his day in court, and yet at the same time in the drunk-driving arraignment court where the defendants practically all plead guilty, after they have pleaded guilty their cases are handled in a matter of minutes or seconds. It is, of course, important that people have trials in which their rights are fully protected but it is also important that proceedings in the arraignment court should be given adequate time.

[34] For a discussion of one aspect of the problem see Packer, *The Crime Tariff,* 33 American Scholar 551 (1964).

procedures to collect them, should be substituted to handle those offenses which do not involve moral considerations and where future compliance with the law is more important than punishment for past conduct. In a related direction, we should pay increasing attention to expanding medical, psychiatric, and other treatment facilities so as to reduce by cure the volume of persons processed through the criminal courts because of addiction to alcohol or drugs.[35]

Fourth, we need to pay more attention to improving the administrative mechanisms through which the system of criminal justice operates. Much is now being done by the courts themselves through the establishment of administrative offices at both municipal and state levels. But the system of criminal justice should also be surveyed by administrative experts from outside the legal profession. Those with fresh viewpoints may be able to devise ways and means of expediting the handling of criminal cases without impairing the fundamental values expressed in our notions of due process of law. Basic administrative reforms may be needed before we can afford to conform our system to the due-process ideals which now are often lost in the day-to-day processing of large volumes of cases.[36] The challenge here is enormous—and the need for imaginative work is far too great to leave the process of reform entirely to lawyers and judges, encrusted as they are with the barnacles of legal tradition.

[35] Compare Judge Clifton's colorful language in a recent letter:

> Certainly if an auto repairman had a business in which one-half of the customers were there for bad brakes or for brake repairs, he would have a large brake department, or if a merchant were selling a number of things, but one item comprised one-half of his sales, he would certainly devote some time and money in handling this type of customer or sale. The courts in the United States should wake up to the fact that they are not properly handling the majority of the intoxication arrest cases which compose one-half of the arrest cases and devote sufficient time and personnel to them so that not only the legal aspects of the cases are inquired into, but also persons who are alcoholics, or beginning to become alcoholics, can be directed to treatment through court-imposed sanctions.

[36] For an imaginative discussion of the tensions between due process values and administrative imperatives, see Packer, *Two Models of the Criminal Process,* 113 University of Pennsylvania Law Review 1 (1964).

Harry W. Jones

5

The Trial Judge
—Role Analysis and Profile

"In the long run," wrote Judge Cardozo, "there is no guarantee of justice except the personality of the judge." Each of the four preceding chapters of this book point to and support Cardozo's conclusion. Basic reforms in court organization and sound and imaginative new procedures for handling the mounting flow of civil claims and criminal prosecutions are indispensable conditions for meeting today's crisis in the courts. But law can never be much better than the men who administer and apply it. Legal rules and procedures do not operate automatically, nor cases decide themselves.

This chapter deals with trial judges, the work they do and the intellectual and personal qualities required for genuinely effective performance on the trial bench. There is very little in legal literature on the nature of the judicial process in the lower courts, even in trial courts of general jurisdiction. A few thoughtful trial judges, notably Joseph C. Hutcheson, Curtis Bok, and Charles Wyzanski, have provided sensitive interpretations of their own experience, but there is practically nothing available by way of systematic examination of the role of the trial judge in the administration of civil and criminal justice. This chapter is certainly not the comprehensive analysis that needs to be written, but it may serve to make the crucial point that in the work of the courts, as in every other aspect of our culture, the quality of the craftsman is fully as important as the efficiency of the tools with which he works.

HARRY W. JONES *is Cardozo Professor of Jurisprudence at Columbia University. In 1954 he edited* The American Assembly *book,* Economic Security for Americans, *and he is co-author of casebooks in legal method and contracts. In recent years, most of his writing has been in the fields of*

*jurisprudence, legal philosophy, and church-state relations. He is a mem-
ber of the American Philosophical Society.*

A certain Bishop of Paris, known throughout Europe for his
great learning and humility, came to the conclusion that he was unworthy of his high place in the Church and successfully petitioned the
Pope for reassignment to service as a simple parish priest. The legend is
regrettably vague as to whether this happened in the twelfth century or
the thirteenth, or indeed as to whether our almost unbecomingly humble
prelate was bishop in Paris or some place else, but it is perfectly clear as
to what came of the reassignment. After less than a year of parish work,
the former bishop was back in Rome with another petition, this one
praying for his restoration to episcopal status, and for good and sufficient
reason. "If I am unworthy to be Bishop of Paris," he said,

> how much more unworthy am I to be priest of a parish. As bishop, I was
> remote from men and women of lowly station, my shortcomings and weak-
> nesses concealed from them by distance and ecclesiastical dignity. But as
> parish priest, I move intimately each day among the members of my flock,
> endeavoring by comfort, counsel and admonition to make their hard lot on
> earth seem better than it is. I *am* the Church to them; when my faith flags
> or my wisdom fails or my patience wears thin, it is the Church that has failed
> them. *Demote* me, Your Holiness, and make me bishop again, for I have
> learned how much easier it is to be a saintly bishop than to be a godly priest.

The trial judge is the parish priest of our legal order. The impression
that prevails in society concerning the justice or injustice of our legal institutions depends almost entirely on the propriety, efficiency, and humaneness of observed trial court functioning. "Important as it is that
people should get justice," said the Victorian chancellor, Lord Herschell,
"it is even more important that they be made to feel and see that they
are getting it." This profound truth about law in society is deeply rooted
in the common-law tradition, and it fully justifies the focus of this book
on trial courts and what they do. The typical citizen will never see an
appellate court in action, but there is every likelihood that he will sooner
or later be drawn into the operation of one or another of our trial courts,
whether as litigant, witness, or juryman.

The Trial Judge as a Representative of Justice

Aristotle was surely right when he said that members of the
public look upon the judge as "living justice," that is, as the personifica-
tion of the legal order. For better or worse, it is the trial judge upon
whom this representative responsibility falls in our society. He *is* the law

for most people and most legal purposes. Whenever a trial judge fails in probity, energy, objectivity, or patience, his failure is observable and cannot but impair public fidelity to law. This is true even and particularly of the minor magistrate in a police court or a small-claims tribunal. He may be at the bottom of the judicial totem pole, but it is there that the exposure is often greatest and the strains of the judge's role manifest for all to see.

Indeed, a case can be made that a judge's importance as a justice representative varies inversely with his rank in the judicial hierarchy. There is a public welfare perspective in which the personality of the appellate-court justice seems less significant than that of the trial judge of general jurisdiction, and the personality of the police-court magistrate more significant than either of them. Thoughtful citizens are concerned and apprehensive about the decreasing respect for law and social order evidenced by mounting crime statistics, particularly by the sharp rise in arrests for petty offenses, narcotics addiction, drunkenness, and juvenile delinquency. These are offenses of social alienation. The juvenile delinquent and the narcotics addict are not professional criminals, at least not yet. It is a great task of the legal order to win back for society as many of the alienated as are not irretrievably lost to it.

Scholars of society advise us that great symbolic importance, for good or for harm, can attach to the juvenile offender's or the alcoholic's early encounters with the institutions of the legal order, and particularly with the judge in his case. As to this, Edward Barrett's essay (Chapter Four) describes an intolerable situation. When the young or petty offender's first encounter with the legal order takes the form of a mass shape-up, with each subject for adjudication taking his place in a long queue for split-second disposition of his case by a tired, bored, or irascible magistrate, the social effects can be disastrous. If organized society treats a petty offender or a neglected child as if he were a blank for machine processing, there may be no getting him back from social alienation into useful citizenship.

To be sure, unbearable time pressures are imposed on our so-called "inferior courts" by the quantitative explosion in criminal law administration. It is reckless parsimony for an affluent society to withhold the modest expenditures that would be necessary to create the reality and appearance of compassionate deliberation in the operations of our lower criminal courts. Available judicial manpower there must be increased at least threefold, and speedily before further irremediable damage is done. But the problem calls for more than in increase in undifferentiated units of judicial manpower. It is equally important that the new judges brought to the lower criminal courts not be professional misfits or clubhouse hacks, but men and women of understanding, firmness, and imagination, genuinely concerned about the social consequences of their adjudicative work and earnestly determined to do something constructive about it.

There are all sorts and conditions of trial judges, ranging in professional status from prestigious United States district judges and state judges of general jurisdiction to lowly magistrates whose social importance is hardly grasped at all by the legal profession or the public at large. There are many areas of judicial specialization, each requiring that its judges be persons of unusual and particular competence and experience: divorce courts, probate or surrogate's courts, children's courts, and many others. What these sorts and conditions of trial judges have in common is that they are all engaged in bringing law's general principles and commands down to the people law governs and serves. A legal order without trial judges of high professional and moral qualifications is like an army without dependable field-grade combat officers or a school system without able and devoted classroom teachers. Planning and policy coordination must come from headquarters (in law from the appellate courts) but it is out in the field that the day-to-day work is done.

It will be a thesis of this essay that genuinely effective service as a trial judge calls for qualities of mind, heart, and character that may differ from but are in no way inferior to the qualities required for effective service on a high appellate court, even a state court of last resort or the Supreme Court of the United States. When and how can it be brought home to the legal profession and to the public generally that a man unworthy by character and temperament to be an appellate judge is, in a real sense, even more unworthy to be entrusted with the highly visible powers and responsibilities of a trial judge? There is a growing recognition of this in the selection of judges for high-prestige trial courts of general jurisdiction and for courts charged with responsibility in delicate matters of juvenile behavior and family law. But the recognition has been slow in coming and has still not been extended to awareness of the importance of far higher standards than now prevail in the recruitment of personnel for the inferior courts at the bottom rung of the judicial hierarchy.

The Central Importance of Trial Courts in Adjudication

Suppose that we were to get the appraisal of a thoughtful and experienced trial judge on what has been said so far about the role of the trial judge as a kind of justice representative. In all probability, he would concede that he inevitably carries a certain responsibility as one of the law's principal representatives and witnesses to society, although it might make him a bit uneasy in his daily courtroom work if he thought too much about it. But he would insist that his role as representative of public justice is only incidental to his main job and that his main job is the business of adjudication. This is a sensible and thoroughly professional way of looking at the matter, and no one could quarrel too much with it. Certainly judges are appraised by their peers not in terms of their sensitivity to human relations but in terms of their effectiveness as adjudicative officials. We turn, then, to an analysis of the trial judge's basic role as a decision-making and decision-influencing officer of the legal order.

COMMON MISCONCEPTIONS OF THE JUDGE'S ROLE

How important, really, is the work of the trial judge qua adjudicative official? The question is not as fanciful or simple-minded as it might seem to be on first impression, and it is often pressed by non-lawyers, even by behavioral scientists of considerable legal sophistication, at conferences on judicial selection and law administration. Such doubts as to whether a particular trial judge's qualifications, or lack of them, make any genuine difference as to the ultimate outcome of a case seem to proceed from two more or less related preconceptions: *First,* that ours is a "government of laws and not of men," from which the inference is readily drawn that one judge will read the law's mandate about the same way as another will, if it be assumed that both of them are men of probity and learned enough in formal legal sources to have passed a bar examination; and *Second,* that a trial judge, in any event, has several tiers of appellate courts above him, and his appellate betters will surely catch and correct any misreading of the law of which he may be guilty at the trial stage of a controversy. On this showing, say the doubters, how can a civil suit or criminal prosecution be affected, as to its final result, by the circumstance that the particular trial judge before whom it comes is, or is not, a man of resourcefulness, wisdom, and uncommon professional skill?

The question just put is, of course, a crucial one for the current proposals, described and appraised by Glenn Winters and Robert Allard in Chapter Six, that are designed to improve prevailing standards of judicial selection in the United States. If the intellect and personality of the trial judge make relatively little difference on how cases are finally decided, why should the public generally be too much concerned about judicial selection, at least about the qualifications, questions of elementary honesty aside, of aspirants for the trial bench? In fact, the prevailing public attitude, even among leaders of community opinion, may be about as suggested. If this is not the prevailing attitude, it is curious that reasonably alert citizens and civic groups should be as acquiescent as they are about the not infrequent appointment of second- or third-rate lawyers to first-rate trial courts and that intelligent people should go to the polls and vote for a party-leader-nominated slate of trial-court judges, without having the foggiest notion of the intellectual and moral qualifications of the candidates.

The conceptions that contribute to this widespread under-appraisal of the work of the trial courts have no support whatever in the realities of the adjudicative process. A trial judge's intellect, energy, and character, or his deficiencies in any of these qualities, will make a great difference, can make all the difference in the world, on how the cases tried before him are finally decided. The trial judge is the key man in our system of adjudication. In the great bulk of litigated cases, he is by far the most important and influential participant, and this whether or not the case at hand is a jury case, whether or not it is appealed from trial-court judgment to one or more higher appellate courts, and whether or not the legalities of the controversy involve the interpretation of a federal or state statute or a question of common law.

LEGAL RULES AND CONCRETE CASES: THE INESCAPABILITY OF CHOICE

We need not pause too long to dispose of the hoary fiction that judges have no discretion, no choices between alternative decisions, in "a government of laws and not of men." The notion that a judge merely pronounces results already preordained and fixed by the rules of the legal system is the long-discarded "slot machine" theory of the judicial process and almost as misdescriptive of the trial judge's work as it is of the work of appellate courts. This is not to say that the established substantive law is always or usually uncertain in its application to the particular controversies that reach the courts for decision. In most cases it is doubtless true that there is little room for argument as to the legal rule that controls the dispute between the parties, once the facts of the case are "found" by the judge, or by the jury under the judge's guidance and supervision. Legislative foresight is finite, however, and there is no limit to the variety of situations that can arise in a complex and dynamic society. No legal code, no aggregate of statutory directions and judge-made precedents, can ever furnish explicit and unambiguous commands for every conceivable case.

If the law were truly and everywhere as certain as the "government of laws and not of men" formula would have it, why would businessmen of good sense hire lawyers of distinction to advise and represent them, at fees running into six figures, when the services of a low-status professional might be secured for a few hundred dollars? Why, for that matter, would the Supreme Court of the United States divide as often as it does, by five to four or six to three? No, on any account of the judicial process, there is a substantial incidence of cases in which the law is unclear, that is, in which the judge has no clear mandate to decide one way or the other and must choose between the alternative decisions open to him on the basis of his own best judgment as to which decision is fair between the parties and sound as a matter of generally applicable public policy. Whatever the incidence of these hard or "unprovided for" cases may be —even if it be calculated very conservatively at no more than one-fifth or even one-tenth of the cases that reach the courts—it is indisputable that the work of a judge involves the high art of prudential judgement. To quote Cardozo:

> It is when the colors do not match, when the references in the index fail, when there is no decisive precedent, that the serious business of the judge begins.

A trial judge lacking in social insight, prudence, and intellectual resourcefulness is incapable of measuring up to the challenge of this aspect of his serious business. It must be kept in mind that in any hard case in which his decision on the troublesome question of law is not appealed to a higher court, the trial judge's error of law and wisdom can effect an irremediable miscarriage of justice.

THE UPPER COURT MYTH

What of the other preconception that underlies public discounting of the importance of the trial judge's role as an adjudicative official? What merit is there in the suggestion that the center of gravity of American adjudication is really in the appellate courts and that the determinations of trial judges are provisional only and subject to ready correction on appeal? The realities of the American judicial system have been obscured, in scholarly writing as in public discussion, by the stubborn persistence of what the late Judge Jerome Frank called the "upper-court myth," the notion that everything will be all right in the house of justice so long as appeals from trial-court decisions are freely available and the upper courts manned by judges of wisdom, experience, and professional competence. In this view, which has been contributed to by the almost exclusive preoccupation of American legal education with the reported opinions of appellate courts, the trial-court stage of a civil suit or criminal prosecution seems a mere preliminary bout; the main event will not begin until the case reaches the appellate court of last resort. Political scientists have absorbed the upper-court myth as uncritically as their scholarly brothers in the law schools. For every book or article analyzing the functioning of the trial courts as agencies of government and large-scale public administration, there are a dozen or more given to charting the batting averages of individual justices of the Supreme Court of the United States on this or that issue of constitutional law or to developing the logical or policy subtleties of striking pieces of rhetoric in Supreme Court opinions.

The extent to which the upper-court myth distorts the relative significance of trial-court functioning and appellate-court functioning is manifest even if we put aside, for the moment, the assembly-line operations of police courts, traffic courts, small claims courts, and the like and consider only the traditional and substantial civil and criminal cases that are heard, as of first instance, in trial courts of general jurisdiction. It is a safe guess that at least 90 per cent of even these blue ribbon controversies are determined and controlled, as to practical outcome, by rules of law applied and facts "found" at the trial-court stage, as against 10 per cent at most that are controlled in result by what happens to them in the appellate courts. It is in the appellate courts that precedents are forged for the future and statutes given their authoritative interpretation and effect, but, as concerns the ultimate adjudicative fate of litigated controversies, the trial courts outweigh the appellate courts by at least nine to one.

Relatively Few Cases Are Appealed. The quantitative appraisal just recorded may be surprising to a non-lawyer reader. Since a right to appeal is generously, perhaps too generously, afforded in our judicial system, how can it be maintained that the practical outcome of a substantial lawsuit is set and determined, ninety times out of a hundred, by what happens to the controversy in the trial court? The first and obvious point in the explanation is that relatively few cases, perhaps 10 per cent at most, are ever appealed at all. Although our procedural system does not discourage appeals, as the English system does by assessing heavy fees and costs against an unsuccessful appellant, appeals are expensive and time-consuming, and the statistical evidence warns sufficiently that incomparably more trial-court decisions are affirmed on appeal than reversed. Even in jurisdictions where the ratio of appeals to trials is far higher (as in the federal courts) than one in ten, a substantial number of appeals are taken with no great expectation of success, either as a delaying tactic to impose pressure for settlement of the case at less than the amount of trial-court judgment or as a means of assuring a disappointed and indignant client that every possible step is being taken in his behalf.

Findings of Fact Can Be Decisive. The rising incidence of appeals dealt with in Geoffrey Hazard's essay (Chapter Three) suggests this question: Would the work of the trial courts become less significant if a full third or more of trial-court decisions were taken on appeal to a higher court? Even this would require no drastic modification of the proposition that the ultimate fate of most cases, whether appealed or not, is determined by what happens to them at the trial stage. It is in the trial court that the facts of a case are "found," and for most cases the findings of fact are decisive. Of the mine-run of controversies that reach the courts, relatively few—one in five, perhaps, as we have seen—turn on questions as to what the "law" of the case is. The usual dispute is as to what the true facts are. Consider, for example, the automobile accident-personal injury cases that have inundated trial courts of general jurisdiction throughout the United States. The central issue in dispute between the plaintiff and the defendant (or the defendant's liability insurance company) is rarely an issue of substantive law, that is, rarely a question whether, on some agreed or conceded set of facts, the law of the state concerned would or would not authorize a judgment for damages in the plaintiff's favor. The crucial issues are far likelier to be factual in character: Was the defendant driving sixty-five miles an hour in a thirty-five-miles-an-hour speed zone, as the plaintiff asserts, or was the defendant proceeding at a cautious thirty-miles an hour, as he contends he was? Had the red light changed to green before the plaintiff started to cross the intersection, as he and his witnesses swear that it had, or was the green light still in defendant driver's favor, as he and the passengers in his car swear that it was? Is the injured plaintiff permanently disabled for his former employment, as he and his physician testify, or is his injury temporary and capable of simple surgical correction, as the defendant's medical witnesses declare?

Similarly, in commercial litigation and in criminal prosecutions, the central issue in dispute is far more often what lawyers call an "issue of fact" than an "issue of law." What precisely did the property owner say when the contractor came to his office and told him that the construction would not be ready by the date fixed in the contract, or could not be completed for the originally agreed contract price? Did the seller call the buyer's attention specifically to the presence of an arbitration clause embedded in the fine print on the back of the seller's standard contract form? The seller says yes, the buyer says no, and which of them is to be believed? Or, in a criminal case, was the accused really in Peoria on the day of the bank robbery, as his alibi witnesses swear that he was, or are the prosecution's eyewitnesses testifying truthfully and accurately when they say that they saw him that day running out of the held-up bank? Questions like these are the grist of the adjudicative mill, even in cases of first magnitude to the parties involved. Once the factual dispute has been resolved, the facts "found" in favor of one party or the other, the result of the case, more often than not, is foreordained.

When injustice occurs in our legal system, it is less often because of some archaicism or unfairness in the general law than because of some error in the ascertainment of facts, that is, from some failure in the reconstruction at the trial of what had actually happened outside the courtroom. Here is Judge Frank's appraisal:

Trained lawyers know the "jurisprudence" relevant to murder trials or automobile accident trials and can prophesy with a high degree of reliability what rules will be applied in such litigation. But what of it? The layman wants to know whether these rules will be applied to the actual facts. . . . If a man, defeated in a suit because of a mistake about the facts, goes to jail or the electric chair or loses his business, will it solace him to learn that there was no possible doubt concerning the applicable legal principles?

The trial court, as the agency of the state for the hearing and determination of disputed issues of fact, holds the central position in the practical administration of justice.

Findings of Fact Not Reviewable on Appeal. As Milton Green's essay (Chapter One) makes clear, appellate courts rarely undertake to review trial-court findings of fact. The appealing party may be able to secure reversal of a trial-court judgment against him if he can persuade the appellate court that the trial judge was wrong on his "law," as where the jury was given an instruction embodying an erroneous view of the substantive law, or inadmissible and prejudicial evidence was admitted at the trial over the appellant's objection. But there are relatively few situations in which an appellate court will listen to an argument that the version of the facts accepted as true by the jury, or by the trial judge sitting as trier of the facts without a jury, was a false version or one against the weight of the evidence at the trial. Reasons both of tradition and of good sense explain this general limitation of the appellate process to legal (as distinguished from factual) issues. There would be no end to litigation if factual disputes could be recontested at each successive tier of the judicial hierarchy, and appellate judges, having only a printed record before them, are properly reluctant to second-guess a trial judge or a panel of jurymen who observed the demeanor of the witnesses at the trial and heard their examination and cross-examination. Thus the factual element in a case, the element which, as we have seen, is the decisive one in most litigated controversies, is decided with substantial finality in the trial court. This should be enough to dispose of the upper-court myth.

RELATION OF THE TRIAL JUDGE TO JURY FACT-FINDING

Nothing a trial judge does in his role as an adjudicative official is more important than his work in relation to the determination of disputed issues of fact. This is clear enough when the trial judge is himself the sole trier of the facts, as he often is when the case is of a category which, historically, does not call for the summoning of a jury (e.g., a suit for an injunction or other "equitable remedy") or when the parties to a civil suit or the accused in a criminal case "waive" the right to jury trial and

consent to have the case's issues of fact as well as its issues of law determined by the court without a jury. But how important is the judge's role
when the issues of fact are for the "twelve good men and true" in the
jury box? In a jury case, is the trial judge much more than a keeper of
order and master of ceremonies?

The institution of the jury trial retains greater vitality in the land of
its transplantation than in the land of its historical origin. In England,
jury trials have been abolished for almost all civil litigation; in the
United States, federal and state constitutional provisions preserve the
jury institution not only for serious criminal prosecutions but also for the
generality of civil cases. Even in this country, however, the trial judge is
far from a passive bystander in a jury case. Through his rulings on
questions of the admissibility of evidence, he controls or largely influ-
ences the testimonial data from which the jury will draw its inferences
as to the truth of the plaintiff's and the defendant's competing versions
of the facts of the case. The trial judge, within certain more or less
defined limits, may set aside the jury verdict in a civil suit and order a
new trial of the case when he believes that the verdict at which the
jury arrived was capricious or wholly unsupported by the evidence before
it. He may do this, too, in a criminal case if the jury comes in with a
verdict of guilty, although our legal system, for reasons of fairness sym-
bolized by the phrase "double jeopardy," gives conclusiveness and finality
to a jury verdict of not guilty. Most important of all the forms of the
trial judge's participation in jury fact-finding is his "charge" or instruction to the jury, in which he expounds the law to be applied by the jury
in reaching its verdict, telling the jurymen, in effect, the facts they must
find to be true (beyond a reasonable doubt in criminal cases or, in civil
cases, supported by the preponderance of the evidence) before they can
bring in a verdict for one side or the other in the controversy.

If the personality of the trial judge is such that he can establish a
working rapport with the juries empaneled in his courtroom, the judge
becomes the jury's effective guide and counselor, virtually a full partner
in the jury's discharge of its decisional responsibility. Top flight trial
judges have always been able to establish close working relations with
their juries, but this achievement requires that the judge be possessed of
unusual talents of communication, talents not widely shared by members
of the legal profession. The high art of charging a jury furnishes a good
illustration of the point at hand. A run-of-the-mill trial judge will phrase
his instruction to the jury in impenetrably technical terms; a charge so
worded is a pure ritual, hardly more influential on the jury's deliberations than it would have been if delivered in classical Greek. A genuinely
qualified trial judge has the capacity to translate legal jargon into English intelligible to lay jurymen and can, without endangering the legal

soundness of his instruction, give the jury a useful analysis of the task it has ahead of it. Sensitivity to jury relations and skills at communication are among the qualities that are most imperative for effective service as a trial judge. It is regrettable that these attributes are taken account of as infrequently as they are in professional and public discussions of the qualifications for judicial office.

Strains and Demands in the Role of the Trial Judge

A lawyer raised to the bench by appointment or election comes at once under the influence of a great and continuing tradition of craftsmanship and social accountability, perhaps the most powerful craft tradition that survives in contemporary society. If the lawyer was a good man before his elevation, he will almost certainly be a better man after it, at least as goodness is measured in the legal universe. If he was mediocre before, appointment or election to the bench is likely to make him less mediocre. Even if he was the kind of lawyer who should never have been made a judge, and many such unpromising candidates reach the bench every year, his temperament and character will probably show at least some improvement after he dons the robe.

This demonstrable fact about the tendency of judicial office to elevate the moral and intellectual standards of the men and women who attain it is sometimes drawn on to support a kind of argument that there is no reason for great concern about the professional and moral qualifications of judicial hopefuls, that the tradition will somehow ennoble even the least qualified man. This wildly overoptimistic suggestion claims too much even for the great adjudicative tradition of our common law. To be sure, the tradition can transform an indifferent lawyer into a somewhat less indifferent judge, but in law, as elsewhere in life, one cannot make a silk purse out of a sow's ear. Nowhere in the whole range of public office are weaknesses of character, intellect, or psychic constitution revealed more mercilessly than in the discharge of the responsibilities of a trial judge. The strains and demands of the role could be illustrated in a dozen different contexts; we will consider two of them, the tensions involved in the trial judge's relations with the lawyers appearing before him, and the burdens he must sustain in the sentencing of persons convicted on criminal charges.

JUDGE-LAWYER RELATIONS IN AN ADVERSARY SYSTEM OF LITIGATION

American court procedure, like the English system from which it springs, is adversary in character both in its approach to the determination of contested issues of law and in its approach to the even more important matter, for most cases, of determining the truth of disputed issues of fact. The opposed parties appear in the trial court through advocates, professional champions, each of whom is pledged to present the legal theory, or the version of the disputed facts, favorable to his client's side of the case. It is only in a limited sense that the trial lawyer is an "officer of the court"; actually the advocacy model embodied in the common law canons of professional ethics is that of the honorable partisan who fights honestly and fairly but wholly in his client's cause. This trial by forensic combat strikes most laymen as a curious, even eccentric, way of going about the hearing and determination of controversies. Most lawyers feel, as I most assuredly do, that the adversary system, with all its conceded shortcomings, is a better procedure than any other yet devised for arriving at the sound development of legal principles and the substantial justice of particular litigated cases. There are certain postulates, however, on which even we lawyers base our confidence in the adversary system. The premise of our system of adjudication is that the adversary performance will go on with a cast of characters composed of an equally powerful advocate for each side and a trial judge who is at least the equal of either of them in legal acumen, energy, and force of character.

Defects of Resolution. In American procedural theory, the conventional description characterizes the trial judge as the "umpire" of the contest. Few American judges intervene as actively as their English common law predecessors did in the examination of witnesses and other aspects of trial management. This is true today as concerns jury trials in criminal cases in the two countries; it is suggestive of the difference that the English idiom speaks of a criminal case as tried *by* the judge, while we speak of it as tried *before* the judge. But the role of umpire in an adversary court proceeding is not one that can be played effectively by a judge who is mediocre in intellect or professional skill, lacking in decisiveness, or in any way emotionally insecure. Courtroom decorum has to be maintained with a firm hand if cases are to be tried fairly and expeditiously, and as a case proceeds the trial judge is called upon to make many rulings that are of great strategic and tactical importance for the outcome of the litigation. These rulings, characteristically, have to be made by the trial judge "from the hip," that is, under the pressures of the trial and without opportunity for extended consultation of the formal authorities in the law books. Many trial judges who have later moved up to high appellate courts have spoken gratefully of the more relaxed pace and opportunity for reflection they found in appellate work after years of the hurly-burly of trial court proceedings. It is as if a teacher had suddenly been translated from a classroom assignment in a problem high school to the relative tranquility of a post as assistant superintendent of schools.

Former President Truman's classic injunction, "If you can't stand the heat, get out of the kitchen," applies superbly to trial judges and particularly to judges of the trial courts of general jurisdiction. The trial judge who is shaky in professional understanding, imperfect in moral resolution, or unduly conciliatory in personality will inevitably be overpowered and overborne by forceful and aggressive trial counsel. The evil that weak judges do, less often from partiality, as commonly supposed, than from simple psychic inability to stand up to abrasive or stronger willed leaders of the trial bar is a bitter but largely untold story in the administration of justice. If the adversary system is to work justly, the trial judge must command the respect, not necessarily the affection, of every advocate who may appear before him, however powerful or distinguished the advocate may be. This status he can never attain unless he has every resource of self-respect: confidence in his judgment, willingness to act on the balance of probabilities, and inner assurance of his authenticity in the role he has undertaken. The umpire who thinks himself inferior to any player on the field will never be able to call 'em as he sees 'em.

The Sin of Arrogance. In inadequate men of other psychic constitutions, the tensions of the trial judge's role can be manifested in a quite different way but one equally violative of the postulates of the adversary system. Every multi-judge trial court of general jurisdiction has at least one tyrant in residence. Sometimes he is a short-tempered man of professional ability and irascible disposition. If his technical qualifications are outstanding, they may compensate in large degree for the unpleasantness of his personality, although the excessively crusty judge will leave a bad taste with litigants, witnesses, and jurymen, however impressive his technical endowments may be to the lawyers in the case.

Far more often, as would be expected, the judicial tyrant is a man of inferior intellect and professional skill whose impatient and overbearing manner reflects deeply rooted feelings of his own inferiority. In any metropolitan community, arrogant judges of this second category are readily identified by experienced trial lawyers. There are regular ways by which the sophisticated advocate manages to avoid having his cases assigned to them for trial, with the ironical consequence that the worst judges are likely to get more than their ratable share of the cases in which trial counsel are inferior or inexperienced, and so least able to cope with impatience, oppression, or undue interference from the bench.

The very real values inherent in the adversary system of litigation are undermined when the trial judge in a case is a man of arrogant and abusive temperament. The lawyers in the controversy find it impossible to develop their cases in an effective and orderly way. Witnesses become confused or defiantly resentful. They expect harsh treatment on cross-examination by opposing counsel, but not from the judge, to whom they look for comfort and support in their unusual ordeal. The clarity and accuracy of their testimony suffers accordingly. Jurymen are estranged and disinclined to follow the instructions of their heavy-handed preceptor. The entire trial process is distorted, and the parties, certainly the losing party and often the winner, leave the courtroom with a distinct impression that their dignity has been assailed and their claims and grievances inadequately heard. In the administration of justice, Roscoe Pound once wrote, "men count more than machinery." His text applies perfectly to the trial of a civil action or criminal prosecution.

The Strains of the Role on the Best of Judges. It has been seriously suggested now and then that aspirants to the bench should be required to go through some kind of psychoanalytic screening, as is now required of psychoanalysts themselves and gradually being extended to students preparing for the ministry, candidates for certain sensitive government positions, and a few other socially critical employments. This is not a derogatory suggestion or in any way unflattering to the men and women who now preside over American trial courts. It is rather a recognition of the critical social importance of the work of the courts and of the strains imposed by judicial office not only on problem personalities like our unduly conciliatory judge and his tyrannical opposite number but also on men and women of average or better than average patience and psychic endurance.

As claimants, defendants, and accused persons pass before him, a trial judge meets and has to put up with many more scoundrels, cheats, and liars than most other men encounter in their vocations. His work is not calculated to make him excessively optimistic concerning the natural inclinations of human nature. The lawyers who appear as counsel before him are often incompetent or barely competent, and the trial judge of first-rate intellectual and professional attainments has the good craftsman's proper impatience with shoddy work and wishes that the sorry advocates before him would get on with their business. It is hard for an able man to suffer fools gladly when they are certified members of his own profession. Sometimes the trial judge has the even more painful awareness that one of his fellow professionals of the practicing bar is trying to mislead him into acceptance of a fraudulent claim or defense or trying to badger him into some error that will cause the reversal of the trial court judgment on appeal. And, all the while, the conscientious trial judge is striving to maintain unbroken concentration on a flow of complex and conflicting evidence that may extend over many days.

The strains and psychic demands of the trial judge's role were illustrated dramatically some fifteen years ago when the leaders of the American communist party came up for trial before Judge Harold Medina, now a judge of the United States Court of Appeals, for violation of the Smith Act. The trial lasted for months, and the several counsel for the defendants did everything they could, day after wearying day, to break Judge Medina down or to taunt or exhaust him into some reversible error of trial procedure. We have wondered since whether any other lawyer of our time would have had the resilience and psychic durability to complete that trial as Judge Medina did, or even to survive it. The case was out of the ordinary, but it serves admirably to make the point that our adversary system of litigation can on occasion impose burdens that challenge the patience, spirit, and endurance of the strongest of trial judges.

THE BURDEN OF SENTENCING IN CRIMINAL CASES

Severe demands are made on a trial judge's moral resources, in this case on his sensitivity and compassion, by his duty to determine and impose the sentences of persons found guilty of a crime. The judge's discretion and responsibility are large, since the general statutory precept, more likely than not, will authorize a wide range of permissible treatment of the offender: "Punishable by fine not to exceed $10,000 or by imprisonment from one to five years, or by both such fine and such imprisonment" is not an untypical sentencing provision of our day. In short, the legal rule merely fixes the outside bounds for the inescapable act of judicial discretion. Shall the offender before the court be sent to prison for five years, or one, or for some period in between, or is it perhaps appropriate that he be put on probation during good behavior and not sent to prison at all? The trial judge must decide. Nowhere else in our society is one man invested with so awful a power over the life and freedom of another man.

Two things must be understood at the outset if the trial judge's role as sentencing official is to be seen in full perspective. The first of these is that the overwhelming majority of the persons up for criminal sentence plead guilty, as Edward Barrett's essay (Chapter Four) has noted. When the accused enters a plea of guilty to the charge against him, the determination of the sentence to be imposed is the only significant decision made by a court in his case. Thus, by any quantitative standard, the trial judge's exercise of his sentencing authority far outweighs everything else he does as a participant in the administration of criminal justice.

The second essential insight is that the severity of the punishment that will be imposed on a convicted criminal offender depends in very large measure on the personality and social attitudes of the particular judge before whom the offender comes for sentence. A crime that strikes one judge as deserving of a long prison term may seem appropriate for far milder punishment to another judge on the same bench. Contemporary sentencing statistics demonstrate that there are dramatic differences from judge to judge in the imposition of penalties in similar criminal cases. This is no news to persons familiar with the realities of criminal law administration. A study made fifty years ago of the records of the then forty-one criminal magistrates of the City of New York revealed that the percentage of cases in which the accused person was discharged without any penalty at all varied from 74 per cent for the most permissive of the magistrates to less than 7 per cent for the most punitive and austere of the forty-one. In disorderly conduct prosecutions, one magistrate heard more than five hundred cases and discharged only one of the accused without penalty. Another magistrate, in an adjoining court, discharged more than half of the disorderly conduct charges brought before him. The criminal court as a whole convicted and imposed penalties on 92 per cent of the 17,000 persons brought up on charges of drunkenness, but one sympathetic magistrate convicted only 20 per cent of the drunks summoned to trial before him. It would be useless to belabor the point with additional statistics. The social view of the particular judge can be the most important single factor in the sentencing equation.

In the literature of law and criminology, penal sanctions are analyzed and appraised from many different perspectives, sometimes as instruments of deterrence, sometimes as means of treatment and social rehabilitation of the offender, occasionally as measures of retribution visited on the offender for the moral and social wrong of his unlawful act. However one may interpret the purpose or purposes of the criminal law, it is evident that sentencing determinations are socially critical decisions. What qualities of mind and character would we want our sentencing judge to have, and how should he go about the demanding and often painful task? There is no simple answer to either of these questions.

The sentencing burden will be easiest on the judge if he can find some way to routinize it, to make punishments fit categories of crime without too much attention to the particular offender and his personal and family circumstances. This seems, superficially at least, a technique for administering equal justice, and there are trial judges whose sentencing practice is more or less along these lines—so many years for embezzlements, so many days in city jail for drunken and disorderly conduct, and the like. But this way of easing the strain of sentencing is barred to the thoughtful judge by his awareness that discriminating individualization in the handling of specific cases is an essential element in our tradition of justice. Shall the sentencing judge, then, avoid or minimize the burdens of his responsibility by making it his practice to impose whatever penalty may be recommended in the probation report on the offender? Conceivably, some time in the future, the judicial function in criminal cases may be cut down so that only issues of guilt or innocence are left for determination by judge or jury and decisions as to punishment referred to boards of experts in criminology, psychiatry, and other relevant fields of knowledge, as parole matters are handled under modern procedures. Over the years a good many judges and scholars have urged that our system of criminal justice would operate more fairly and effectively if the guilt-determining function were separated from the sentencing function and all issues concerning a convicted offender's penalty resolved less hurriedly and by specialists better qualified for the task than most judges are. But this is not the existing situation. The judge still carries ultimate sentencing responsibility, within the bounds fixed for the offense by the legislature, and he must exercise that responsibility as best he can.

The demands and strains of the sentencing role bear hardest on the sensitive and compassionate trial judge, who cannot help seeing the patterns of human tragedy in the cases that come before him. Would it be better if all the judges of our criminal trial courts were as detached and hard boiled as many of them are, or make out to be, in sentencing matters? There is respectable authority, tracing back at least to Thomas Hobbes, that charity and compassion are no part of legal justice and that the sentencing judge must learn to steel himself against humanitarian impulses. But would we be content with a trial bench of judges who, by personality and character, find no burden or psychic strain in the sentencing task? Is a man worthy of judicial office, whatever his other qualifications, if he is entirely insensitive to the searching implications of the chastening injunction, "Judge not, that ye be not judged"?

And Who Is "Qualified"?

Bar associations and other civic groups undertake from time to time to determine whether particular candidates for appointment to the bench are or are not "qualified"—variously, "well qualified" or "exceptionally well qualified"—for judicial office. No person or organization has yet been rash enough to offer an authoritative definition of the crucial word "qualified" or even an all-inclusive checklist of the attributes to be kept in mind in appraising the qualifications of a lawyer who aspires to join the company of the judiciary. This essay was certainly not designed as a systematic analysis of judicial qualifications, but our examination of the role of the trial judge in the administration of justice should suggest at least a few of the attributes of mind, heart, and character that are essential to the task.

PROBITY

To be authentic in his role, the trial judge must be an unusually honest man, a man of exceptional integrity financially, politically, and socially. This is usually put first in discussions of qualifications for judicial office, and rightly so. But honesty is hardly a sufficient qualification or even one unique to the judicial branch of public service. It has been taken for granted throughout our analysis of the trial judge's role that a judge who is susceptible to bribery in any form, or who favors his relatives, cronies, or political sponsors either in the conduct of litigation or in the award of lucrative commissions like guardianships and receiverships, is unworthy of his post and, for that matter, unworthy of membership in the legal profession. The ugliest words in the administration of justice are "the fix is in" or any remote equivalent.

The stress on personal honesty in most discussions of judicial qualifications seems quite unflattering to the legal profession, and one searches for an explanation of the prominence of the theme. Certainly a list of qualifications for appointment as a superintendent of schools or director of a scientific laboratory would not put comparable emphasis on elementary probity as a *sine qua non*. There are several possible explanations. Insistence on personal integrity as an indispensable qualification, almost as *the* indispensable qualification, for judicial office reflects an apprehensive awareness in the legal profession of the immensity of the damage that can be done to the legal order by judicial corruption. If a physician or a professor or a businessman is discovered to be a thief or an influence peddler, the disclosure will not put medicine, higher education, or business into general disrepute. But judges are different and more representative; revelations of judicial corruption create suspicion and loss of confidence in legal processes generally and endanger public respect for law.

The further explanation of the heavy emphasis usually put on personal honesty as a judicial qualification is, I think, that it reflects a great and continuing uneasiness, in the legal profession and in the public generally, about the dominance of political considerations in judicial selection. These considerations weigh heavily, and are known by the public to have this weight, even when judicial offices are filled by executive appointment, as in some states by the governor, and in the federal court system by the President on recommendation of the Attorney General. In states where judges are elected, it is common knowledge that party politicians are the effective nominators of judicial candidates, and there is ground for concern, or at least for suspicion, that judges so chosen may be vulnerable to political pressures in the performance of their high social duties. Perhaps we worry as much as we do about the personal honesty of candidates for the bench because of a certain feeling in our society that a man who has been active enough in party politics to have earned the reward of a coveted judgeship may not be as righteous as he ought to be. The greatest single objection to our prevailingly political system of judicial selection is that it makes our judges subject to the suspicions that members of the public entertain about politicians and political processes generally. If there were a flat rule that no one would be eligible for judicial office if he had ever been active in party politics, many of our ablest trial judges would have been lost to the administration of justice. But it is unlikely that as much would be heard as is heard today about personal honesty as the indispensable requirement for judicial office.

PROFESSIONAL SKILL AND ACUMEN

Only a good lawyer, a genuinely good one, is qualified for service on a substantial trial court. This was plain at every step in our analysis of the importance, difficulty, and strain of the trial judge's role, and it would be unprofitable to repeat the points already made in that analysis or readily inferable from it. Civic groups and bar associations have been far too generous, by and large, in their ratings of judicial candidates. "Qualified" has come to be used much as teachers use the *C* grade, as signifying a passable minimum of proficiency; the grade *B* candidates are characterized as "well qualified" and the *A* men as "exceptionally well qualified." If such in-group appraisals of judicial candidates are to have political value and influence, "qualified" must have the signification of professional excellence, a degree of intellect and technical proficiency equal to that possessed by the best members of the practicing bar. A man who is pretty good but not good enough is not "qualified" for appointment or election to the trial bench.

Professional excellence on a trial court of general jurisdiction means at least: 1) wide ranging analytical power comparable to that of the qualified internist in medical practice; 2) mastery, or the intellectual capacity to achieve mastery, of the intricacies of legal procedure and evidence; 3) unusual discernment in dealing with facts and weighing conflicting testimony; and 4) unusual skill at communication with jurymen and witnesses. The judge presiding over a juvenile court, family relations court, or other court of specialized jurisdiction does not have to be a "generalist" to this extent, since his cases will involve fewer different areas of substantive law and formal trials will be less important in his work, but he has the corresponding intellectual burden of the specialist, familiarity in depth with a relevant and ever increasing body of medical and behavioral-science knowledge. Professional excellence of the specialist sort is called for, too, in the lower criminal courts. Only a man of first rate capacity can make sound split-second decisions on questions of criminal law and procedure, exercise sentencing responsibilities thoughtfully and wisely under exhausting pressures of time, and improvise procedures to make assembly-line law enforcement seem less cut and dried.

In this connection, the creation, less than two years ago, of the National College of State Trial Court Judges in Boulder, Colorado is one of the happiest developments in the recent history of legal institutions. The new College extends to recently selected trial judges opportunities for intensive study of their role comparable to the educational opportunities that have been provided to appellate judges for some years by the School of Law of New York University. There are other significant signs of serious interest in the study of trial-court processes by the men and women who actually conduct them. The ambitious and well planned judges' training program of the National Council of Juvenile Court Judges is an important recent enterprise in point.

Judicial education can help greatly in improving trial-court processes but, as in education generally, as much depends on the innate ability of the students as on the quality of the instruction. A great university can keep its student quality high by selective admission procedures. This form of quality control is manifestly unavailable to a college for judicial education; the prospective student is already in office, and the less qualified he is the greater his need for the training. The programs for improving judicial selection described by Glenn Winters and Robert Allard in Chapter Six are, in this context, proposals for genuinely selective admission to the great university of the trial judiciary.

CHARACTER, ENERGY, AND PERSONALITY

In any sizeable community there will be many lawyers of complete financial probity and genuinely first rate professional skill and acumen. Some of these able men would be very bad trial judges. It has been a central thesis of this essay that the role of the trial judge calls for uncommon qualities of personality and character. The demands and strains of his courtroom task require unusual emotional stability, exceptional firmness and serenity of temperament, and not infrequently great intellectual and psychic endurance. In his relations with jurymen, witnesses, and litigants, the trial judge has to be empathetic and endlessly patient. As a sentencing official, his action must be compassionate without being mushy-headed, and his demeanor must be at once sensitive and austere. These are not attributes that can be measured on a quantitative scale or in any precisely objective way. But they are essential to performance of the role in accordance with the best traditions of common law adjudication.

By these criteria, has any lawyer ever been "qualified" for selection as a trial-court judge? *Fully* qualified? Of course not, any more than men are every fully qualified in mind, heart, and character for the ministry, or for high military command, or for management of a great governmental or business enterprise. But every lawyer knows at least a few trial judges who have come wonderfully close to the ideal, partly through their own natural qualities as human beings and partly through the influence and support of the common law judicial tradition. And the statement of an ideal provides a standard to measure the extent to which particular aspirants to judicial office approach or fall short of the ideal.

Only a brave and good man, or a stupid one, will put himself forward as worthy of designation as a representative and witness of public justice. There is much talk in contemporary literature about improving the "image" of justice. Justice is not a commodity to be marketed by such means. The way to improve the image of justice is to improve the reality of justice in the trial courts of the United States. That depends, above all, on the intellectual, moral, and personal quality of the men and women who are called to serve as our trial judges.

Glenn R. Winters and Robert E. Allard

6

Judicial Selection and Tenure in the United States

The preceding chapter has demonstrated sufficiently that only men and women of intellectual and moral excellence are qualified for service as trial court judges. The practical question remains. How, in view of existing political realities, can judges of this quality be secured for the trial courts, and how can they be kept in office once they have ascended the bench?

There are many approaches to the problem of judicial selection and tenure. In most "civil law" countries, judges constitute a separate branch of the legal profession; judicial posts are filled not from the practicing bar but from a separate career judiciary. In England, judges are appointed for life from the ranks of the barristers. In the United States, largely as a legacy from the creed of Jacksonian democracy, popular election is the prevailing procedure, although judges are chosen by executive appointment in some states and in the federal courts.

In despair at the experienced domination of judicial elections, and state judicial appointments, by partisan political considerations, a small but increasing number of states have turned to the plan of "merit selection and tenure," first adopted in Missouri in 1940. This chapter examines the theory and practice of "merit selection" and provides a critical comparative analysis of the elective and appointive alternatives. The chapter also considers several problems closely related to judicial selection and tenure, including judicial compensation, procedures for the removal and disciplining of judges, and trends in specialized judicial education.

GLENN R. WINTERS *is Executive Director of the American Judicature Society and the editor of the Society's influential journal. He has written widely on judicial selection and court reform and is one of the country's most respected crusaders for improved judicial administration.* ROBERT

ALLARD *is Assistant Executive Director and Director of Special Projects for the American Judicature Society. He is the author of numerous articles on the work of the courts and has been active in the organization of recent "Citizens Conferences on the Courts" in many major cities of the United States.*

The selection and tenure of judicial personnel is one of the most critical issues of government in the United States. It is also one of the most neglected.

The judicial branch of government has neither purse, sword, nor sufficient patronage to attract consistent public attention. Other than the Supreme Court of the United States, the judiciary has received no systematic treatment at any level of the American educational system. The parochialism of American state-organized legal systems, together with the case method of legal education and the client-centered adversary approach of most lawyers, has prevented the legal profession and its organizations from giving effective attention to the administration of justice. As a consequence, the general public is exquisitely uninterested, its educated leadership is functionally illiterate, and the legal profession is profoundly phlegmatic about the issues involved in judicial selection and tenure in the United States today.

At some time in American history there may have been a general understanding of the critical role of the judiciary as the final rampart for personal freedom and public welfare. If so, it was before the onslaught of industrialization, urbanization, impersonalization, and population explosion in the first half of the twentieth century. Today, courtrooms are as empty of informed spectators as school textbooks are empty of information about the operation of justice under law and the central role of the judge in that operation.

Many American lawyers regard the judge as merely an umpire of an adversary contest between lawyers to see which one is more proficient in legal one-upmanship. The concept of the judge in other legal systems is that he has no power to declare law other than as it appears in statute or code. But the role of the judge in America and other countries using the legal system known as the "common law" is actually that of a lawmaker. He has obligations in every controversy to preserve the accumulated experience of the past and anticipate the consequences to future generations, even as he seeks to dispense justice in the particular case before him. He must be, in the words of Justice Brennan of the Supreme Court, "the active agent of justice guiding the trial and the protagonists so that right and justice may truly prevail." [1]

[1] Brennan, *Efficient Organization and Effective Administration for Today's Courts— The Citizen's Responsibility*, 48 J. Am. Jud. Soc. 145, 149 (Dec., 1964).

Emphasis upon trial judges, federal, state, and local, is a recent development in American jurisprudence. Traditionally, the appellate bench has received whatever little attention was given to the courts by political scientists, sociologists, and legal scholars. Law-school texts have been predominantly filled with appellate opinions. The trial judge has been neglected in spite of the fact that he makes final disposition of virtually all of the legal disputes which come to the courts.

The demands of the trial bench are markedly different from those of the appellate bench, as Harry Jones (Chapter Five) makes clear. Many observers believe that the trial courts require a different type of judicial personnel. There has been little scientific exploration of this hypothesis to date. Without regard to the merits of this position, however, it is clear that the functions of a trial judge in modern American society, particularly in urban areas, demand special decision-making skills within an adversary setting and the ability to make such decisions under extreme pressures.

This essay will focus primarily on the judges of state trial courts of general jurisdiction, although reference will be made from time to time to federal trial judges and to judges of courts of special and limited jurisdiction. Courts of general jurisdiction (referred to in this essay as *trial courts*), are those in which all types of civil and criminal disputes are decided, except those specifically designated by constitution, statute, or court rule to be heard in some specialized court. It is in these courts of general jurisdiction that the dramatic backlog of untried cases is most apparent, and it is on them that the inevitable growth of judicial work will initially fall. It is for these reasons that the selection and tenure of these judges should receive the most attention.

The Historical Background

During colonial times, judges were appointed by the British Crown. After the Declaration of Independence, six of the new states vested the responsibility for judicial appointments in the governor; none, however, was willing to give its governor that power without restrictions. Chief of these was that the appointment should be subject to approval by some group of citizens. In Pennsylvania and Delaware this approving authority was the state legislature; in Massachusetts, New Hampshire, and Maryland it was the governor's council; and in New York there was a special "Council of Appointment," consisting of the governor and certain members of the legislature. When the federal government was organized a few years later, the Constitution provided for appointment of federal judges by the President, "by and with the advice and consent of the Senate." In contrast, seven of the original states entrusted the selection of judges to their respective legislatures. These were Connecticut, Rhode Island, New Jersey, Virginia, North Carolina, South Carolina, and Georgia.

Five years was enough for Georgia to allow its legislature to make judicial appointments; in 1793 that state became the first to adopt the principle of popular election of judges. During the next two or three decades, and especially during the 1820s, known as the era of Jacksonian democracy, popular election of officials for short terms was idealized as the solution of all governmental problems. Resistance to change of any kind was strong, but Mississippi discarded appointment of judges for election in 1832, New York did the same in 1846, and thereafter, one by one, many of the original states and all of the newly created ones swung around to the elective method. By the time of the Civil War, judges were elected in 22 of the 34 states of the Union.

Not all of the older states were satisfied with the choice of judges by election. Seven of them—Connecticut, Delaware, Massachusetts, New Hampshire, New Jersey, Rhode Island, and South Carolina—never got into it at all, and Maine only with respect to probate judges. Virginia went back to legislative appointment after 14 years of the elective system. Vermont began electing judges of inferior courts in 1850, but gave it up for legislative appointment of all judges in 1870. Florida first tried electing circuit judges and appointing supreme court justices and then reversed itself, electing supreme court justices and appointing circuit judges. Even Mississippi went back to appointment of judges in 1868, and stayed with it until 1910.

By 1962, some or all judges were appointed by the governor with confirmation, approval, or consent by a legislative body, council, or commission in nine states: California (appellate judges), Connecticut, Delaware, Hawaii, Maine, Massachusetts, New Hampshire, New Jersey, and Rhode Island. In addition, initial appointments in Maryland were made by the governor but the judges so appointed had to stand for election on a partisan ballot at the first election one year or more after appointment. In four states—Rhode Island, South Carolina, Vermont, and Virginia— some or all judges were chosen by the legislature. *The elective method of judicial selection was still in force for some or all judges in 36 states.* In 16 of these "elective" states, a separate nonpartisan ballot was used for voting on judges; in the other 20, judicial candidates were listed under their party designations and took their chances with the rest of the party ticket.

The Idea of Merit Selection

How are judges to be selected? Until 1913, American practice furnished four basic answers:

1. Executive appointment, with or without confirmation;
2. Selection by the legislature;
3. Partisan political election; or
4. Nonpartisan political election.

How are judges to be retained in office? Until 1913, American practice furnished three basic answers:

1. At the will of the appointing authority;
2. For life, during good behavior; or
3. By competitive election for a fixed term of years.

ORIGINS OF THE MERIT SELECTION IDEA

In 1913, Professor Albert M. Kales of the School of Law of Northwestern University conceived a method of judicial selection and tenure which has since become known as the "Missouri Plan," from the first state to adopt it. He proposed that an elective officer of the state appoint judges from lists of qualified candidates selected by an impartial commission and that the judges so appointed go before the voters at periodic intervals, on a *noncompetitive* ballot, on the sole question of whether or not they should remain in office. If a judge were rejected by the voters, the vacancy would be filled by the same procedures. The heart of the proposal was, of course, that the appointing authority would be restricted in his choice to the candidates proposed to him by the impartial commission; he could appoint one of them but no one else.

This plan became an essential element in the comprehensive program for court reform of the American Judicature Society, founded in 1913 by Professor Kales along with Dean Roscoe Pound, Dean John H. Wigmore, Herbert L. Harley, and others. The purpose of the Society was expressed in its full corporate title, The American Judicature Society to Promote the Efficient Administration of Justice. It was the first systematic attempt by a small segment of the American legal profession to seek reforms of what Pound had characterized, in an influential address delivered in 1906, as "The Causes of Popular Dissatisfaction with the Administration of Justice." [2] In this address Pound had said of existing methods of judicial election: "Putting courts into politics and compelling judges to become politicians, in many jurisdictions, has almost destroyed the traditional respect for the bench."

Kales's plan of judicial selection and tenure was embodied in A State-Wide Judicature Act, a model state court system published in 1914 by the American Judicature Society. Herbert Harley, the Society's principal

[2] 46 J. Am. Jud. Soc. 55, 66 (Aug., 1962).

founder, became the advocate for merit selection of judges and provided continuing leadership for more than thirty years in the campaign to win acceptance for it. Through correspondence, personal conferences, interviews, and speeches, he promoted a broad program of judicial reform, but always with primary emphasis on merit selection and tenure for judges. Through the Society's journal, which he founded in 1917 and edited for many years, Harley reached a nationwide audience of leaders of the legal profession.

The First Step Towards Merit Selection. In 1934, after twenty years of hard work by Harley and others, a partial victory was achieved in California. In a 1932 speech before the Los Angeles Bar Association, Judge John P. Wood, a friend and convert of Harley's, had pointed out the sorry spectacle of judicial elections in Los Angeles and had challenged the organization to find a remedy. A committee of the Association produced a proposal patterned after the Kales-American Judicature Society plan, and this proposal was approved by the state bar association and submitted to a popular referendum. The state chamber of commerce submitted a rival plan, which substituted a confirming body for the proposed nominating commission but retained the noncompetitive re-election feature of the original merit selection plan. A further modification was that the plan was made to apply only to appellate judges, although counties of the state could adopt it for trial judges of general jurisdiction by local option. The compromise plan was adopted by referendum vote in 1934. Complete victory for merit selection of judges did not come until six years later in Missouri.

1913 AND 1962—TWO CRUCIAL YEARS FOR COURT REFORM

Nineteen-thirteen and 1962 can safely be described as two of the outstanding years in American judicial reform. In 1913, the American Judicature Society was organized, and in the years immediately thereafter accomplished the great work of drafting its major patterns for merit selection of judges, sounder court and bar organization, and modernization of court procedure. In 1962, the essential elements of the Society's State-Wide Judicature Act, including its provisions for merit selection and tenure of judges, were adopted by the House of Delegates of the American Bar Association in its Model Judicial Article. This action of the Association reaffirmed an earlier endorsement, in 1937, of the proposals concerning judicial selection and tenure.

In 1962, voters of Illinois and Colorado adopted state constitutional amendments providing for reorganization of their courts into unified systems with effective managerial controls; voters of Iowa and Nebraska adopted merit selection and tenure plans for all state court judges. Also in 1962, the Joint Committee for the Effective Administration of Justice, a cooperative effort of fifteen national legal organizations under the chairmanship of Justice Tom C. Clark of the Supreme Court, began an intensive educational program on the necessity of state court modernization. In short, 1962 was the year in which the movement for adoption of the 1913 reforms caught fire.

The acceleration of court reform activity after 1962 explains why we have occasionally used that year as our point of departure in examining the prospects for improvement of judicial selection and tenure. The reader is cautioned, however, that the present build-up of reform activity means that the 1962 picture is of historical interest only, as a measure of progress achieved since then. In 1962, bar associations and other civic groups in more than twenty states were beginning serious efforts to improve their methods of selecting judges. By 1965, six states had advanced as far as introduction of merit selection proposals in their state legislatures, this being, of course, the first step in a long-range campaign that may take as much as ten years to complete.

Merit Selection in Action—the "Missouri Plan"

The first complete triumph of the idea of merit selection came in 1940, when Missouri adopted it for the selection and tenure of all the state's appellate judges and for the trial judges of the City of St. Louis and Jackson County (Kansas City). In 1945, probate judges and judges of the court of criminal correction of St. Louis were also included under merit selection.

The Missouri Plan, as it has become known, provides for a nominating commission empowered to select three nominees for any judicial vacancy in the appellate courts, both supreme and intermediate. From this slate of three nominees, the governor must appoint one to fill the vacancy. The appellate commission is composed of the chief justice of the state as chairman, three lawyers elected by members of the state-wide bar, and three non-lawyer citizens appointed by the governor. Commission members, other than the chief justice, are prohibited from holding public office or political party office. Terms of the lawyer and non-lawyer members are six years and staggered.

Trial judges in the two metropolitan areas are selected by two similar commissions. Each includes the presiding judge of the intermediate court of appeals for that area as chairman, along with two lawyers and two non-lawyer citizens. The lawyers and non-lawyers must be residents of the area and are selected in the same manner as those on the appellate commission. Terms of service and restrictions on office holding are also the same.

HOW A NOMINATING COMMISSION OPERATES

A concrete example of how a nominating commission operates in practice has been set forth by Judge Elmo B. Hunter of the Kansas City Court of Appeals, who, as presiding judge of that court, acted as chairman of the commission to select trial judges for Jackson County. Judge Hunter wrote:

Just a few months ago two of our trial judges retired because of a combination of age and illness. This created two judicial vacancies. Our judicial nominating commission issued a public statement carried by our press and other news media that the nominating commission would soon meet to consider two panels of three names each to be sent to the governor for him to select one from each panel to fill the vacancy, and that the nominating commission was open to suggestions and recommendations of names of those members of our bar best qualified to be circuit judges.

It received the names of many outstanding and highly qualified lawyers who were willing to be considered by the commission because of the nonpolitical merit type of selection involved. The commission on its own surveyed all eligible lawyers in the circuit to see if it had before it the names of all those who ought to be considered. From all sources the commission ended up with 57 names.

After several weeks of careful study by the commission, the list of eligibles was cut to 12 then to nine and finally to those six whom the members of the commission sincerely believed to be the six best qualified of all. Those six names, three on each of the two panels, were sent to the governor, who, after his own independent consideration of them, made his selection of one from each panel. His selections were widely acclaimed by the press and the public as excellent choices from two very outstanding panels. The commission was glad to see the governor get this accolade, but its members knew that no matter which one of the three on each panel he selected, the people of Missouri would have been assured an outstanding judge.

It might be noted in passing that each of the two panels of three names submitted to the governor happened to contain the names of two Democrats and one Republican. The governor was a Democrat. He appointed a Democrat from one panel and a Republican from the other. I do not think this was deliberate. I am convinced that our plan has so proven its merit that our governor, who is oath-bound to follow the constitution, shares its spirit as well as its letter. He selected the two he thought best qualified, irrespective of political party.

This is not an isolated instance. Another rather dramatic example occurred just a few years ago when our legislature created three new judgeships for the Kansas City area to meet the increasing cases resulting principally from population growth. The judicial selection commission sent three panels of three names each to another Democratic governor. On each panel there were two Democrats and one Republican. The governor appointed two Republicans and one Democrat.[3]

Retention in office for these judges is by noncompetitive re-election. Sixty days prior to the general election preceding the expiration of a judge's term, he may file a declaration to succeed himself, in which case his name is submitted without party designation to the voters on a separate ballot, reading "Shall Judge ——————— of the ——————— court be retained in office? Yes ——— No ———." If the majority of votes are negative, or if he does not file for retention, there is a vacancy which is again filled by appointment.

Acceptance of Merit Selection. Public confidence in the "Missouri Plan" was strong in that state at the time of its adoption and continued to be so despite early efforts to repeal it. Originally adopted by a majority of 90,000 votes in 1940, it was resubmitted in 1942, at the insistence of opponents who argued that the people had not understood the plan. The voters re-endorsed it by a majority of 180,000 votes. The plan came up for consideration by the people again in 1945, as a part of a new constitution, which was approved by a majority of 150,000 votes. Subsequent attempts in the 1950s by special interest groups in Missouri to alter or abolish the plan never got beyond the legislature.

JUDICIAL SELECTION IN MISSOURI BEFORE 1940

The effects of the plan in Missouri can be assessed most clearly against the background of the pre-1940 conditions in that state. In the 1930s judicial selection had suffered chiefly from the introduction of "machine" politics into the state's competitive election of judges. In campaigns for appellate and trial courts, the pressure of the political machines and intraparty conflicts deprived the judiciary of the essential element of independence and prevented selection of judges on the basis of their qualifications for the office.

In the famous case of Judge Padberg, the politically dominated system had brought a person judged to be incompetent to the bench. The politicians selected Mr. Padberg to run in the 1934 Democratic primary for nomination to the circuit court, despite the fact that in his eight years of so-called private law practice he had been the filing attorney in only nine law suits, eight for divorce and one for annulment. Actually, during

[3] Hunter, *A Missouri Judge Views Judicial Selection and Tenure,* 48 J. Am. Jud. Soc. 126, 130 (Dec., 1964).

that time, Mr. Padberg's chief occupation was as a pharmacist in a St. Louis hospital. In a pre-primary poll of lawyers conducted by the St. Louis Bar Association, Mr. Padberg was ranked nineteenth out of twenty-one candidates. Because of the efforts of the political boss of his party, Mr. Padberg was nominated at the primary and elected in the general election, despite a second bar poll ranking him last of the eighteen candidates on the ballot. Judge Padberg's record was what could have been expected. When he offered himself for re-election in 1940, the St. Louis *Post Dispatch* characterized his six years on the bench as "a humiliation to the law and to the city," and had harsh criticism for Judge Padberg's handling of a grand jury charged with investigating election frauds. A fellow member of the bench, Judge McAfee, had summarily discharged the grand jury when it failed to act and subsequently resigned, stating that he no longer wanted to remain a judge under the political system.[4]

In another pre-1940 Missouri case a supreme court judgeship became a political football for the Pendergast machine of Kansas City, and, as a result, a highly competent jurist was very nearly removed from the bench. In the 1938 Democratic primary, Judge James M. Douglas of the state's supreme court was a candidate for renomination. Because of his vote in a fire insurance rate decision which offended Democratic boss Tom Pendergast, the politicians slated an opponent to run against Judge Douglas, even though he had shown himself to be well qualified and had an excellent record in office. The primary campaign became a spectacle of a knockdown, drag-out political fight in which both candidates campaigned in all the counties of the state, an effort which required Judge Douglas to devote much time away from the bench. Though he was successful in the election, Judge Douglas was required to spend between $10,000 and $25,000 on the campaign, a very considerable sum in 1938.

EXTENSIONS OF MERIT SELECTION TO OTHER STATES

The record of the Missouri Plan during the first quarter of a century of its operation has vindicated the expectations of its early supporters. This favorable experience led to adoption of the plan for some or all state court judges in six other states by 1962. Three states adopted all the provisions of the plan for the entire state judiciary above the minor court level. On its admission to the union in 1958, Alaska made the plan a part of its new constitution, applying its provisions to cover its supreme, appellate, and trial courts. In 1962, Iowa and Nebraska joined Alaska in

---

[4] Accounts of Judge Padberg's term in office can be found in Crowdus, *Twenty Years of the Missouri Nonpartisan Court Plan*, J. Mo. Bar, p. 124 (March, 1962) and in an unpublished paper by Charles P. Blackmore, *Has Missouri Found the Answer?* (1959).

providing for the selection of their appellate- and trial-court judges under
the plan. Kansas adopted all the provisions of the plan in 1958 for its
supreme court. In addition, Alabama put the judges of its largest trial
court, Birmingham, under a merit selection plan in 1950 and Oklahoma
adopted it by statute in 1961 to fill juvenile court vacancies in Tulsa.

Voluntary use of this selection plan was adopted by governors and
mayors in at least five states in the years immediately following 1962, and
continuing efforts for its adoption were under way in twenty or more
states. It has proven itself, in the opinion of such men as Judge Samuel
I. Rosenman to be a "better way to select judges."

Election of Judges

Speaking from an intimate association with elective judicial
selection for more than thirty-five years, Judge Rosenman has said:

> It is practically impossible for the public, especially in large centers of pop-
> ulation, to know anything about the qualifications for judicial office of those
> who practice at the bar. . . . The voters, as a whole, know little more about
> the candidates than what their campaign picture may reveal. Nor do they have
> any great desire to get to know much more—although bar associations do try
> to give them information. Their concern is centered on the executive and
> legislative candidates because they are identified with the only issues and
> causes which interest the voters. Most often, when they reach the judicial
> candidates down on the ballot, they vote blindly for the party emblem.[5]

Sources of Voter Information. Judge Rosenman's observation was forcefully documented in a poll made by the Elmer Roper organization within
ten days after the New York general elections of November 1954. The
poll, conducted in three areas of the state, New York City, Buffalo (an
upstate urban area), and Cayuga County (a semi-rural upstate area), revealed that a shockingly large percentage of those who had voted for any
judicial candidate (61 per cent in New York, 48 per cent in Buffalo, and
75 per cent in Cayuga County) had paid no attention to judicial candidates before the election. Even larger percentages (81 per cent in New
York, 70 per cent in Buffalo, and 96 per cent in Cayuga County) could
not name one of the judicial candidates for whom they had voted.[6]

The causes of voter apathy and inability to make an informed choice
among judicial candidates are apparent. The physical length of the election ballot itself makes any careful investigation by even the most conscientious voter virtually impossible. The New York City ballot in the

[5] Rosenman, *A Better Way to Select Judges,* 48 J. Am. Jud. Soc. 86, 88 (Oct., 1964).
[6] *How Much Do Voters Know or Care About Judicial Candidates?* 38 J. Am. Jud. Soc.
140 (Feb., 1955).

1954 general election is a vivid example. On that ballot, voters were requested to choose from among ninety candidates listed under six political parties. Voters were requested to assess the qualifications and choose among sixty-two candidates for judicial office alone.

Moreover, voters are confronted with a lack of nonpartisan public information on most judicial candidates. There is very little about judicial service which brings an incumbent judge into the public eye. Even the candidates for the highest judicial posts are apt to be strangers to the public. While the organized bar in many states has undertaken efforts to evaluate judicial candidates and communicate their results to the public, the Roper poll indicated that, of those who paid attention to judicial candidates prior to the election, only 1 per cent or less had received their information directly from the organized bar and only 7 per cent (Cayuga County) to 18 per cent (Buffalo) had read newspaper accounts of information obtained by the press from the organized bar. The source of information most relied upon by the voters was the political party. Half of those who paid attention to the judicial candidates in New York City and one-third of those in the other two areas relied on the advice of their political parties.

Even where there is sufficient voter initiative and where information is readily available, laymen are able to assess intelligently only a part of all the qualifications required of a competent judge. While the lay voter can, if he knows the candidate, assess his personal characteristics, including his honesty and initiative, the lay voter is largely unqualified to assess candidates in terms of judicial independence, impartiality, and legal ability.

Domination by Political Leaders. Not only is elective selection characterized by voter apathy and inability to make informed choices, but it also suffers from domination by politicians. Observers agree that in popular competitive election, it is the politicians who select the judges. The voters only ratify their choices. In Judge Rosenman's words:

> The idea that the voters themselves select their judges is something of a farce. The real electors are a few political leaders who do the nominating. . . . Political leaders nominate practically whom they choose. Sometimes the districts are so overwhelmingly dominated by one political party that the nomination by these leaders must result in election; even in doubtful districts, interparty political deals often deprive the voters of any real choice.

In a similar vein, Herbert Brownell, former Attorney General of the United States, has said:

> As a matter of hard fact, judges are in most instances picked by political leaders. This is quite obvious in the case of elected judges. The party con-

ventions and primaries that nominate judges are managed by professional politicians. This is what politicians are for. Sometimes they have good candidates nominated, but most often their favor . . . shines on mediocre candidates.[7]

For several reasons, the competitive-election process dominated by political considerations cannot assure selection of judges on the basis of their judicial qualifications. First, judicial candidates are frequently placed on political slates for reasons other than their judicial qualifications. Politicians repay political debts with judgeships. They make nominations in order to balance a ticket as to ethnic group or geography. Second, the election process requires that the would-be judge be qualified not only for the office but also as a political campaigner. No matter how well qualified he may be, a judicial candidate may fail to be elected for lack of political appeal and campaigning know-how.

THE MIRAGE OF NONPARTISAN ELECTION

Many states have attempted to avoid political domination in the election of judges by having judges chosen at nonpartisan elections in which political parties do not make the nominations or sponsor the nominees. In those states the candidates' names appear on a separate nonpartisan judicial ballot or on the regular ballot but without party designation. Obtaining a place on the ballot is left to the initiative of the would-be candidates themselves, usually by means of petitions circulated by their friends.

While this device appears to free judicial nominations from control by politicians, it often leaves the candidates in a worse position than under partisan election. It nullifies whatever responsibility political parties feel to the voters to provide competent candidates and thereby closes one of the avenues which may be open to voter pressure for good judicial candidates. Indeed, experience indicates that where appeal to the voters on political grounds is made impossible by the nonpartisan ballot, other considerations equally irrelevant to a candidate's qualifications for judicial office are injected into the election. This is what Raymond Moley has called the "politics of nonpartisanship" and described in these terms:

> More recent attempts to keep out party politics by a nonpartisan ballot have roused the dogs of another kind of politics. Appeal to the people by a judge of anything except a very high court means appeal to race, religion, and

[7] Brownell, "Too Many Judges are Political Hacks," *The Saturday Evening Post* (April 18, 1964).

other political irrelevancies. It means cheap stunts for gaining publicity and slavery to the news-gathering exigencies of the city desk.[8]

Nonpartisan election also withdraws from the judicial candidate any financial and campaign support his party may provide, thereby requiring him to rely solely on his own means and campaign efforts or to become beholden to his friends for contributions. If he is an incumbent judge he must take time away from his judicial duties to mount his own campaign. And the nonpartisan ballot tends further to reduce popular interest and participation in the election itself. Statistics collected by George E. Brand indicate that where the separate nonpartisan ballot was used, just over half as many people on the average voted for the highest judicial officer as voted for the highest executive officer.

Executive Appointment of Judges

While a majority of states still provide for election of their judges, most judges initially go on the bench by appointment. This occurs because of the usual provision, even in elective states, that when a judicial vacancy occurs, the governor may appoint someone to serve for the unexpired term. Since these appointments usually are not subject to confirmation by the legislature, the process amounts to what may aptly be called "one-man judicial selection."

In appointive judicial selection, whether of the unrestricted one-man variety or of the restricted type in which legislative confirmation is required, the appointing officer is better able, if he chooses, to obtain information and make intelligent assessments of judicial candidates than can the electorate at large in popular elections. But the appointing officer has neither the time nor the personal knowledge to do the task alone. He must rely on individual advisers, within or outside his political party, and on the voluntary efforts of community organizations, and he, too, is subject to political pressures which cannot but influence his choices.

THE ADVISORY ROLE OF THE ORGANIZED BAR

The organized bar has undertaken a major role at the federal level and in certain cities in advising on judicial appointments. Since 1952 the Committee on the Federal Judiciary of the American Bar Association has worked closely with the Justice Department to gather information on and assess the qualifications of candidates for federal judicial office. In the first two years of the Kennedy Administration, the committee submitted

---

[8] Moley, *Tribunes of the People* (1932), p. 247.

609 reports to the Justice Department in connection with the record number of judicial appointments, 128, during that period. The Chicago Bar Association has a long history of judicial polls, as have other large local bar associations in New York, St. Louis, Cleveland, and other cities.

Unfortunately, efforts of this kind do not guarantee continued high quality appointments to the bench. Their effectiveness depends heavily upon a continued willingness to cooperate from both the appointing officer and the advising organizations, and upon the degree to which the appointing officer heeds the advice given him. Since the ABA Committee was organized, it has received sustained cooperation from Presidents Eisenhower, Kennedy, and Johnson. In the 1960 presidential campaign, it obtained pledges of cooperation from both candidates. Although Presidents have usually appointed only candidates designated by the Committee as qualified, some have been appointed who were rated as "not qualified." [9]

PARTY CONSIDERATIONS IN THE APPOINTMENT OF JUDGES

Failure to select the best qualified judges is caused chiefly by the pressure on the appointing officer to select from among members of his own political party to whom he owes some political debt. Although a chief executive is concerned about maintaining his reputation by appointing qualified judges—since he is primarily and publicly responsible for their selection—pressures within his party tend to control appointments in all cases except those in which the proposed appointee is totally unfit. The dominance of this factor in appointive selection was made strikingly clear in the 1961 annual report of the American Bar Association Committee on the Federal Judiciary:

> Invariably, presidents have made their judicial appointments primarily from the ranks of their own party. Criticism of this practice goes as far back as the presidency of John Adams and Thomas Jefferson. Judicial appointments by Democratic Presidents Cleveland, Wilson, Franklin D. Roosevelt, and Truman ranged from 92 per cent Democratic by President Truman to 99 per cent by President Wilson. Judicial appointments by Republican Presidents Theodore Roosevelt, Taft, Harding, Coolidge, Hoover, and Eisenhower ranged from 86 per cent Republican by President Hoover to 98 per cent Republican by President Harding. These facts do not prove that all the appointments made in this way are bad. What they do suggest is that the best

[9] Eight out of 99 appointees were rated not qualified between August 1961 and August 1962; 1 out of 19 between August 1962 and August 1963; 3 out of 23 appointees between August 1963 and August 1964. Annual Reports of the Standing Committee on the Federal Judiciary of the American Bar Association, 87 A. B. A. Rep. 25 (1962) 88 A. B. A. Rep. 20 (1963) 80 A. B. A. Rep. 20 (1964).

qualified judiciary is apt to be sacrificed for political purposes under an appointive scheme.

Legislative Confirmation. In one-man selection there are virtually no restrictions at all upon the appointing officer. Even where judicial appointments must receive confirmation by some body independent of the appointing officer there is no substantial protection against inferior selections. At best, confirming bodies have only a veto power. While they may reject one appointee, they cannot be certain that the next appointee proposed will be any better qualified. In actual operation, Senate confirmation in the federal system works not so much to improve the quality of appointments as to make them political footballs. Senatorial objection, an important factor influencing federal judicial selection, is often made not on the ground that the nominee lacks the necessary qualifications, but explicitly on the basis that he is "personally obnoxious" to a Senator from his home state.

In brief, traditional elective and appointive selection methods have proved inadequate in furnishing a well qualified and independent judiciary. In competitive elections the voters have neither the interest nor the ability to participate intelligently; they only ratify politicians' choices which, in turn, are made largely on factors unrelated to the qualifications for judicial office; while in appointive selection, although a single appointing officer is better able to choose judges wisely, the system offers no continuing permanent body to advise the appointing officer, and it does not serve to limit the adverse effect of political pressures on judicial appointments.

EXECUTIVE APPOINTMENT AND MERIT SELECTION COMPARED

The "Missouri Plan's" provision for a nominating commission retains the important advantage of the appointive scheme, that is, participation in the selection process of an authority qualified and able to assess judicial candidates. At the same time the nominating commission device avoids the instability inherent in voluntary cooperation between the appointing official and existing advisory groups by providing for a continuing official body to submit candidates to the appointing officer. The composition of the commission can be tailored so as to bring together people well equipped to assess judicial qualifications. A specific number of lawyers drawn from the community bring to the commission's deliberations their expert knowledge of the qualifications required for judicial office and of the legal ability of the candidates under consideration by the commission. Fair representation of all segments of the bar is usually assured by election of the lawyer members of the commission by all the members of the bar itself. The lay members, also drawn from the community, bring to the commission's deliberations their knowledge concerning the equally important non-legal qualifications necessary in a judge. The member of the judiciary usually included on the commission gives it insight into aspects of the judicial function with which outsiders could hardly be familiar.

In addition to creating a permanent body of well qualified persons to nominate candidates for judicial office, the nominating commission arrangement insulates judicial selection from the adverse effects of politics inevitable in appointive selection of judges. Since the appointing official's choice is limited to the nominees on the list submitted to him by the commission, it is largely unimportant if he chooses to select only nominees from his own political party, so long as the nominating commission submits only the best qualified possible appointees. Nonpartisanship on the commission itself is accomplished in a number of ways. The commission members are prohibited from serving as officers of a political party during their terms on the commission, and, if deemed necessary, it can also be required that a nominating commission be equally representative of both political parties, thereby achieving nonpartisanship through establishment of strictly equal bipartisanship.

It is for these reasons that a governor of Missouri recently wrote: "The present system has resulted in a better administration of justice than previously prevailed." [10]

Judicial Tenure and Compensation

An adequate selection method meets only a part of the problem of maintaining an able and independent judiciary. Each of the basic methods of judicial selection has traditionally been accompanied by a method of retaining judges in office.

PATTERNS OF JUDICIAL RETENTION

Retention of judges for life during good behavior is the method used in the federal courts and in several of the states. Although such a system assures security of judicial tenure, it is open to the criticism that it tends to produce a judicial autocracy over which effective control is difficult. The unethical or incompetent judge is frozen into office as well as the good one.

Re-election and Its Problems. By far the most widely accepted retention provision calls for the re-election of judges for short terms in parti-

[10] Letter from John M. Dalton to the Texas Civil Judicial Council, 12/9/64.

san or nonpartisan competitive elections. Many of the criticisms already made of selection by popular ballot apply to this method of retention. Here again the voter has neither ability, information, nor inclination to assess the qualifications of a long list of judicial candidates, and the polls of state and local bar associations have proved largely ineffective. Judge Rosenman, who had served as chairman of the Judiciary Committee of the Bar Association of the City of New York, could report only "meager results" from that association's published reports on the qualifications of incumbent judges and other judicial candidates. The influence of politics is fully as strong in the retention of judges by election as in their initial selection.

Judicial retention by election, combined with short terms, operates to discourage able men from seeking judicial office, and once they achieve the office it may operate to remove them despite their doing a good job on the bench. Judicial elections are often affected by issues entirely unrelated to the qualifications of the incumbent judge. The late Fred L. Williams, an eminent Missouri jurist, is reported to have said that he was elected to his state's supreme court in 1916 because President Wilson kept the country out of war, but was defeated for re-election in 1920 because the President did not keep the nation out of war. Results like this can make an able lawyer reluctant to seek election to the bench because of the real possibility that, once he has given up a valuable law practice, he may be turned out of judicial office on the basis of quite irrelevant political issues.

Judicial elections, whether partisan or nonpartisan, may well be decided on a point as small and absurd as the name of the candidate. Justice W. St. John Garwood, now retired from the Supreme Court of Texas, recalls that in one campaign his opponent, little known in the state, received substantial support at the polls merely on the strength of his name, Jefferson Smith, which happened to be the same as that of the leading character in a then-popular movie, "Mr. Smith Goes to Washington." [11] A highly regarded judge in the state of Washington was almost defeated in 1962, in a so-called nonpartisan election, by an opponent with the politically significant name, Robert Kennedy. In the 1964 elections in another nonpartisan election state, a state supreme court judge was defeated by Paul Brown, a good name for football fans in that state. A jurist with sixteen years of experience was defeated in an election during the presidency of Lyndon B. Johnson by an opponent whose last name just happened to be Johnson.

In some states attempts to achieve greater security of judicial tenure are made by encouraging political parties to give preference to incumbent

[11] Garwood, *Judicial Selection and Tenure—The Model Article Provisions,* 47 J. Amer. Jud. Soc. 21 (1963).

judges when making up slates of nominees. For the most part, this scheme is inadequate because it is only voluntary. Sidney Schulman, writing of the Pennsylvania experience, has indicated the scheme's ineffectiveness in that state:

> The policy of bipartisan, political support for "sitting judges" who have conducted themselves well in office has been accepted only to a limited degree by the political leaders in Philadelphia County. In most other counties this principle has been rejected and judicial contests are bitter fights.

Noncompetitive Re-election. The third basic method of judicial retention and tenure, a companion to the Kales selection plan, attempts to retain the best features of both appointment for life and political re-election. Under this plan, an incumbent judge seeks retention in office at the end of his term by simply filing a declaration to that effect. His name is then placed on a ballot without opposition and the voters are asked whether he should be retained in office. The judge is required to submit to this type of noncompetitive re-election within a short period after his initial appointment and thereafter at the end of each successive term.

This periodic merit retention plan serves a twofold purpose. There is no need for political campaigns. The only step the incumbent must take is the filing of his statement of intention to remain in office; his total expense is the price of a postage stamp. No judicial time is lost in campaigning, and qualified judges are not prevented from remaining in office simply because they lack political appeal on the campaign trail. Since the retention election is disassociated from political campaigns for other public offices, the chances that a judge will be removed from office on political grounds unconnected with his ability as a judge are greatly reduced. Judicial tenure is secured against purely political tides.

The second underlying purpose of the periodic merit retention provision is to reserve to the people a veto on judicial candidates, a privilege which is thwarted under appointment-for-life tenure. The public is rarely in a position to know in advance how good a judicial candidate is, but if his record as a judge is outstandingly poor, the voters can ascertain the facts, and in the merit retention election they have a means of removing him.

The Missouri Experience with Merit Retention of Judges. The Missouri experience has shown that the merit retention provision secures judicial tenure while at the same time reserving to the voters the possibility of removing unqualified judges.

In the first four elections under the Missouri plan, it became clear that issues between political parties were no longer decisive on the tenure of judges. In the first election, in 1942, the state went Republican, but two

Supreme Court judges, both Democrats, were retained by two-to-one votes. St. Louis went Republican but retained, by two-to-one votes, six circuit judges who were Democrats and at the same time confirmed for a full term the first circuit judge, a Republican, appointed under the then-new plan. In 1944, the state went Democratic, as did both Kansas City and St. Louis, but two supreme court judges, one from each major party, received substantially the same favorable vote, three-to-one for retention, and two court-of-appeals judges, again one from each major party, were retained. In Kansas City, a Republican probate judge was retained and, in fact, received fewer "no" votes than any of the six circuit judges, who were all Democrats.[12] Subsequent Missouri elections have shown substantially the same results, and experience in other states has been similar. There was a Democratic landslide in Iowa as elsewhere in 1964, but all incumbent judges, both Republicans and Democrats, were retained in office.

It has also been proved that the procedure of merit retention of office is effective in accomplishing the removal of unsatisfactory judges. A Kansas City judge who had first taken office during the reign of the Pendergast political machine in that city came up for re-election on a merit retention basis in 1942. A committee was organized to campaign for his removal from office, and he was defeated.

Judicial Compensation. For substantially the same reason that it is important to provide means of judicial selection and retention which do not place unnecessarily high demands on the financial resources of a would-be or incumbent judge, it is also important that judicial office carry with it financial rewards equal to those of comparable positions in the practice of law. One of the common measures of success of the practitioner is his income during his active years, and the financial provisions for his retirement.

The state, as an employer of judges, is only one of several buyers in the legal job market. To attract to the bench the high quality of personnel required, it must be able to compete on a financial basis with corporate employers and private-law practice. Unfortunately, since World War II, judicial salaries have lagged behind compensation for comparable positions in the practice of law.

Judicial Salaries. Figures on the comparative incomes of experienced lawyers and trial judges in three representative states reflect the present situation. According to a State Bar of Michigan survey of lawyer income in 1962, private practitioners with five or more years of experience received an average income substantially higher than the lowest paid ($12,500) trial judge. A 1964 survey showed that lawyers in the city of Boston with ten or more years' experience earned $1,000 to $10,000 more

[12] Hyde, *The Missouri Plan for Selection and Tenure of Judges,* 9 F. R. D. 457 (1950).

than trial-court judges. Boston suburban lawyers' incomes exceeded the income of trial judges by even greater amounts. A survey by the Oklahoma Bar Association indicated that the 1959 average gross income of self-employed lawyers with ten or more years of experience exceeded the salary of the highest paid trial judge by amounts ranging from $1,000 to $13,000.

It would be a mistake to try to pay judges as much as the highest-paid lawyers earn. The state could not afford it, the salaries would be out of line with the compensation of other public officials, and there would be unseemly political scrambling for judicial posts. But salaries no higher than the earnings of lower-level practitioners cannot be expected to bring high-level talent to the bench. The judicial salary range should be somewhere well above the average or median of lawyer earnings.

Pension Benefits. A judicial compensation system adequate to attract well-qualified lawyers to the bench must include some provision for pension benefits after termination of service. All states now have such plans for some or all of their judges, but many of these plans are inadequate as to coverage, or benefits, or both. The plan, at minimum, should provide retirement benefits computed on the basis of a judge's earning level during active service and be payable upon retirement at a certain age and after a certain minimum term of service. In addition, the plan should provide for benefits in the event of some disability which causes termination of active service before the judge's normal retirement age, and make some provision for the dependents of a deceased judge who would have been qualified either for disability or retirement benefits. Federal judges, on retirement, receive a pension equal to the full amount of their regular salary at the time of retirement. Most states are less generous, providing 75 per cent or 50 per cent or less, and some require contributions by the judges of more than 7 per cent of their salaries.

MANDATORY RETIREMENT OF JUDGES

Related to retirement benefits but designed essentially to protect the legal system from extreme advanced age and senility in judges are the commonly adopted provisions for mandatory or voluntary judicial retirement at a specified age. A simple voluntary retirement plan can do little to protect the legal system against judicial incompetence because of mental or physical incapacity due to age. A voluntary retirement plan can, however, be so designed as to encourage voluntary retirements, by reducing benefits if the judge chooses to retain his office after he has passed a certain age. Such a modified voluntary retirement plan is now in force in California.

Nearly half the states have provisions for mandatory retirement of judges at ages ranging from seventy, the large majority, to eighty in Louisiana.[13] Mandatory retirement requires a judge's withdrawal at an age after which his efficiency and productivity can reasonably be expected to decline. Many states have arrangements by which a judge's post-retirement service is allowed, by call of some judicial officer. This device has been effective as a source of valuable judicial service in times of unexpected increases in judicial business. Mandatory retirement at a fixed age is sometimes objected to on the ground that it frequently deprives the state of competent judicial service that might still be given. The provision for post-retirement service as needed adequately disposes of that objection.

REMOVAL AND DISCIPLINING OF JUDGES

Provisions for mandatory retirement and for periodic review by the voters of a judge's performance in office are both designed in large part to safeguard against incompetence or unethical conduct in judicial office. These measures provide only limited protection, however, since they permit removal of unfit judges only at specified times.

Procedures for the removal and disciplining of judges can furnish additional safeguards of the quality of the judiciary. In most states these traditional means include *impeachment,* that is, indictment by one house of the legislature, trial by another, and removal upon conviction; *address,* that is, trial by a legislative body and request to the executive for removal; and *recall,* that is, a popular petition requiring a judge to run in a special election if he is to continue in office.

Defects of the Traditional Procedures. All three devices have glaring defects. They provide an inflexible remedy, outright removal, and hence are unsuitable for dealing with the most common types of judicial misconduct, which warrant some form of discipline short of removal. The infrequent use of impeachment and the other devices is due largely to this inflexibility in sanction. And these traditional measures are cumbersome because they require either the mobilization of entire legislative bodies or the preparation and circulation of popular petitions. In situations involving anything less than the most flagrant violations of judicial ethics or indisputable incompetency, legislators and citizens hesitate to take the trouble to initiate removal procedures.

Florida's experience with the impeachment of two of its trial court judges vividly exemplifies these problems. There were two trials by impeachment, one in 1957, the other in 1963. In each instance, special legislative sessions had to be called, since the legislature was too busy to dis-

[13] Ala., Conn., Fla., Hawaii, Idaho, Kansas, Maine, Md., Mich., Minn., Mo., Neb., N.H., N.J., R.I., Va., Wisc.—age 70; Iowa, S.C.—age 72; Ore., Va., Wash.—age 75.

pose of the charges during its regular session. The cost of the two trials ran to approximately a quarter of a million dollars, over half the annual budget of the state's supreme court. Chief Justice Drew of the Supreme Court of Florida, who presided at one of the trials, noted that the forty-four-member legislative body that heard the impeachment charges was extremely unwieldy. His rulings during the trial were always subject to reversal by vote of the senate, only one-third of the members of which were lawyers. In addition to the excessive cost and the unwieldy nature of the proceedings, the remedy available proved to be too harsh in both cases. Despite the fact that many senators believed that the judicial conduct involved merited some kind of censure or discipline, the legislators acquitted both judges.

Impeachment and address suffer from an additional serious defect. Both are essentially political and not judicial proceedings, and political considerations tend to take precedence. Because of the manifest defects in the traditional removal measures, those who have considered the subject carefully have long urged the adoption of additional procedures that will be both workable and flexible as to the measure of discipline to be imposed.

Disciplinary Procedure in California. California has adopted one of the more successful of these procedures and has now had substantial experience with it. A constitutional amendment adopted in California in 1960 created a Commission on Judicial Qualifications, composed of nine members: five judges selected by the state supreme court, two lawyers elected by the board of governors of the state bar association, and two laymen appointed by the governor with the advice and consent of the state senate. The commission is empowered to investigate a complaint submitted by any person concerning the incapacity or misconduct of a state judge and to recommend to the supreme court that he be retired or removed. All complaints, preliminary investigations, and formal hearings are kept confidential unless and until a recommendation for retirement or removal is filed with the supreme court, when the record becomes public.

In its first four years of operation the commission considered 344 matters, most of which were dismissed, after initial investigation, as groundless. Twenty-six of the investigations led to voluntary resignation or retirement without formal removal proceedings. In the one case carried to the state supreme court, the court reviewed the evidence and declined to remove the judge concerned. In the remaining cases, questionable activity was found which, in the commission's judgment, did not merit removal. In these instances—which included unjudicial participation in a case, insufficient industry, and faulty courtroom demeanor—a simple notice to the offending judge that the investigation was being conducted usually prompted him to reform his conduct voluntarily.[14]

The benefits of the California procedure are clear. It allows flexibility of remedy to cope with all types of judicial misconduct and incapacity. A commission composed largely of judges preserves the independence of the judiciary from political forces, and lawyer and lay membership on the commission assures representation of all public interests and provides a basis for balanced judgments. In its 1963 report, the California commission said of its work:

> The Commission is mindful that it is exercising a significant and sensitive attribute of state sovereignty. By operating carefully and unobtrusively a practical contribution to jurisprudence is being forged. It has now been demonstrated that an independent commission, possessing the authority to investigate and hold hearings, can act for the maintenance of judicial fitness without infringing on the essential prerogatives of the judicial branch.

The strict confidentiality of the commission procedure until the very final stages preserves the integrity of the good judge against unwarranted public attack and lets the incompetent or unethical judge resign without public disgrace that might reflect unfairly on the bench as a whole.

Procedures in Other States. Comparable measures for removal of judges and for investigation of complaints of judicial misconduct exist in other states. In New Jersey a judge can be removed for cause or retired for incapacity by the state supreme court, and Alaska empowers its judicial council to recommend "early retirement" of trial judges on grounds of incapacity. Since 1947, New York has had a Court on the Judiciary, with power to remove judges for cause or retire them for mental disability, although the special court, so far, has acted in only a few instances. In Ohio, by a 1957 rule of the state's supreme court, a board of commissioners has authority to investigate complaints of judicial misconduct and make recommendations to the supreme court as to disciplinary action, and a 1959 rule of the supreme court of Michigan requires the court administrator, on direction of the state's chief justice, to conduct similar investigations. The amended judicial article adopted by Illinois in 1962 provides that a judge can be retired for disability, suspended without pay, or removed for cause by a commission convened on order of the supreme court or the state senate and composed of a supreme court justice, two appellate court justices and two judges of the state's trial court of general jurisdiction.

[14] Frankel, *Removal of Judges: California Tackles an Old Problem,* 49 A.B.A.J. 166 (1960). See also the current annual reports of the Commission on Judicial Qualifications of the State of California.

The developments just listed reflect widespread and increasing aware-ness of the importance of fair and workable procedures for the investiga-tion of complaints against judges and for the retirement, removal, or dis-ciplining of unfit members of the judiciary. Since 1962 there has been a marked acceleration of efforts to provide effective methods of disability retirement and removal. Within five years after adoption of the Califor-nia plan, a dozen states have moved to follow suit, and as many more now have similar proposals under study.

The Minor Courts

Up to this point, we have dealt primarily with state trial courts of general jurisdiction, with some reference in passing to the appellate courts. We turn now to the many courts of special and limited jurisdic-tion with which average citizens are most likely to come in contact: traffic courts, small-claims courts, police courts, probate courts, and domestic-relations courts.

The Surviving J.P. A large majority of the states still have Justice-of-the-Peace courts operating in some or all areas of the state. In only a few of these states is there a requirement that Justices of the Peace be lawyers or have any legal training or experience. In some states, the Jus-tices of the Peace perform only ministerial functions like administering oaths or performing marriages; in others the Justices of the Peace have been replaced in more populous areas by city or municipal courts pre-sided over by judges who are required to be lawyers. Several states have taken the more drastic step of doing away with the Justice-of-the-Peace courts altogether and setting up a system of minor courts with law-trained judges or magistrates.

Minor Courts in the Rural Areas. Although a state-wide system of minor courts with law-trained judges is highly desirable, it has not always been possible in certain rural areas to find a lawyer who wants to be a judge. Stringent residence requirements, if coupled with a requirement that all judges be lawyers, may leave some rural courts without judges. In at least two states, legislatures have recognized this problem by pro-viding that in the absence of qualified personnel a judge may be chosen from non-lawyers or from lawyers in another part of the state.

When Justices of the Peace are replaced by trial courts of limited jurisdiction this change is rarely accompanied by a change in the method of selecting minor court judges. In Missouri and Iowa, for example, the appointive-elective plan when adopted was limited to judges of the ap-pellate courts and trial courts of general jurisdiction.

Juvenile Courts and Family Courts. Recent modifications in the structure of minor-court systems have brought about little change in the methods of selecting judges for most of these courts, but, when we turn to juvenile and family courts, a trend toward an appointive judiciary is apparent. In 1962, more than fifteen states had separate juvenile or family courts for all or part of the state. In many of these states the method of selection differed from that used to select trial judges generally. For example, judges of the Juvenile Court in Tulsa are selected by the nominating commission method, as are family-court judges in New York City. The requirement of legal training or experience is usually the same for juvenile-court judges as for other trial judges. In Florida, Delaware, Georgia, and the District of Columbia, there is an additional requirement that juvenile-court judges shall have had some special experience in children's problems, juvenile delinquency, and family welfare.

Minor Courts in the Cities. There is a sharp contrast between the qualifications of minor-court judges in metropolitan areas and those in rural areas. A 1964 survey of the minor courts in the one hundred largest metropolitan areas in the United States showed very few in which judges were not required to be lawyers. In several cities judges could be chosen only from members of the bar who had practiced a prescribed period of years. The terms of office of judges in these courts were usually longer than those of the judges of courts in rural areas.

Salaries and Benefits. Compensation for judges of courts of special and limited jurisdiction tends to be substantially less than that provided for other state trial judges. A 1963 survey revealed that thousands of Justices of the Peace and probate judges still depend for their compensation on fees collected from the parties in cases before them. Justices of the Peace on salary received from $3,600 annually in North Dakota to $13,200 in Florida. Juvenile-, family-, and municipal-court judges' salaries tended to be lower than those paid to trial judges of general jurisdiction in the same community. This is also true of retirement benefits. As compared with state trial judges generally, these judges received minimum retirement benefits, or none at all.

Movements toward unification of state court systems, such as those accomplished in Colorado and Illinois during 1962, have tended to bring about higher qualifications, longer terms of office, and more adequate compensation and retirement benefits for judges who perform these special or limited functions. To the extent that there is greater recognition of judging as a life career, with a consequent emphasis on judicial experience, a practice may develop of selecting higher-court judges from the ranks of these minor-court judges. If so, then the initial selection of judges of these minor courts will require far more attention than has been given in the past.

Judicial Education

Recent efforts to modernize the judicial personnel system have been accompanied by a growing awareness that certain additional developments are needed to obtain the highest quality of performance of judges, particularly trial judges. The first is the creation of a program for educating judges in the craft of administering justice under law as judges. The late Karl N. Llewellyn made explicit what all thoughtful judges recognize early in their careers, that good judging requires more than a sound legal education and experience as an advocate. Good judging is itself a unique craft.

> The existence of a craft means the existence of some significant body of working know-how, centered on the doing of some perceptible kind of job. This working know-how is in some material degree transmissible and transmitted to the incomer, it is in some material degree conscious, it is to some degree articulated in principles and rules of art or of thumb, in practices and dodges or contrivances which can be noticed and learned for the easing and the furtherance of the work.[15]

Because the craft of judging is neither taught in the course of university legal education nor learned by experience as a lawyer, the new judge upon coming to the bench must begin the process of developing his craft. Justice Tom C. Clark has put the point this way:

> . . . Ascendancy to the bench is the beginning, not the end, of one's professional striving. . . . On donning the robes one must continue to be a student. And he must be sure that the school in which he has enrolled has a curriculum as current as the most recent slip opinions and law review.[16]

PROBLEMS OF THE LAWYER NEWLY BECOME JUDGE

The newly selected judge often lacks both the knowledge and the technique that are essential elements of the craft. The lawyer newly selected for the bench may find that, due to the specialty of his practice, he has lost touch with recent developments in many areas of substantive law. With the growing specialization of the profession this problem is increasing. The experienced trial lawyer may be current on the law of evidence and procedure but less acquainted with the law of corporations, trusts, and taxation. The office lawyer, skilled in drafting contracts, wills, and trusts, may be deficient on evidence, procedure, and the recent developments in the law of torts and crimes. Both the former trial lawyer and

---

[15] Llewellyn, *The Common Law Tradition: Deciding Appeals* (1960), p. 214.
[16] Clark, *Progress of Project Effective Justice,* 47 J. Am. Jud. Soc. 88 (Oct. 1963).

the former office practitioner will soon be called upon, as members of the bench, to make decisions covering all areas of law and must be prepared to do so as the occasions arise.

Even lawyers coming to the bench from a background of advocacy are unprepared to deal with problems of judicial decision-making, writing, and the mechanics of the internal court operations. For the trial lawyer who becomes a trial judge, problems in many of the following areas must be faced: inferring the truth or falsity of material facts; interpretation of rules of law in a nonadversary fashion; sentencing techniques; supervision of the presentation of evidence to a jury; instruction of the jury; and supervision of the work of lower courts, administrative agencies, and offices.

Traditionally the new judge has been left to cope with the problems created by his deficiencies and to correct these deficiencies by his own efforts. This accumulation of personal experience has been far from ideal. The process is expensive in social and economic costs, and the experience of an individual judge will tend to be limited to what he can gain by his own intuition, as augmented by whatever advice he can get from his brothers on his particular bench.

The growing realization of the need for some type of formal education of judges to supplement traditional experiential development of the judicial craft has fostered the hope that a body of knowledge and techniques of the judicial craft can be assembled into pedagogical form. This hope has been given substance by important initial steps in the pooling of the experience of judges across the nation.

In the fields of jury supervision and instruction, motion practice, pretrial and discovery, administration of courts, and review of administrative agencies, valuable learning and insight have been and are being developed. In addition, scholarly fields once thought wholly unrelated to the administration of justice can provide valuable material to the judge. The disciplines of semantics and psychology, for example, contain information which is important for understanding and control of the process of drawing conclusions from facts and the process of reasoning from rules of law. Psychology, psychiatry, and social work are rich with learning that is invaluable in the rehabilitation of adult criminals and juvenile offenders.[17]

SEMINARS FOR JUDGES

The first steps toward formalized learning of the judicial craft were taken in 1956, when the Appellate Judges Seminar was founded under

[17] Friesen, *The Judicial Seminar: Foundation for Judicial Education,* 46 J. Am. Jud. Soc. 22 (Oct., 1962).

the auspices of the Institute of Judicial Administration of New York University. At its first meeting in 1956 and annually thereafter some twenty "student judges" have participated in three weeks of concentrated full time summer study of problems of judicial technique, opinion writing, and internal administration of courts, as well as recent developments in basic areas of substantive law. Before coming to the seminar, the judges are given reading lists to provide a common frame of reference for each subject to be studied. At the seminar, experienced judges and law teachers form panels which present each subject and then engage the student judges in discussion.

While the founders of the Appellate Judges Seminar were exploring the means of teaching the appellate judicial craft, another organization, the National Conference of State Trial Judges, was founded in 1957 to promote the exchange of ideas among judges of trial courts of general jurisdiction. The Conference's services to its state trial-judge members came to include the publication of the *Trial Judges Journal* and the sponsorship of some twenty committees which have been actively working on such problems as the relationship between fair trial and free press, the treatment of the sociopathic offender, and the drafting of a code of judicial decorum.

Between 1959 and 1961, three states, Washington, Florida, and Colorado, developed seminars for trial judges patterned along the lines established by the Appellate Judges Seminar. During this same period a judicial seminar program was established for the federal courts. The first of a series of sentencing institutes for federal judges was held in 1959, and in the following three years similar institutes were conducted in connection with the judicial conferences of many of the federal judicial circuits. In 1960, the first federal judicial seminar was held in Boulder, Colorado. With the appointment in 1961 and 1962 of approximately one hundred new federal judges, the need for additional federal judicial seminars became urgent. The United States Judicial Conference arranged for a series of three seminars for new judges, which were held during 1962 in three widely separated cities across the nation.

THE NATIONAL COLLEGE OF STATE TRIAL JUDGES

At about this time, the Joint Committee for the Effective Administration of Justice was developing an important judicial seminar program to implement its concern with the attitude of judges toward the problems encountered in their work. In its three years of operation, late 1961 to 1964, the Joint Committee sponsored or assisted forty judicial seminars conducted on a state or regional basis. Some three thousand state judges attended and discussed topics in eight basic areas: civil pre-trial and discovery, criminal pre-trial proceedings, judicial responsibility in domestic-relations cases, judge-jury relationships, judicial control of demonstrative evidence, sentencing and probation, court delay, and jury instructions.

The Joint Committee's seminar program culminated in a most significant development in judicial education, the founding of the National College of State Trial Judges. The College, sponsored by the National Conference of State Trial Judges, held its first session in July 1964, on the campus of the University of Colorado in Boulder. During its four-week session, 96 new state trial judges devoted 190 class and study hours to a curriculum closely following that of the Joint Committee seminars. The format of instruction followed the seminar system in which the group and its instructors both contribute to the interchange of ideas and problem solutions. The 1964 teaching staff of the College was composed of law teachers and experienced judges, many of whom had served on the faculty of the Joint Committee seminars. Because of the success of the College's first session, funds were secured for two additional years of operation preparatory to its establishment on a permanent basis.

OTHER EDUCATIONAL PROGRAMS

Teaching of the judicial craft through seminars and meetings has not been limited to judges of appellate and trial courts, but has been found highly useful in the education of judges of courts of special or limited jurisdiction. For more than a decade, the Traffic Court Program of the American Bar Association has reached judges of traffic courts across the country. New York has offered special two-day training courses to give non-lawyer Justices of the Peace a basic grounding in judicial procedures that may better the administration of justice in those courts.

In another important effort, the National Council of Juvenile Court Judges initiated in 1962 a training program for juvenile court judges. In this program's opening twenty months of operation twenty state and regional meetings were staged. Week-long regional programs and shorter state meetings involved 550 judges and 150 allied professionals in the areas of law, probation, psychiatry, and public welfare. The focus of the meetings varied. Some dealt with substantive areas important to judicial competence and court work; others stressed problem-solving techniques and interview skills in human relations; still others focused on the exchange of data and exploration of problems in areas of common professional concern

JUDGING AS A LIFE CAREER

The need for formal education in the judicial craft to which all of these programs attest carries with it a corollary about judging itself. This second development, which began to find expression about 1950, is the increasing conviction that once a judge comes to the bench both he and the public should regard his judicial service not as a phase in an advocate's career or stepping stone to other public office, but as a life-long commitment to the giving of justice according to the best practice of the judicial craft.

Because the judicial craft is developed slowly, honed against years of experience on the bench and in more formal learning experience where available, the public—including both taxpayers and litigants—makes a substantial investment in it. At the beginning, the judge must move more slowly and carefully until he has sharpened his craft. During the initial period, the public has to accept a judicial work product less efficiently and effectively done, in order to obtain a highly skilled judiciary in the future. Hence an expert judiciary, a body of judges equipped with the best tools and techniques of the judicial craft, is an asset belonging to the public as a whole.

Such an asset is too valuable to be wasted either by the judge who chooses to retire and return to private law practice with the prestige of having been on the bench, or by public action voting a judge out of office without good grounds. The loss in both these instances is double. Not only is the investment in the retiring judge lost, but the public must make a second investment of similar proportions in a new judge. Only if the judge and the public think of judging as a life career can the social costs of maintaining a well qualified judiciary be minimized.

Even more importantly, the acceptance of judging as a career will maximize the effective administration of justice. The very purpose of developing the judicial craft is to resolve society's disputes in as just and efficient a manner as possible. Once the judge has refined his craft sufficiently, he is endowed with a unique capacity to resolve social disputes. Should he leave office or be rejected by popular vote, justice and efficiency of dispute settlement are bound to suffer until his replacement has attained an equally high level of craftsmanship.

It is conceivable that by the beginning of the next century a pattern may develop of providing formal professional education and training for career judges that will be separated, at least in part, from the education provided for lawyers. While this is contrary to past American practice, it is the practice in many other countries including France, Japan, and

Brazil, and the recent judicial education devices here considered are perhaps a step in that direction.

The Courts and the Future

The quality of judicial personnel, particularly of the trial judges who dispose of something like 99 per cent of the judicial workload in American courts, becomes increasingly important as American society grows more complex, impersonal, and urbanized. In 1914, the authors of the American Judicature Society's State-Wide Judicature Act anticipated the shift from a rural to an urban society. Today, 70 per cent of our national population live in urban areas. With the expected population explosion in the next fifty years, it is anticipated that 80 per cent (320 of 400 million Americans) will be urban dwellers.

Throughout history, cities have always been the predominant source of work for the courts. The traditional transmitters of values and rules such as the family, the school, and the church have never been as effective in urban as in rural societies. Increased proximity of large numbers of persons breeds legal disputes. Individual freedoms are continually restricted to accommodate to the demands created by urbanism. Public welfare is often threatened by impersonalization and irresponsibility which characterize the urban scene.

To the extent that this becomes true, the function of the courts in protecting individual freedoms and the public welfare within an ordered society becomes one of the most critical issues of government in the United States. Ultimately, the success or failure of the courts to meet these emerging challenges rests on the judges of these courts. Courts and judges should become a national concern.

Discerning judges and lawyers have long advocated the establishment of a ministry of justice to, in the words of Justice Cardozo, "watch the law in action, observe the manner of its functioning, and report the changes needed when function is deranged." [18] The crisis in our courts together with what can easily be predicted in the foreseeable future should create a renewed demand for such ministries of justice at both the national and the state level, and the issues of judicial selection and tenure should be the first order of business.

[18] Cardozo, *A Ministry of Justice,* 35 Harv. L. Rev. 113 (1921).

The American Assembly

American Assembly Books in the Spectrum Series

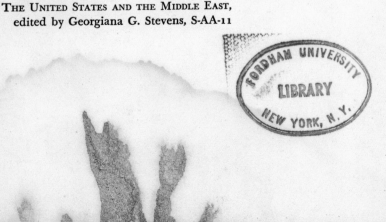